# Praise for MARKETING ONLINE

"*Marketing Online* takes the mystery out of the information superhighway and makes it easy to turn your computer and modem into powerful marketing tools."

—Lisa Kanarek, author of
*Organizing Your Home Office for Success*

"If you've been intimidated by online marketing—or just procrastinating—Marcia Yudkin's book will get you going. She shows you that the digital marketplace is no more exotic than a Middle Eastern bazaar. This is easily the most user-friendly book on the subject."
—Barbara J. Winter, author of *Making a Living Without a Job*

"Marcia Yudkin fills this book with practical advice that comes only from having done one's homework online."
—Paul and Sarah Edwards, authors of *Making Money with Your Computer at Home*

"Yudkin offers time- and money-saving advice for maximum use of the new online medium. Don't get 'flamed' as a Cyberspace 'newbie' . . . read this book."
—Jim Cameron, sysop, The Journalism Forum, Compuserve

"*Marketing Online* is chock-full of ideas and helpful examples that show you *exactly* how to get your name in front of potential customers without alienating online service users or sysops."
—Janet Attard, forum leader, The Small Business Center, America Online; The Business Know-How Forum, Microsoft Network; The Home Office/Small Office RoundTable, GEnie

"Marcia Yudkin brings practicality, insight, and logic to the world of online marketing. She has a good sense of what works, what doesn't, and what readers can do to generate business in the emerging world of online communication."
—Peter Miller, creator and host,
Real Estate Center, America Online

"Marcia Yudkin has towed me out of the breakdown lane of the information superhighway. Her chapter on responding to authors' appeals is luring me toward the high-speed lanes."
—Alan Weiss, Ph.D., author of *Million Dollar Consulting*

"This book is packed full of practical techniques that will enable you to get the word out in cyberspace about your business."
—Alice Bredin, author of the syndicated column "Working at Home"

"I thought I knew the online world, but with her entertaining anecdotes Yudkin has given me many new insights and planted dozens of intriguing new ideas in my head."
—Herman Holtz, author of *How to Succeed as an Independent Consultant*

"Whether you sell to a publisher or publish yourself, *you* must promote the book. *Marketing Online* is full of opportunities for book authors and publishers."
—Dan Poynter, author of *The Self-Publishing Manual*

"A wise and useful book, enabling you to learn from the successes—and mistakes—of entrepreneurs who have been there."
—Angela Gunn, contributing editor, *Home Office Computing* and *Computer Shopper*

# VOICES FROM THE INTERNET

Before publication, we posted Chapters 6, 7, and 8 of *Marketing Online* on the World Wide Web and asked for comments. Here are a few of the online marketing success stories that turned up.

"When I joined forums, bulletin boards, and Usenet newsgroups and did as you outlined in your book, I began receiving public and private inquiries about my services. This led to picking up several new clients. I also came in contact with someone who offered me a position as V.P. of Marketing along with an equity position in a new business, which is taking off because of the principles you write about."
—Mike McBride, Smithfield, Rhode Island
mmcbride@ix.netcom.com

"I help students with essays for college and grad school, and when I saw someone in the student section of the Legal Forum looking for help one day, I responded. This student became one of my best clients. A few weeks later, he referred someone else looking for help in the forum to me. Two others saw the exchange, and they too became clients. In addition, I received wonderful testimonials for my marketing literature."
—Linda Abraham, Santa Monica, California
72604.551@compuserve.com

"Marketing and information technology will be strategic alliances for competitive survival in the '90s. Thanks for sharing your book via the Web site and allowing people to think as entrepreneurs and be agile to the use of Web sites and see how change can benefit them and their organizations. And oh . . . check out the Oakland Coliseum's Web site at http://www.cyberzine.com/raiders for a sneak preview of things to come to the online world."
—Steve Koss, Information Systems Manager, Oakland Coliseum
skoss@netcom.com

"I am the publisher/editor of *Scenes of Vermont*, a cyberspace magazine focusing on specific areas of the state (http://www.pbpub.com/vermont). I published an article warning motorists of a 25 mph speed limit in Woodstock and about Lisa, the parking lady, who can write a ticket and have it on your windshield in 30 seconds. This news is now all around the area. The merchants are far more willing now to buy advertising since I've proved people are reading the stuff."　　　　　　　　　—Tim Palmer-Benson, PB Publishing
publish@databank.com

"One of our best online marketing techniques was to look up listings of AOL members in our local area, and then email them a polite and nice letter with information about our BBS, Cyberia. We were able to locate people in our area with modems who really wanted to find out about our services. To visit our BBS, telnet://cyberia.com, and visit our home page at http://www.cyberia.com."
　　　　　　　　—Adam Viener, Cyberia Communications, Inc.
adam@cyberia.com

"At this point, sheer marketing budget volume alone does little to provide a competitive advantage in a medium that rewards ingenuity (and maybe a little design sense), not repetition and size. I'm sure General Motors and Coca-Cola will find a way to crush us little guys, but for now we're on equal footing . . . and it feels great! To see what this particular 'little guy' has done, take a look at http://www.mindspring.com/cbi—information headquarters for children's book writers and illustrators."
　　　　　　　　　—Jon Bard, Fairplay Colorado
cbi@mindspring.com

MARCIA YUDKIN is a speaker, consultant, and writer who specializes in helping people communicate creatively. Her articles have appeared in magazines ranging from the *New York Times Magazine* and *Psychology Today* to *Ladies' Home Journal* and *Cosmopolitan*. She is the author of *Six Steps to Free Publicity* and co-author with Laurie Schloff of *Smart Speaking* and *He and She Talk* (all Plume). She lives in Boston.

Other books by Marcia Yudkin

*Six Steps to Free Publicity*
*He and She Talk* (with Laurie Schloff)
*Smart Speaking* (with Laurie Schloff)
*Freelance Writing for Magazines and Newspapers*

# MARKETING
## ONLINE

### Low-cost, High-yield Strategies for Small Businesses & Professionals

---

## Marcia Yudkin

A PLUME BOOK

PLUME
Published by the Penguin Group
Penguin Books USA Inc., 375 Hudson Street,
New York, New York 10014, U.S.A.
Penguin Books Ltd, 27 Wrights Lane,
London W8 5TZ, England
Penguin Books Australia Ltd, Ringwood,
Victoria, Australia
Penguin Books Canada Ltd, 10 Alcorn Avenue,
Toronto, Ontario, Canada M4V 3B2
Penguin Books (N.Z.) Ltd, 182–190 Wairau Road,
Auckland 10, New Zealand

Penguin Books Ltd, Registered Offices:
Harmondsworth, Middlesex, England

First published by Plume, an imprint of Dutton Signet,
a division of Penguin Books USA Inc.

First Printing, October, 1995
10  9  8  7  6  5  4  3  2  1

LIBRARY OF CONGRESS CATALOGING-IN-PUBLICATION DATA:
Yudkin, Marcia.
    Marketing online : low-cost, high-yield strategies for small businesses & professionals /
Marcia Yudkin.
        p.  cm.
    ISBN 0-452-27529-6
    1. Internet marketing—Cost effectiveness. 2. Small business—Management.   I. Title.
HF5415.1265.Y83   1995
658.8'4—dc20                                                                  95-23587
                                                                                  CIP

Printed in the United States of America
Set in Times New Roman
Designed by Leonard Telesca

For Chen, again

"What, you want to get on the information highway—*you??!*"
You see, readers, if I can do it, so can you.

# Acknowledgments

Special thanks this time around to Fawn Fitter, Peter Kim, Barb Tomlin, and Jennifer Starr as well as my usual literary partners, Diana Finch and Deb Brody. And a big round of gratitude to everyone mentioned in the book who took the time to share technical or strategic information, or to tell their online success story.

# Contents

# PART I

# Orientation
# and
# Overview

# 1 | How Online Activity Produces Business

"My sole purpose in going online was to use it as a marketing channel," says Paulette Ensign, a professional organizer in Bedford Hills, New York. Within her first three days on CompuServe, the most international of the major commercial online services, she had connected with a publisher in Milan who decided to release an Italian translation of her organizing-tips booklet. Within her first four months online she landed spots on several radio shows, enticed people to sign up for a seminar in Seattle, sold numerous special reports, found two producers interested in an interactive CD-ROM of her work, and got herself interviewed for this book— all direct results of dialing up CompuServe from her computer and exchanging messages from her home with people located anywhere from Anaheim to Zurich.

Ensign's coups are far from a fluke. Consider the successes of these other folks:

- Mike Bayer, a Laguna Hills, California, public relations consultant who specializes in working with lawyers, estimates that he did twenty-five to thirty half-hour introductory consultations last year for CompuServe members who sought him out after reading informative files he had provided online. Two of those prospects became clients with billings totaling more than $10,000 each.
- Every day Jan Melnik, who runs a home-based desktop publishing business in Durham, Connecticut, receives one or two

credit-card orders in her electronic mailbox and two or three checks in the U.S. mail for her books or her newsletter because of her participation on America Online, another commercial online service. The fan mail she has received online helped convince her publisher to offer her a contract for another book.

- Christian Martin, marketing director of Rail Pass Express, Inc., in Columbus, Ohio, generated $55,000 in sales of Eurail and Britrail passes from an investment of $400 in fees for the time it took to post travel information and answer questions for Europe-bound travelers on America Online.

- Shortly after setting up shop on the unowned, international grandmother of all computer networks called the Internet, Singapore-based Asia Online began receiving inquiries from browsers all over the world who had stumbled across its site. One company wanted to find an Asian source of plastic gloves, another to sell cement mixers in Asia, reports cofounder Hoo Shao Pin. Worldwide magazine advertising can't touch the Internet's cost effectiveness.

- Stefan Kolle of Trust Services Benelux in Amsterdam, Holland, has lined up writers, producers, and sources of financing for several feature films through CompuServe. Signing up projects like these normally happens only at film festivals and markets such as at Cannes, Berlin, or Las Vegas, Kolle notes.

In the mid-1990s, electronic communication is no longer just for computer whizzes. Anyone who can compose a business letter using a word processor can negotiate the technology necessary for online connections. And while hooking up with other computer users can be a source of fun, it has also evolved into a serious business tool. Night and day, all over the world, smart, creative business owners and professionals are swapping information and sending messages that lead to lucrative deals of almost every imaginable sort. You don't need any expensive equipment. Paulette Ensign makes do with what she calls an "archaic" IBM system with two floppy drives and no hard disk, the kind you might pick up at a tag sale for $50. And best of all, getting business online needn't eat up your entire marketing budget. Just $30 a month can cover the online access and fees necessary for successful electronic marketing.

Whatever your line of business, whether you're just starting up or well established in your field, you need some method of attracting new people into the orbit of being your customers or clients. Going online offers numerous advantages over other methods of marketing.

*It gives you an enormous geographic reach.* If Joni Spence Smith, a professional fund-raiser, were to rely on personal word of mouth, she would only be serving clients within a forty-five-mile radius of her hometown of Butner, North Carolina, "so small it has just one stop light," she says. But by announcing her availability on Prodigy's Service Clubs Board, she can gather leads and secure work from Girl Scout chapters and Lions Clubs all over the United States.

*It bypasses gatekeepers and puts you directly in touch with important decision-makers.* Lawyers, business owners, and executives who are active online look around and participate in exchanges on their own, not through a subordinate. A woman who was trying to launch a newsletter for doctors showed up on the Prodigy Business Board bemoaning how hard it was to get her telephone calls past the receptionist or her mail onto the doctor's desk. I advised her that her problem might be solved if she sought out places where doctors congregated online, like CompuServe's Medsig forum.

*It enables you to zero in on prospects with highly specific needs or interests.* Retired engineer and inventor Pat March's greatest expertise lies in mold-making for plastic parts. "I'm good at cutting down the total number of parts and designing for low-cost production," he says. On Prodigy's Hobbies Board, he offers suggestions to people designing and manufacturing model airplanes and has ended up being hired on a consulting basis by several.

*It can save you gobs of money.* When Joyce DiBacco of East Brookfield, Massachusetts, decided to start a consignment crafts shop, she received hundreds of responses from a notice on Prodigy's Crafts Bulletin Board titled "Crafters Needed." "I needed that quantity of response in order to find quality crafters," DiBacco says. "Just one ad in the right magazine would have cost me fifteen hundred dollars. This way I spent nothing beyond what I was paying anyway to be on Prodigy."

*Compared with face-to-face networking, it's time effective.* Instead of having to get into the car at a specified time, drive, find a parking space, and maybe suffer inedible chicken and boring speeches, you can meet peers and prospects whenever you happen to have time and as often or seldom as you like. Online networks are available for your participation twenty-four hours a day. "When my kids are asleep and I don't have anything to do, I can go online and promote my book in parenting forums at two a.m.," says Bill Adler, author of *Tell Me a Fairy Tale* and other books.

*Because the millions of people who might come across any particular message each know hundreds of others, your reach goes far beyond the online universe.* Through participating in FoxPro and computer consulting forums on CompuServe, Christian Desbourse, a Belgian software developer, landed five months of work in Istanbul, Turkey, with a company that itself was not online. "Another consultant, who was working onsite in Turkey at the time, put us together," he explains.

*Its speed and efficiency of communication are unparalleled.* Compare the zap, zap, zap of electronic messaging with the days it might take to end a desperate game of telephone tag or the weeks it takes for a series of letters to cross the oceans. Unlike faxes and telephone calls, you can send as detailed an electronic message as you need—even an entire software program—without inconveniencing yourself or your recipient. "You don't need to know when your correspondent is available," says Desbourse. "It's noisy receiving faxes in the middle of the night, but you can pick up E-mail anytime that suits you." From his home in the woods forty kilometers south of Brussels, it costs him a local call to send a message to a client in Taiwan.

*Compared with the telephone and in-person communication, you don't need to be quick-tongued.* "I like the fact that online I can take time to reflect on what I want to say," says Gary Ellenbogen, a computer consultant in Winooski, Vermont, who has been active on CompuServe for the last two years. "I always try to review my responses to people's questions before I send them off, and sometimes I'm astonished by what I see. I'll see that I didn't address the question after all, or said something that could be construed as condescending, or wrote something that now looks to me like gibberish. This way I get the chance to clarify my thinking."

*You can quickly build a reputation.* It took just one month, says Jan Melnik, before others in the desktop publishing area on America Online began spreading the word that she was the expert to direct questions toward, and that her book, *How to Open and Operate a Home-based Secretarial Services Business,* was the thing someone wanting to get started in her business should buy. "Simply leave pleasant, well-informed notes on your topic," says mystery writer Lary Crews, who quickly gathered fans first on Prodigy and then in America Online's Writer's Club, "and pretty soon people are saying, 'Gee, Ostrich Man seems to know about ostriches.' "

*You can bypass prejudices that may come into play face to face.* "I'm a fat guy with a beard," says Lary Crews, "and when I meet people online there's no initial opinion about that that I have to fight against." Cathryn Conroy, a senior writer for *CompuServe Magazine,* told me an unfortunate variation on this theme: A man in the graphic arts business who had found a lot of clients online agreed to an interview with her. After his picture appeared in the magazine, however, several clients who had been working with him by phone and E-mail dropped him, sending his business into a tailspin. They had had no idea he was black.

*It helps you find prospects you may not be able to reach through other media.* Literary agent Wendy Zhorne of Pasadena, California, was thrilled to have found through Prodigy's Books and Writing Board two highly qualified, prolific authors whom she has taken on as clients. "They don't read writers' magazines, go to writers' conferences, or know about the publishing-industry directory *Literary Market Place,* so I wouldn't otherwise have had access to them. They were impressed by the way I answered questions, so they came to me rather than asking around for some other agent," she says.

*It keeps you in touch with the beliefs, assumptions, and preferences of your market.* Online, you can easily and quickly eavesdrop on thousands of conversations among members of the population you are attempting to serve. Helen McGrath, a literary agent in Oakland, California, says she has as many clients already as she can handle. Nevertheless she too finds Prodigy's Books and Writing Board useful because "it tells me how writers feel about agents—what drives them crazy, how they think, what misconceptions they have, what they really do and don't understand about the business."

*If you travel a lot, you can stay plugged in with that line of communication.* When Nicholas Negroponte, director of the Media Lab at MIT, flies to distant parts of the globe, he keeps up with his electronic correspondence without anyone needing to know he's left Massachusetts. "People are sending messages to me, not Tokyo," he says, adding that unstandardized plugs throughout the world— twenty different types in Europe alone—do present a challenge.

Despite all these advantages of the online medium, it has been difficult for small-business owners and professionals to find much guidance about how to round up customers online. Newspaper and magazine articles here and there have profiled successful electronic networkers but without nitty-gritty dos and don'ts. The online services don't offer many tips, either, beyond an official policy forbidding outright offers, except in isolated areas set aside for advertising. On the vast unowned and ungoverned stretches of the Internet, a ritual of scorn called "flaming" punishes transgressors of its informal code of protocol. Newcomers in cyberspace have thus had to use trial and error to understand which tactics receive a green light and which earn them a rap on the knuckles, deleted messages, megabytes of abuse, or threats of getting locked out of a service.

As I was gathering examples for this book, several people told me they were just beginning to catch on to what they had to do to exploit the marketing potential of their participation online. It had dawned on them that either instinctively or consciously, they could use certain techniques to make themselves well known and credible online. With close observation and creative risks, they could discover where the invisible boundaries of acceptability lie, and position themselves just a hair's breadth away from behavior that would attract criticism. Here, as in many other aspects of business, effectiveness depends on the details.

Up to now, a confusing situation has confronted electronic novices: If they barrel in trying to drum up business, they get castigated. Yet they can see deal-making going on around them right up to the point at which money has to change hands. Even more perplexing, the very same rule—no solicitation—is implemented strictly in one place and loosely in another. Joyce DiBacco, for instance, was firmly reprimanded when she tried to place the notice on CompuServe's crafts forum that was working so well for her on Prodigy. What gives?

The best analogy I can think of is American speed limits—the official ones versus the real ones. A visitor from abroad told me she couldn't understand why she was stopped for speeding on a country road when everyone traveled that fast on the interstates. I explained that police were much more likely to stop someone going seventy miles per hour on an isolated stretch of road than when car after car was driving at that speed. I also told her about small-town speed traps. On the information highways as well, the posted rules don't necessarily correspond with what actually happens. But with an anthropological curiosity, you can learn how to attract business quickly and consistently without collecting tickets or losing your license.

Consider this book your guide to the cultures and customs online and the strategies that allow you to profit from your appearances there and remain a participant in good standing. You'll notice as you read along that I give very little attention to electronic advertising, as compared with online networking and publicity. Instead, I've concentrated on personal marketing, with which you can make a large impact on a small budget, and in which you have an advantage over larger companies that are prepared to dump megabucks into electronic marketing. As I'll soon explain, with electronic schmoozing, in place of establishing a corporate presence and an image somewhere in cyberspace, an individual or small company can use expertise and personality as a powerful magnet for attracting customers.

Although cyberspace has been growing and changing month by month, I doubt very much that the strategies I recommend in this book will go out of date. Too many people have become accustomed to—and have benefited from—interacting electronically for online communication to dwindle and die with some new technology or some cultural innovation. More likely, opportunities for meeting up with potential customers online will simply grow as more and more people begin using the modems and communications software preinstalled in the new computers they buy. Of course, some will try out the equipment and fail to have any interest in continuing to use it, while others, media hype having ratcheted their expectations to the breaking point, will ˙ quit in disillusionment. In my opinion, bandwagon arguments like "It's the cool thing to do," "Listen to these numbers," and "Don't be left behind" constitute poor reasons to go online. If you lack patience, consistency, even-temperedness, and an average or above-average ability to express yourself in words, traditional methods of marketing may pay off better for you. Indeed, even if you surpass the results of those I've profiled in this book, I don't recommend forgetting about time-honored marketing methods like targeted mailings, print advertisements, attending professional meetings, and contacting the media by phone.

I originally thought I would be able to include some criteria here to help you decide whether marketing online would suit your line of business. Yet the more my research progressed, the more my assumptions exploded. I believed a prerequisite for taking advantage of cybermessaging was being able to serve or sell to a national, if not international, clientele. But lawyers licensed to practice only in one state told me that hanging out online brought them referrals from lawyers in other parts of the country whose clients had matters that needed to be taken care of in their territory. Similarly, it's hard to imagine a less likely candidate for information superhighway marketing than take-out food, with an area of service circumscribed by the reach of a fifteen-minute drive. Yet when Pizza Hut in Santa Cruz, California, made it possible to order pizza delivery through the Internet, lots of local college students apparently found it easier or more fun to zip an order in on their computer than to drag themselves across the room to a phone. I also thought you'd have to be set up to accept credit cards if you set out seriously to round up customers online. But out of twenty-five people I surveyed on CompuServe who had found a significant amount of work online, only ten accepted credit cards. The rest managed fine with invoices, contracts, retainers, bank transfers, purchase orders, or sending merchandise COD.

In the same way I think it's important to suspend any assumptions about demographic groups that you can and can't reach online. For example, impressed with the consensus that 80 to 90 percent of regular modem users are male, you might conclude that a product or service aimed at women had no chance of succeeding electronically. Take quilting, for example, a craft going back hundreds of years whose enthusiasts are mainly female. Would you imagine that quilters gather online in any great numbers? In fact, they do! Sharon Orella, a quilter in Wilsonville, Oregon, got the idea of selling so-called charm packages, assortments of five-by-five-inch or six-by-six-inch pieces of fabric that quilters use in their creations. Through notices in areas set aside for crafters on Prodigy and Delphi, another major service, she asked if there was a demand for this sort of product. Enough responded with their names and addresses to enable her to get her business off to a rousing start. Bill LaSalle, owner of a Lakeland, Florida, crafts-supply business called Craft King, theorized, "A lot of people involved with computers also have an interest in working with their hands—or someone else in their family does."

But as I'll explain in greater depth in Chapter 4, these days you don't need to be heavily "involved" with computers to link up via modem with people in your target market. I'm not even moderately adept with computers. "I operate strictly on a need-to-know basis," I explain whenever someone gets incredulous at the holes in my knowledge (about once a week). Don't worry if you're one of those who still can't program a VCR. Like me, you can profitably pursue online networking and publicity without going into training to become a techno-nerd. I've kept technicalities to a minimum in this book, and because of the countless ever-changing interface variations, I've avoided pictures of what going online might look like on your computer screen. Still, if you ever get lost in bauds and bytes, refer to the back-of-the-book glossary. To understand and apply the marketing maneuvers that form the meat of this book, though, you need very little technical sophistication.

In the chapters ahead you'll learn:

- How to choose the most promising online areas for your business and begin creating relationships that lead to business

- How to make the most of your online participation by under-standing the medium of electronic messaging
- The crucial differences between CompuServe, America Online, BBSs, and the Internet
- How to convey your marketing message without violating online customs and rules
- Ways to set out bait online and, over time, reel in clients
- Ethical, legal, and practical danger areas you must consider
- Why and how to set out the welcome mat for international customers
- How to prevent your online activities from taking over your life
- Ways to meet the press online and get invaluable offline publicity

But before we get to strategies you need some perspective.

# 2 | Personal Marketing for Fame and Fortune

Let's say you restore pianos—you take an upright or a grand that's been knocked around and neglected and make it look and sound more wonderful than the day it first stood in the showroom. Your fundamental, never-ending challenge, as for anyone who offers a service or product, is to persuade the people with the means and motivation to buy to contact you to trade money for your goods or skills. Those who own damaged or neglected pianos or want to buy one you've refurbished need to know that you exist and need to have a positive impression of you and your competence. Much of your business comes through referrals from people you've helped in the past, but you see a lull coming up in your schedule and wonder if there's an inexpensive way you can rustle up more customers.

Advertising, of course, is an option but requires a lot of money and a few months' lead time for the publications most likely to reach the piano owners who need you. Reaching out to the media for publicity might work, but you'd have to think of a creative angle to earn TV or newspaper coverage in the near future. Showing up at some professional and networking groups and handing out business cards might yield some leads, but the odds don't seem that promising. You decide to look into direct mail, since it allows you to target a fairly precise audience on your own schedule, and you get a quote from a local direct-mail specialist. Then, almost by accident, you discover a marvelous computer-age marketing procedure.

## Magnetic Messages in Computer Space

Your teenaged son belongs to GEnie, a commercial online service, and has showed you the Music Roundtable, where people interested in pianos (among other instruments) hang out. But today, shocked by the quote you received, you sign on to the service through his modem, make your way to the Home Office/Small Business (HOSB) Roundtable, and post this electronic message:

> To: All
> From: Dianne Weinman
> Re: Direct Mail Costs?
> Can somebody tell me if $3,900 is totally outrageous for the following or not: a mailing to 1,700 music directors at American private schools and colleges—? Supposedly that breaks down to $1,200 for copywriting and design, $150 for list rental, $650 for printing of envelopes, so-called lift letters and inserts, $550 for postage, $470 for mailing house fees, and $880 for "project management," whatever that is.
> I'm in Indianapolis, by the way, and the mailing is about our reconditioned and restored pianos.

An hour and a half later, in Ojai, California, Jerry Naylor is at his computer, modem on, scanning the headlines of new messages in GEnie's HOSB Roundtable. Noticing DIRECT MAIL COSTS? he reads the whole message and quickly enters the necessary command to reply publicly:

> To: Dianne Weinman
> From: J. Naylor, Creative Marketing Consultants, Inc.
> Re: Direct Mail Costs?
> Dianne, the quote you got is not out of line for top-notch talent to create a traditional direct-mail package. But our clients have gotten excellent results with simpler, cheaper, and more eye-catching postcards. A mailing of 1,700 postcards done by us from start to finish would

cost you something like $1,425, including list rental.
Which option is better for you has to do with whether
you're looking for immediate orders or, as I suspect, just
promising leads. Let me know if you'd like more
information.—Jerry

Because you prefer dealing with someone local, you use this message to bargain your direct-mail consultant to a more palatable
price—not exactly what Jerry had in mind. Nevertheless, both you
and Jerry round up new customers because of this exchange. Two
days later, Mr. Ji Ling Su of Singapore comes upon your post and
responds by private E-mail:

To: Dianne Weinman
From: JLS/Republic of Singapore
Re: Direct Mail Costs?
Ms. Weinman: Indianapolis is not far from the University
of Purdue, is it not? If my geography is correct, would
you kindly E-mail me your address, telephone, and fax
number. My niece attends graduate school there and
says she is very unhappy without a piano.
(Mr.) Ji Ling Su, President, JLS, Ltd.

Jerry is equally fortunate. A real estate lawyer in Hartford, Connecticut, reads his response to Dianne and sends a public message
back that she likes the idea of the postcards, and don't they take
much less time to get out into the mail as well? A few more exchanges and phone calls later, the lawyer is sending a deposit check
to Jerry by Express Mail to design, prepare, and send an urgent
20,000-piece mailing.

And the dance of needs and possibilities does not end there. A
week later, she posts a comment in response to someone else's
question in the Music Roundtable and receives this private reply:

To: Dianne Weinman
From: Hank Glontlewitz
Re: Business Deal?
Dianne: Are you the lady who reconditions pianos? I do

the same for brass and woodwind instruments, and
have a lot of connections in elementary and junior high
schools. If you're interested in talking about how we
might work together, give me a call at 208-555-7779.
(That's Idaho Falls, Mountain Time.)

Two months later, the lawyer whom Jerry helped spots his name in
the newsgroup and decides to thank him publicly for his help, telling him about her very gratifying 5.5 percent response. Jerry picks
up three new prospects—who do not personally know the
lawyer—as a result of her thoughtful gesture. He also receives an
E-mail from someone putting together a seminar series on cost-
cutting marketing for small businesses.

You can't *count* on these sorts of results, but they occur plenty
often, especially to those who use the techniques in this book and
who hold the attitudes described in Chapter 23. Surprisingly,
though, this electronic sashay right and allemande left among business people only works for individuals, not for corporate entities.
And there lies a key advantage for small business owners and professionals in going online to find and attract business. When an organization or company tries to do what you and Jerry did, it's like
an elephant trying to fit into ballet slippers.

## The Personal Advantage

Soon after I first signed on to Prodigy, a response to one of my
messages in a discussion group appeared from someone named
"Home Office Computing." Although I understood it came from
some representative of the magazine by that title, I felt affronted at
not knowing who I was dealing with. My irritation grew as I received more messages from this masked entity, until I stated that I
refused to communicate any longer with someone who wouldn't
identify himself or herself. This corporate entity, I eventually
learned, was *both* a "him" and a "her"; contributing editor Angela
Gunn and researcher Charles Pappas took turns answering questions on behalf of *Home Office Computing* magazine. "According
to the terms of the contract between Prodigy and *Home Office*

*Computing,* we had to sign off exactly as 'Home Office Computing/Prodigy Service/Home Business Expert,' on three lines," Gunn recalls. "Instead of generating discussion threads, however, we tended to end them. And we weren't gathering any sort of a following. Finally, after we negotiated an agreement that allowed Charles and me to use our names, a lot of people who had never mentioned their discomfort with the previous arrangement commented positively on the change."

As I'd sensed almost immediately, online discussion areas are an intrinsically personal medium. In this they resemble letters, telephone communication, and in-person meetings. That is, when we receive an unsigned letter, or one signed only with a company name like National Bank, we feel vaguely affronted. When we receive a phone call from a person who refuses to provide a name, we tend to feel vulnerable, angry, or frightened. If we were trying to schmooze at a professional conference with a person whose name tag read just CREATIVE MARKETING CONSULTANTS, INC. who claimed his name was irrelevant, we'd probably walk away. We're used to person-to-person communication in these situations, so that being confronted with a faceless or nameless corporate presence comprises anywhere from a minor to a major violation of our expectations. Advertising, of course, is a totally different story—we know it's never directed to us alone. And significantly, Angela Gunn points out that the only online vehicle conducive to an anonymous voice is the World Wide Web (see Chapter 13), which most resembles traditional advertising. "The bulletin-board analogy is unfortunate," says Gunn. "You always need to establish that there's a human being behind a posting who's aware that other human beings will read it." Wherever dialogue gets going online, communication is always between *Jerry Naylor of Creative Marketing Consultants, Inc.,* and *Dianne Weinman of Weinman Pianos,* not between Creative Marketing Consultants, Inc., and Weinman Pianos, or between Jerry Naylor and Weinman Pianos.

Even where you can put yourself forward with a company identity, as on America Online or the Internet, people assume that whenever they interact with, say, "CreaMktCon," they are interacting with the same person, not sometimes Jerry and sometimes Jim and once in a while Alexandra. Sharing one corporate ID as

"Home Business Expert" led Gunn and Pappas to bizarre situations, as when Pappas posted a reply to a question that Gunn didn't believe was completely accurate. "I'd have to write something like, 'I'm sorry, folks, I misspoke fifteen minutes ago,' " says Gunn. These contortions and the messy maneuvers necessary when someone asked a follow-up question that was clearly intended for just one or the other of them show why the kinds of marketing I'm focusing on in this book can't be neatly delegated or handled by a group. For that very reason, however, they offer exceptional potential for solo practitioners and those piloting the progress of a small company.

With online marketing, your personal identity becomes the instrument for building business relationships. Who you are—your skills, experience, expertise, communication ability—along with your personality traits like generosity, patience, tolerance, and wit, and moral qualities like integrity all take on as much relevance as the specific services and products you have to offer prospects. Factors like your personal hygiene, accent, body language, and speaking and listening rhythms have no influence online, but everything that can come through in words does have an impact, as a way of building up a picture of who you are, what you stand for, and the value embodied in your products and services. Although the channel of information appears limited online, everything that does come through attaches to your name and influences whether or not people pursue business with you.

In part the prominence of the whole human impression accounts for the complaint of a newsletter publisher in CompuServe's Smallbiz forum. "No one out there with a paid staff of more than five is making money in electronic marketing," he wrote. "It doesn't 'scale upward.' That is, you should be able to make $100 a day, then double your effort or hire a couple of people and then make $200 a day and then move to $800 a day. You quickly hit a point of diminishing returns, like with your first employee. Online marketing is greatly oversold." In my view, it's not that online marketing doesn't "scale upward," it's that it doesn't transfer from boss to employee or from one staff member to another at all. If you, Dianne, get to know Jerry Naylor, Ji Ling Su, and others online, so that they become willing to recommend you to friends who need a piano fixed up, you can't hand GEnie back to your son George and expect him to carry on the marketing where you left off. All the momentum you built up gets lost, because it attaches to you, not to Weinman Pianos.

It's easy to miss the significance of this point because a trend in the business world called "relationship marketing" involves a very different vision of customer-company relationships. According to this perspective, if FedEx keeps track of the fact that I prefer packages delivered on the side porch and does so on future visits without being asked, the company has cemented a relationship with me. Well, perhaps I would indeed continue to choose them as my overnight courier, but that's good customer relations, not a relationship. On the other hand, I have a relationship with a particular FedEx driver who knows I'm a writer and whom I wouldn't hesitate to wave to a halt if I saw him on his route and had a question. I don't know his name, but I know his smile and his friendly, slightly pushy manner. Person to person, we know each other at some level. If this driver gets a new route or I move, though, FedEx loses the benefit of our cordial feelings for one another.

However, given the intrinsically personal nature of online communication, it's tailor-made for situations where you *are* your business. There the distinction between your behavior toward customers and prospects and marketing disappears. If I come to respect your knowledge, from cordial feelings toward you, and figure that we know each other, we have a relationship that inevitably feeds directly, although not necessarily immediately, into your business. For instance, New York City venture capitalist Lee Kaplan and I discussed life/business philosophies online numerous times. Even before we spoke on the phone, I knew him to be intelligent, intuitive, and empathetic. No money has changed hands between us, but he helped me find people to interview for this book, and I would definitely send him opportunities that might interest him when they come across my path.

Still, things need not get that chummy for you to get the benefit of the personal factor online. Simply showing up in a way that announces that you're open to contact encourages the start of a conversation that leads to a purchase or a deal. "Ironically, with electronic networks we're reverting to the pattern of preindustrial times, when you bought shoes from the guy around the corner," says Wally Bock, publisher of *Cyberpower Alert!* newsletter. "There's a lot of sharing on the side of the seller before the sale. For instance, on the Internet people can get information about my newsletter from the autoresponder that robotically sends back information to them. Yet most of those who end up buying ask me a question by E-mail to which I respond, and then they order. The questions are legitimate, but they're also a way of 'sniffing me out' and starting a relationship. It wasn't obvious to me a year ago that the way to tell a good subscriber was that they ask me questions." According to Angela Gunn, this dynamic did not play out successfully with *Home Office Computing*'s presence on Prodigy. "Conversation" with an organization does not have the effect that it does with an individual. "When a large organization tries to become your friend it often comes across as phony or Big Brother–ish," says new-business development consultant Jennifer Starr. "But where a person is concerned, if you feel you've gotten to know the person, you're more likely to buy."

Remember too that most of the online conversations we've been considering occur in public, readable by onlookers. If you're trying to build a reputation, no medium can match the power, speed, and accessibility of online participation. Here's how and why.

## Visibility + Competence + Word of Mouth = Reputation

Advertisers and marketers of all sorts have proven that the sheer number of times someone runs across your name or the name of your product has an enormous impact on their likelihood of doing business with you. When your name turns up on someone's desk or computer screen once, it's rarely enough to make that person remember you. But appear before the right audience at least seven times within eighteen months, says Jeffrey Lant, author of *The Unabashed Self-promoter's Guide,* and you'll find yourself on the other side of the familiarity barrier. Richard Ott, author of *Creating Demand,* adds that because of the familiarity factor, a greater number of small impressions adds up to a larger effect than a smaller number of bigger impressions. In other words, five one-paragraph notes have a greater impact than one five-paragraph note. Wally Bock confirms this with his observation that when he participates frequently in an Internet newsgroup, the number of newsletter inquiries traceable to any one appearance there goes up. In Chapter 5, I discuss choosing the right places to put out your name online, but here the important point is a rider to Woody Allen's remark that "Eighty percent of success is showing up." Online, don't show up once—do so again and again and again and again and again and again and again.

Frequency is only one factor in business visibility, however, notes Jennifer Starr. The value of the medium in which your name appears—*The Boston Globe* versus your high school reunion booklet—has an influence, as does the reach of the medium—the number and characteristics of the people exposed to the message. Being quoted in *The Boston Globe* might appear to have greater value than posting your own online message in a "Creative Management" discussion group, but there's a trade-off. With the newspaper article you receive a valuable implicit endorsement from having been chosen to be quoted. However, the press filters your message for its own agenda and may not present your comments in the context that you would. When you go online, you not only have complete control over your own content, its timing, and its placement, but you'll also find yourself in an environment that encourages responses. I've had photo features about my work in the Sunday *Boston Globe* three times and know indirectly that they've helped my local credibility and reputation, but few readers of that medium trouble to track down my phone number and give me a call—many fewer than I hear from online. And while the Sunday *Boston Globe* may have more readers than a "Creative Management" discussion group on the Internet, the latter is likely to contain more of the people I wish to be visible *to*.

Getting your name out often to the right people builds name recognition, but for that to bolster your *reputation,* your name needs to be linked to some evidence of your competence. The newspaper article can satisfy that requirement by citing your position and accomplishments and quoting your comments. Online it's awkward for you to go into as much horn-tooting detail as an article about you might, but you have a powerful ongoing opportunity to demonstrate your competence. Instead of telling about your competence, you can show it, by giving precise, up-to-date answers to others' questions, offering hard-to-find resources, and making nonobvious distinctions—rather than always being corrected by folks who appear to know better. "It's deadly to give out bogus information," says Christian Martin, who answers questions online about travel to Britain for Rail Pass Express, Inc. "If you say, 'Do such-and-such in London,' and that's inaccurate, someone will come on who's from London and set you straight. On the Internet, someone will *always* one-up you if they can."

Dan Kohane, a trial lawyer in Buffalo, New York, who has been active in CompuServe's Lawsig forum for years, says, "If you're well spoken and informed on your subject, people start to call on you for advice in that area. If there's a legal question about insurance in the forum, for instance, people say, 'Ask Kohane, he's the insurance guru.'" That third-party word of mouth is the final ingredient that cements a reputation, according to Starr. Ideally, word of mouth builds on both visibility and competence. "If other people your prospect knows say they know you, or even better, say good things about you, she's more likely to buy from you," Starr says. Indeed, a study by the Canadian Congress of Advertising showed that two-thirds of the adults surveyed relied for product information on "talking to friends/family/colleagues." Far below that was newspaper advertising, key information for just 44 percent, trailed by flyers, magazine ads, TV commercials, radio spots, and direct mail. In Chapter 8, I talk about online word of mouth as the "fan club" phenomenon, explaining how it's possible to gather a group of champions in as little time as one month.

If you want to play the fame game, keep in mind that success takes on momentum over time, and that there may be a threshold before which it looks like nothing is working. That's the worst time to give up! As Richmond, Virginia, marketer Richard Ott explains it, "The cumulative weight of a number of persuasive impressions can cause the brain to kick into decision-making mode. Like the drops of water that accumulate in a precariously balanced bucket, one more drop and the entire bucket tips over. The latest direct-

mail campaign, the latest billboard campaign [or the latest electronic message] may very well be the drop of water that causes the
entire bucket to tip. You've kicked many people into decision-
making mode at once, and your sales gush forth. This happens
quite often to marketers that maintain a healthy dose of marketing
activity on a regular basis. They have enough people with full
buckets out there who only need one more drop to kick into
decision-making mode."

Another reason to persist is that your prospects have their own
time line of need and their own decision-making process that necessarily remain a mystery to you. Susan RoAne, a professional
speaker and author of the books *The Secrets of Savvy Networking*
and *How to Work a Room,* says she has come to believe in a "Go
Know!" theory of marketing: "I can be doing everything right with
no effect, and then one day my Aunt Yetta is standing next to
someone somewhere who just happens to . . . , which leads to . . ."
For instance, RoAne was quoted in *Newsweek* and *The New York
Times* in connection with her menopause support group, the Red
Hot Mamas, which, she says, triggered bookings that had no connection with the publicity for her books. Another time a meeting
planner who booked her mentioned that it was the smile in her picture by which he remembered her two years after she got in touch.
But the unpredictability doesn't mean you throw up your hands,
only that you pursue every means of staying memorable and visible. "Be patient—eventually they'll call and say, 'We read your
book, we read about you in *The Wall Street Journal,* you sent us an
article, and we just saw you online.' "

As RoAne suggests, whatever you do online meshes with other
marketing methods such as playing golf with prospects, publishing
articles, placing ads, appearing on radio programs, and presenting
your product at trade shows. With all that dovetailing, it might be
hard to pin down how much effect your online activity had in that
mix. And the results might show up offline, so to speak, because
word of mouth can migrate anywhere. Skip-tracer Gerry Gollwitzer
of Menomonee Falls, Wisconsin, received a call from a fellow in
Las Vegas who wanted help finding his buddies from the Vietnam
War. "I found twelve out of fourteen people for him," says
Gollwitzer, "and then I learned that he'd gotten my name and

number from someone who saw it online. He himself didn't even own a computer." Just a few people mentioned in this book market *only* online. But almost everyone finds their online efforts better than painless—even downright enjoyable. You can't overlook the agreeability factor when you're in a position where your personal efforts make or break your firm. And online worlds are exceptionally focused. Let's turn now to the different kinds of electronic enclaves and services that await your participation.

# 3 | An Online Orientation

When my older sister learned to drive a car, she had to master the bone-jarring difficulty of changing gears by working a clutch. Four years later, when I got my learner's permit, the family cars had automatic transmission. I never came face to face with a clutch or a choke until a decade later, when I graduated to Volkswagens and Volvos. The technical concepts my father drilled into me were few: the safe braking distance to remain from the car ahead; the need to check the oil level and tire pressure once in a while; and the imperative to pull over *immediately* if the oil light went on. Once I knew how to merge, parallel park, and avoid spinning out of control on snowy New England roads, I could concentrate on the main purpose of driving: going places. No orientation was necessary on where to go.

In the mid-1990s, the computer world has evolved to the point where you can choose to go online with the equivalent of automatic-transmission software. You still need a little pertinent know-how, like what to do when you crank the starter, so to speak, and the engine doesn't roar on. So I'll give some pointers here to help you solve problems getting connected. But mostly you business folks need an orientation to the kinds of destinations available to you online, and their advantages and disadvantages when it comes to rounding up customers. Unlike the earth geography we know way before we climb into the driver's seat, few of us have the opportunity to cruise around cyberspace as passengers. What's out there, then? Hang on for a quick tour of options, just as soon as I brief you on the essential technical stuff.

## The Mysterious Modem

If you were to open your computer and peer inside, your modem wouldn't look much different from the rest of its innards: colored knobs, beads, and boxes soldered onto a board printed with mazelike numbers and lines. A modem enables your computer to communicate with distant computers through ordinary telephone lines. It does this through two steps of translation: Since computer data exists in digital form and telephone transmission occurs in analog sound waves, a modem makes computer-to-computer exchange possible by changing digital signals into analog signals and then back again. (A "digital" format portrays information as a collection of separate, either-or 0s and 1s, while "analog" data exists in a continuous flow of qualitative information.) "Modem," in fact, stands for "*mo*dulator-*dem*odulator," where "modulate" means the digital-to-analog part of the transmission and "demodulate" means the analog-to-digital transformation.

Got that? If not, don't worry. You really only need to know that a modem doesn't accomplish this double conversion on its own. It needs the aid of communications software, which tells the modem to do things in a certain order, like wait for a dial tone, put the speaker on, dial a number in tone or pulse mode, say "Hello, how do you work?" in &#@*ese to the computer on the other end, and so on. Whether your communications software is proprietary— specific to a service provider—or generic—allowing you to dial up anyone in modem-land—in my experience these modem commands are the tricky part of going online. You may never come into contact with them directly, but if you continually fail to connect properly with your destination, they're usually the cause. Don't assume that you somehow have to decipher the technical manual that came with your modem in order to solve the problem. Call the technical support department of your service provider and describe the symptoms, and they will almost always cheerfully and patiently talk you through to a solution.

I had no problem signing on initially anywhere, for instance, but when I later wanted to switch from the Windows version of Prodigy's software to the faster DOS version, I couldn't connect. For almost an hour, a technician had me entering and testing strings of symbols, letters, and numbers. Perhaps the tenth combination worked. One week later, CompuServe lowered the rates for high-speed access, and I had to go through the trial-and-error process with its technicians to correct the modem strings appropriately for 9600-baud access. One week after that, I was totally mystified when I tried to sign on to GEnie and the modem gave out an unending high-pitched squeal. It turned out that whatever I had changed for CompuServe affected my ability to connect with GEnie. The GEnie technician eventually gave me the command, "AT&F^MATE1L0S7=60S11=60V1X1S0=0^M," which kept all my dial-ins working. If your service provider won't extend such favors to keep you up and running, tell them sayonara, and take your business elsewhere.

Besides encouraging you to feel free to ask for help, I'd like to add just a few technical tips:

- Invest in a good surge protector to guard your computer and modem against electrical power fluctuations.
- Either put your modem on a telephone line without call waiting or find out from your service provider how to turn off call-waiting signals automatically whenever you go online.
- When buying a new modem, get the fastest you can afford. It will save you money and frustration as you cruise around online.

And now to the fun part—destinations for online prospecting.

## The Commercial Online Services

These services, owned by megacorporations, offer news and weather, business, consumer and reference information, and shopping and discussion areas to members who pay a monthly access fee and usage charges. Each service has its strengths and weak-nesses, a distinct personality, and a particular demographic profile. Since each service continually adds features and periodically changes its "look," please take my comments as starting points for your own explorations rather than as the final word. Contact the telephone numbers or online addresses listed in the Resources Section in the back of this book for current prices and, in many cases, a free trial-membership sign-up. My descriptions and opinions pertain to the status quo for the purpose of finding customers in the spring of 1995.

*1. CompuServe Information Service.* This is far and away the top choice if you offer products or services to businesspeople. Owned by the tax-preparation giant H&R Block, it's also the most international of the commercial services—I've encountered (and sold products to) folks here from Hong Kong, Belgium, Great Britain, Saudi Arabia, and Germany. Because CompuServe is short on fun and games and a bit more expensive than the other services, you'll find lots of serious discussions and few kids, teenagers, and adult sex-seekers here. CompuServe will happily furnish you with its mouse-based point-and-click CompuServe Information Manager, but you can also sign on "raw," directly from any communications program. My monthly bills went way down after I started using TAPCIS, an independently sold program that automatically grabs and posts CompuServe mail, messages, and files for you, so that you spend a minimum amount of time with the money-clock ticking.

A potentially overwhelming 600 or so joinable clubs called "forums" await you here. Aside from more than 400 technical support forums, from Adobe Applications to ZiffNet Support, you'll find numerous groups focused on professional interests, such as desktop publishing or journalism, along with leisure-oriented topic areas like bridge, genealogy, and sailing. In the most popular forums, participation is so high that messages scroll off—that is, move up and then disappear completely—in only four or five days. CompuServe thus isn't the place to place a query and then mosey on back a week later. Forum libraries, for information files and software, tend to be well stocked and heavily used, and the classified section gives you one more way to reach out very inexpensively to your target market. There's some access to the Internet (see below), and you can also receive a free subscription to CompuServe's mailed-out magazine, which alerts you to corners of the service you hadn't imagined existed.

## Demographics:

Members: 3 million
Gender breakdown: 83 percent male, 17 percent female
Geographic reach: 150 countries, including Uganda, Latvia, Fiji, and Lebanon
Average age: 41
Median household income: $90,000
Other: 71 percent have at least a four-year college degree, 29 percent a master's degree or doctorate.

**2. America Online.** Judging from the ten free America Online disks that I've received in the mail, unsolicited, this service really wants me as a customer. And if the ease of installing and using its proprietary software were the only criterion, I'd be theirs for life. But I noticed right away that no business, professional, or entrepreneurial areas were among this service's welcome list of its twenty-five most popular spots to visit. Even more seriously, its energetic sex-chat rooms and encouragement of semi-anonymous nicknames cast their shadow on the ambience throughout the service. Four or five women whom I interviewed volunteered comments about having fled America Online because of being solicited for sex when they were trying to carry on business. Their advice for other women: Don't be recognizably female in your America Online "screen name." Nevertheless, you may find participation here worthwhile if you market products or services to consumers or want to take advantage of its easy-to-use live conferencing system. Forums include the Microsoft Small Business Center, Real Estate Online, the Travel Forum, and the Writer's Club.

Compared with CompuServe's sometimes furious rate of public dialogue, on America Online ongoing discussions are rarer and harder to follow. Posted notes may remain up for more than one year, which is wonderful for timeless self-promotion, less beneficial for passing comments. Some of its libraries bulge with useful files, but information seekers can't hunt for treasure there by keyword, only by perusing the titles and descriptions of files. Classified ads on the service have been free, and there appears to be greater toleration here than elsewhere for impersonal business-related announcements.

Overall, I recommend America Online as a great "starter" service to get a taste of the functions you can perform online. With its generous ten free hours upon sign-up and relatively easy access to the Internet (see below), it's worth a thorough checking out.

### Demographics:

Members: 2.5 million

Gender breakdown: 84 percent male, 16 percent female

Geographic reach: Currently United States and Canada only, with plans to expand to Japan and Europe

Average age: 40

Median household income: more than $50,000

Other: 60 percent have graduated college, 26 percent more have attended some college.

**3. Prodigy.** Like America Online, this third giant service, owned by IBM and Sears, requires that you use its proprietary software, which has been, at least recently, free for the asking. If you have an older computer, though, you may not be able to access all of the service's features and may find the speed at which you can move around maddeningly slow. Alfred Glossbrenner, in *The Little Online Book,* characterizes Prodigy as an online entertainment network competing more with the TV networks and cable services than with America Online or CompuServe. Considering the ubiquitous on-screen ads, I think Grossbrenner has a point. To cater to its family-oriented customer base, Prodigy automatically screens all your bulletin-board postings, returning messages that contain obscene or vulgar words. Few techno-nerds bother with Prodigy, but you'll find more women participating here proportionately than elsewhere in cyberspace.

Alone among the major services, Prodigy accepts no file postings at all. But many of its bulletin boards, such as Money Talk and

Travel, offer an excellent chance for visibility and exchange with other members. Postings remain accessible for about a month, activity is high, and threads are easy to follow. On the Business Board, where I have held the position of special contributor, you'll encounter more people casting about for easy ways to make money than business owners accustomed to closing big deals. During the last four months of 1994, for example, the most popular discussion category was Network Marketing, with more than five times as many posts as Marketing a Business or Accounting/Finance/Taxes. Classified ads cost about the same as on CompuServe, but they're alphabetized and you'll be competing with headlines like, AABANDON AD COSTS! With its easy online navigation and comparatively painless access to the Internet, Prodigy represents another good way to get your online feet wet, and if you market to the family crowd or nascent entrepreneurs, it may offer you a perfect home.

*Demographics:*

Members: over 2 million
Gender breakdown: 60 percent male, 40 percent female
Geographic reach: United States and Canada only
Average age: 36
Median household income: $70,000
Note: Unlike other services, Prodigy counts each party in a family membership as one member.

4. *GEnie.* Owned by General Electric Information Services, GEnie gives you the choice of logging in through your generic communications program or using its proprietary software. Since the latter requires a newer computer than I have, I used the former and managed to catch on fairly quickly to GEnie's menus and commands. The slogan that greets you every time you sign on to GEnie, "The most fun you can have with your computer on," seems to announce that it too doesn't cater to business users. And a whopping prime-time surcharge limits most members to evening, night, and weekend usage. But the discussion areas, called roundtables here, cater to an extremely wide variety of specialized hobbies and

business interests, from comics to motorcycling and romance writers to law enforcement. The Home Office and Small Business Roundtable gets fairly decent traffic. Because GEnie keeps messages accessible in topic threads practically forever, this service is especially convenient for studying member concerns on a particular topic all at once. Its information-packed, keyword-searchable file libraries are worth contributing to, and glassblower Strat McCloskey adds that there's "always someone to talk to" on GEnie, which has more live conferencing than, say, CompuServe.

Writer Jack Germain, who is active on all the major services, characterizes GEnie members as "hobbyists and a lot of entry-level professionals." If that matches your target audience, you just might find a niche here.

*Demographics:*

Members: Over 200,000
Gender breakdown: 77 percent male, 23 percent female
Geographic reach: Mostly United States and Canada; some
   members from Japan, Australia, European countries
Average age: Majority are 25 to 44 years old.
Median household income: Almost $50,000

**5. Delphi.** During my first forays online, I found navigating around this service so frustrating that I dreaded the mere idea of another try. Nevertheless, for you, dear readers, I ventured forth again. As with GEnie and CompuServe, you don't need proprietary software to log on. Although I had an easier time this year following its menus or guessing my way around, I found a sparsely populated service. The library of the Business area held very little that had been uploaded in the last four months, and its forum showed just twenty-three messages posted in the previous week. A pioneer in full Internet access, Delphi now makes it easier than any other major service to launch your own forum. I randomly sampled several of its so-called Custom Forums, which showed postings at a frequency of one every few days. Yet because activity is so low, you could post messages or files here and have them remain up until kingdom come. Note that outside of the Boston area, Delphi hits you with a prime-time telecommunications surcharge during week-day business hours.

*Demographics:*

Members: Over 100,000
Other information: Not available from Delphi, although other sources say members hail from more than forty countries

**6. eWorld.** Because I use an IBM machine and not a Macin-tosh, I wasn't able to visit this fairly new Apple Computer–owned service. I'm told that it's colorful and intuitive to use, and will eventually open its doors to IBM Windows users. It has a file library, forum, and conferencing for entrepreneurs, but for now, you might want to bypass it unless you have special affection for a Macintosh interface or some special reason to gravitate to Mac users.

*Demographics:*

Members: Over 80,000
Geographic reach: United States, Canada, Australia, United Kingdom, New Zealand, Singapore, Hongkong, Taiwan, India, South Africa, and Israel
Other information: Not available

**7. Others.** Several heavy hitters in the computer world, like Microsoft and AT&T, have new online services in the works that might prove valuable to small-business owners and professionals. And other upstarts have grown well beyond the local stage, offering specialized memberships you can hobnob with. Beyond the majors, however, the availability of local access numbers or an Internet in-gate becomes an issue, since you normally don't want to end up forking over a monthly membership fee, hourly usage charges, *and* long-distance costs.

*CIX (Pronounced "kicks")—Compulink Information eXchange.* This Britain-based online service, the world's largest outside of North America, offers a staggering 2,910 discussion groups, the majority concerning either computers or business. I spent an hour poking around several of its message areas and found it to be a friendly, informal service. CIX gives you the option of signing on from your communications program and getting around with commands or using a third-party Windows interface called Ameol (which I couldn't manage to install, probably because I didn't have enough memory). If you have a full-fledged Internet account, you can "telnet" there without paying overseas phone charges. It's a good route for North Americans to a more select international group than can be found on the Internet.

*The Well—Whole Earth 'Lectronic Link.* The online service of the counterculture, San Francisco–based The Well carries an influence that reaches far beyond its 11,000 or so worldwide members. Business takes a backseat to culture and the arts here, where members participate in 260 message areas and can post World Wide Web pages (see Chapter 13) visible to Internet visitors for no extra charge. The Well has been exclusively text based and menu based, but this is scheduled to change. Numerous prominent journalists and writers belong here, which makes it prime schmoozing territory. If you sell services or products to the sort of folks who are interested in ecology, holistic medicine, progressive politics, or the Grateful Dead, this is the place to hang out.

## Bulletin-Board Systems (BBSs)

In a sense, all of the services profiled above constitute overgrown bulletin-board systems. But the much smaller, homier versions actually known as BBSs offer such a different feel and such different marketing opportunities that it's important to discuss them as a separate category. More than 50,000 BBSs operate in North America alone, with countless others in almost every country on the planet. Their sponsors range from teenagers obsessed with cracking the secrets of computer games to governmental entities, such as the Edmonton Economic Development Authority in Alberta, Canada. Although the world's largest BBS, Exec-PC in New Berlin, Wisconsin, receives more than 4,500 calls a day and grosses almost $2 million a year, most BBSs represent the hobby of an individual who loves the work involved and doesn't mind losing money. Like an online service, the typical BBS offers chat or conferencing functions, message boards, file libraries, and, sometimes, classified ads. Unlike an online service, however, according to John Hedtke, author of *Using Computer Bulletin Boards,* about 80 percent of BBSs do not charge access fees. From a marketing point of view, however, you may be more interested in those that do charge for participation.

BBSs break down into four types:

1. General. A 1994 survey by *BBS Guide* found 44 percent of BBSs falling into this category. These boards usually draw callers in their local area interested in exchanging software, selling their used cars or computers, socializing, playing games, or downloading sexually explicit materials. Many general boards are staying abreast of the times by offering access to and from the Internet (explained below). If you sell primarily within your local market, you might want to investigate the more popular general BBSs in your area. Information broker Gerry Gollwitzer of Menomonee Falls, Wisconsin, has connected with landlords interested in credit reports and skip-tracing on his local board, which happens to be Exec-PC.

2. Special interest. The *BBS Guide* survey placed 26 percent of boards in this category. These range from boards focused on handicapped issues, genealogy, or cave exploration to those designed for engineers, desktop publishers, or pilots. Because callers to these boards are more likely to come from a wide geographical area, they represent a worthwhile way to spread the word about your business to the specialized group that you serve. The listings in each issue of *Boardwatch Magazine* (see Resources at the back of this book) lead you to BBS "list keepers" for numerous topics.

3. Technical support/customer service. About 12 percent of BBSs fall into this category, according to *BBS Guide,* providing product information and help to customers. Independent computer consultants might find these worthwhile haunts.

See Chapter 13 on why you might want to set up this kind of board for your company.

4. Organizational. The smallest category of BBS, this includes governmental boards like SBA Online, sponsored by the Small Business Administration in Washington, D.C., and those set up by professional organizations or nonprofit groups to disseminate information. I keep in touch with fellow Boston-area members of the National Writers Union on a BBS of this type.

To find out about BBSs that might prove useful for marketing, look for a publication at large newsstands or computer stores called *Computer Shopper.* Another good source of listings, *Boardwatch Magazine,* is more difficult to find if you do not subscribe but posts back-issues online (see Resources). In addition, you'll often find announcements or ads in special-interest or trade magazines serving your target market. More and more BBSs are designed to offer easy entry and intuitive navigation for new users, who connect with their own generic communications program.

## The Internet

Trying to define the Internet reminds me of the ancient story of the blind men groping at the elephant and taking one part for the whole. One person says, "The Internet is a place where you can find out practically anything you want to know and present your wares to millions of people around the world," and we'll have to agree. Another person says, "The Internet is the grand collection of networked computers throughout the world," and she is pretty accurate too. Someone else says, "The Internet is a collection of miscellaneous tools for accessing and exchanging information worldwide," and he is also right. Unlike the elephant, however, which was conceived and born *as* an elephant, the Internet has changed purposes and form as it has grown. So a quick historical overview is helpful for perspective.

In the late 1960s, the United States Department of Defense decided to develop a way to link up military computers so that if a nuclear attack knocked out a few sites or connections, the others would still be able to communicate with each other. ARPAnet, the resulting decentralized governmental network of networks, spawned other networks for nonmilitary and research purposes that eventually merged and spread into an international amalgam of networks using the same communication protocols. Since the U.S. government had directly or indirectly created and maintained the structure for research and defense purposes, commercial traffic was prohibited on the Internet until 1991, when a consortium of independent Internet access providers established new network backbones that bypassed those banning for-profit messages.

The anticommercial traditions of certain sectors of the Internet stem from the days when only academics, government employees, and corporate researchers were allowed to use the network. Right now, however, no one owns or controls the Internet, although it reaches more than 170 countries, plus Antarctica. It works through cooperation on a global scale and evolves through the widespread adoption of individual and group innovations. For example, the electronic system for publicly exchanging ideas known as Usenet was developed by a group of Unix programmers, but once the system was up and running, they and others soon expanded it to cover other interests like computer games, Eastern religions, and fine wines. Similarly, the convenient nested-menu- based method of archiving and retrieving files called Gopher originated in 1991 at the University of Minnesota, where it was named after the school mascot, and propagated quickly throughout the world. Most recently, a high-energy physicist proposed a system for even easier worldwide access to information that materialized in the browsing tools called Mosaic and Cello in 1993, for a new multimedia, linked-by-a-click sector of the Internet called the World Wide Web, now by far the fastest growing part of cyberspace. Who knows what exciting new tools are being conceived and constructed as you read!

Given that background, you're probably eager to know, as with the other sectors of cyberspace that I covered, what you can do on the Internet, how, and with whom. However, because you don't "join" the Internet the way you do an online service, these questions are difficult to answer clearly. Unless you work for a university, company, or other organization that allows you to use its Internet system, you pay a service provider a monthly fee for a connection through its Internet linkup to a vast collection of resources, functions, and features that the service provider has not itself created or collected, including:

- E-mail: Unlimited one-to-one electronic communication with anyone else connected to the Internet, as well as participation in any of thousands of professional or hobby-oriented discussion groups whose posts arrive by E-mail
- Usenet: A decentralized network of more than 7,000 discussion groups comparable to forums on the commercial online services, although here the topics tilt toward computers, recreation, and culture
- ftp and Gopher: Methods of making software or text files available, or of reading and retrieving them
- World Wide Web: An easy-to-navigate multimedia system of linked pages sponsored by companies, organizations, and individuals
- telnet: A way to link up with and use the capabilities of a remote computer by typing on your own computer

These (and a few others) are the features referred to collectively under the rubric of "the Internet." The scale is much, much larger than any online service, and the scope of interests represented ranges from aquarium building to forensic economics to mine clearing. Once you get linked up, you connect with the Internet community as a whole, some subset of it, or with individuals who are also hooked up—*not* with fellow patrons of your service provider. Some service providers furnish you with proprietary software that allows you to navigate with mouse clicks rather than menus or commands, but most give you the choice of either grappling with the rather difficult text-based command system of Unix or installing software on your own computer that makes your online journeys easier.

And who else is out there on the Internet? Unfortunately, no one has a clear idea of exactly how many million people use the Internet, who they are, or how much disposable income they have.

Most analysts put that figure between 20 and 30 million, but that's only an educated guess. As to who Internetters are, I think it's safe to say they include:

At least four times as many men as women

Millions of college students, graduate students, professors, and university staff

Lots of corporate and organizational employees

Growing numbers of entrepreneurs and self-employed professionals who pay for Internet access as individuals

A predominance of North Americans and English speakers

Increasingly the commercial online services I discussed earlier in this chapter are offering access to some or all of the above aspects of the Internet, while restricting their own features to subscribers. That doesn't mean that online service subscribers get the better deal, because they always have an hourly meter running and sometimes a quota of free E-mail messages. Those getting on the Internet through a service provider, though, often pay a flat monthly fee for both unlimited E-mail and unlimited online time. They also experience comparatively less control over what they do with their account than do subscribers to the commercial online services. For instance, America Online and CompuServe are much quicker than most Internet providers to suspend or terminate an account upon receiving complaints about someone flouting Internet norms.

# 4 | Overcoming the Fear Factor

While hunting down some juicy nugget of information for this book, I discovered the urgent questions I had listed before I ventured online for the first time. Scribbled across the front and back of a used envelope, in the midst of a lot of doodles, I found the following:

1. If I want to post a message, do I do so in a "forum," on a bulletin board, or what? Do I get private responses? Can I repeat it? Do only the people logged on at one time get to see the notice?
2. If I had "full Internet access," would I be able to get onto CompuServe, etc.?
3. Can I type in an offer for something free? Is that "commercial"?
4. Is it OK to give out my "real" address?
5. Would it cost me money to receive a flood of responses?

I'd gotten the idea that going online might help me quickly find people to interview for my next book. And while wired up electronically, I thought I should try some of the promotions that had worked well for me that year in traditional media. Having read a little, I had a smidgen of confused knowledge and nowhere near enough confidence to plunge ahead. So my next step was consulting someone who taught people about the Internet. An independent researcher with a computing account through Harvard, he knew almost nothing about the commercial networks or finding business leads online. So most of my questions remained.

Shortly afterwards, freelance writer Fawn Fitter showed me the paces she went through to participate on The Well, a smallish service based in San Francisco. Though she too couldn't directly address most of my questions, her real-life demonstration of how she selected topics and retrieved and answered messages gave me enough of a general picture that I felt ready to call CompuServe, give them my credit-card number, and explore the Great Unknown on my own.

If you haven't yet gone online, this chapter is for you. Whether you're worried about the safety of exposing your computer's contents to the outside world or afraid of getting hopelessly frustrated and lost, I'd be the last person to pooh-pooh your concerns. On the contrary, I've collected fears you might have about going online, done my best to respond to them, and added suggestions for overcoming general technical intimidation.

## Do You Recognize These Worries?

*I'm a techno-klutz.* "I'm computer-illiterate," said one consultant to explain why she hadn't yet gone online. Since she has sent me papers she's word-processed, I know that reflects her self-image more than her actual knowledge or aptitude. If you identify with her, get your feet wet with a commercial service that lays out the welcome mat for know-nothings, like Prodigy or America Online. When you call them because you can't get connected, they never betray signs of thinking, Oh God, another techno-idiot! They'll just help you solve the problem in the nicest, most unblaming way. In order for them to help you, you need to know just a few basics: the make and model of your computer (e.g., Macintosh SE or IBM-compatible 386); the make and speed of your modem (e.g., Hayes 2400 bps or Zoom 14,400 bps); and whether you have Windows (the mouse-based point-and-click operating system for IBM-type computers) or just DOS (the nongraphical IBM operating system) installed. Once your account number and password get you onto the system, you've usually put the first technical hurdle behind you forever.

What remains is learning how to navigate—finding the areas where you'd like to spend time—and how to perform functions like sending E-mail and transferring important information to your computer. Again, all the major commercial services have practice areas where newcomers can ask questions and learn by trial and error without either running up the bill or drawing down the wrath of veterans. Even once you're leaving messages for real on the commercial online services, whenever you feel unsure you're doing things right, mention that you're new and you'll rarely attract flak. On the Internet you're expected to practice posting to the newsgroups "alt.test" or "misc.test" and not to expose your fumblings to the millions. But if you've mastered posting messages on America Online or CompuServe, it won't take you long to learn the different details of newsgroup procedures.

*I'll spend a fortune before I realize it.* Then sign up with a provider that offers either unlimited monthly access or at least ten free hours on sign-up. If you're concerned about cost, one of the first things to do online is find out which functions run up your bill and which ones don't, along with how to keep watch on your tab as a month flies along. You might also ask around about the inexpensive add-ons called "offline readers," which allow you to read messages and type responses without the money-clock ticking.

*I have to buy a new computer first.* Not so fast! The free disks you receive by mail and the general orientation of the computer press may have given you the impression that if you don't have Windows, or at least a "386" machine, or a hard disk, you're out of luck. On the contrary, CompuServe, GEnie, Delphi, any BBS, and many Internet providers enable you to connect without installing any software in addition to the communications program that probably came along with your modem. America Online and Prodigy both have DOS versions suitable for older machines, available if you ask.

*Don't you need a credit card for an online account?* No. America Online and CompuServe offer direct debit from United States checking accounts, and CompuServe allows corporate customers to pay by check or money order after receiving an invoice.

Some BBSs will be happy to accept a check for their unlimited access annual fee. For a no-fee option, inquire at your public library about "Freenets." And ask around in your family to see if someone has online access that they never bothered to mention to you. Only after I inquired did I learn that my husband had a computer account, including unlimited Internet access, at the university where he was taking graduate courses.

*I'll make a fool of myself without realizing it.* Well, you may make a few mistakes you'll regret. One woman pressed the button that meant "send to all" instead of the one for "send privately," and her passionate love letter was broadcast far and wide. Even a system operator with years of experience on CompuServe once made this kind of a mistake and had to post a public apology for something either nasty or just private he'd said about another individual. He had deleted the errant message, but after it had been up for three hours. These kinds of bloopers can happen with traditional media too, as when you put letters in the wrong envelopes.

*I already spend enough—or too much—time at my computer.* I gave this as my major reason for not going online the year before I took the plunge. After four or five hours a day writing in front of a screen, I believed I needed a change. In fact, however, I'm not sure my online activities have changed the total time at my desk, because with E-mail I spend much less time writing formal letters than I used to. Although many effective online networkers I spoke with said they spent an hour or so a day keeping up, a few spent as little as twenty minutes a day responding to and placing messages. But since they enjoyed what they were doing and knew the payoff was worth it, even those who spent two hours a day keeping up didn't regret it.

*I already spend too much time alone.* Then spending a little more time alone at your computer can help you feel much less lonely. Nadine Keilholz, a newsletter publisher in Lakeland, Florida, calls GEnie "my recreation and contact with humanity. I've always been an outgoing person, but in the last few years I've needed to stay at home most of the time to take care of my father. GEnie lets me be at home and have all the social contact I used to." Often online cliques develop that lead to grand in-person get-togethers. Attorney Harry Dreier attends an annual lunch in the New York

City area along with about twenty-five other CompuServe Lawsig regulars. "It's fun! I like being able to put faces to the names," he says. "It's actually easier for a person who isn't comfortable in social situations to establish a relationship online. That trepidation you experience when you meet a new person face to face isn't present keyboard to keyboard." Or you might become friendly with a distant colleague you can have dinner with when you travel.

*I'm too late—competitors have probably sewn up the market.* It doesn't seem to work that way. An analogy: After moving to a new city, you begin attending chamber of commerce functions. Although several other chiropractors have long been active in the organization, that doesn't affect your ability to impress and later get referrals from the banker and hair-salon owner you're eating breakfast with. Much the same is true for electronic networking, where personality, communication ability, professional competence, and availability have a great influence. The online arenas I've frequented recognize that even the three-hundredth Internet expert to show up can have valuable insights, questions, and objections to contribute.

*Give me a break—I'm too old.* "I have all the technology in my home-business life that I need or want," wrote home-business expert Barbara Brabec in her newsletter. "I can see sixty from here, and I have no interest in networking with millions of people on the Internet, wasting time browsing computer bulletin boards, or learning new software programs." Of course, if you really don't want to, don't. But plenty of others more seasoned in life than sixty and no more enamored with technology have learned to enjoy what online communication can make possible. My eighty-three-year-old uncle uses Prodigy to research movie and restaurant reviews and CompuServe to check his stocks every day as soon as the market closes. The online business exchanges I'm advocating in this book aren't any more difficult than that to set in motion.

*I can't type.* So? Governor William Weld of Massachusetts has an account on America Online, but his staffers print out his E-mail for him on paper, Weld hand-writes replies, and they type the responses back into the system for him. If you lack a secretary and don't relish the prospect of flailing about at the keyboard, you can learn to type, even at an advanced age. It doesn't take months to build up some speed and accuracy, and you won't need to bother learning fancy formatting stuff.

*I'm too shy!* This one floored me when I heard it because I'd always thought of typing onto a screen as the perfect medium of communication for bashful, retiring folks. But apparently there are several species of shyness. When I asked Laura Fillmore, president of the Online Bookstore, how often she posts to mailing lists and newsgroups, she answered, "Not enough. I get trepidatious putting my thoughts out in front of hundreds of thousands of people." Actually, though, you can benefit from going online just by getting in touch privately with people who do bring themselves to put up public messages.

*Wouldn't I be making my computer vulnerable to hackers?* Usually not. See Chapter 21 for precautions you can take to safeguard your computer and accounts.

*Yeah, but I'd have to invest in a second telephone line.* Given that you can't use call-waiting on a line when you're communicating by modem, I used to think this was a reasonable conclusion. For a home business that needed people to be able to call in, where the owner was planning to spend more than a half hour at a time online, it seemed best to install a second line. I have my modem hooked up on the same line as my stand-alone fax machine, which is separate from my phone line. But I've learned of a good one-line solution: In many areas your telephone company offers voice mail for less than one-third of the cost of a second line. With this setup, if you're online when someone calls you, they get your voice mail, not a busy signal.

*I'm not sure it would be beneficial to my business.* Louise Kursmark, owner of a desktop publishing service in Reading, Massachusetts, uses America Online mainly for E-mail communication with far-flung colleagues. Occasionally she answers questions in the Desktop Publishing section of the Microsoft Small Business Forum, but points out that unlike her friend Jan Melnik (see Chapter 1), "I don't have a product to sell." If Kursmark's business weren't keeping her busy, though, she could try seeking out locales where prospects like dentists or lawyers who wanted to start a newsletter hang out. As I previously mentioned, I'm reluctant to rule out any sort of businesses as noncandidates for electronic leads, referrals, and sales. The only way to know for sure is to try.

## How to Splash On In

If you're game to get started with your online marketing adventures, here are some ways to reduce frustration and shorten your learning period.

*Take a class.* Check out the low-cost adult education programs in your community. If they don't offer a class in getting online, call them to suggest one. If they do list such a class, make sure you'll have the chance to watch the instructor go online, or better yet, do it yourself. Otherwise the class is no improvement over the next option.

*Get a book.* I particularly recommend Alfred Glossbrenner's *The Little Online Book* and Sherry Kinkoph's *The Complete Idiot's Guide to Modems & Online Services* (see Resources), but you'll probably find others at the bookstore, including comprehensive guides to CompuServe, America Online, or the Internet. Before buying, either check the back of the book to confirm that it's recommended for beginners, or open it up and make sure you can follow its explanations. Many public libraries do their best to stay up to date with computer books, or offer regional interlibrary loan programs that widen your access to books.

*Find a coach.* The old barter system comes in handy here— show me how to get online and I'll give you one of my paintings or repair your back stairs. As I mentioned earlier, even a live demonstration of getting onto a different service or using a different software program than you'll use can be mighty helpful.

*Find a public terminal.* "Internet cafés," where you can drink cappuccino and go online by the minute or hour, are beginning to open in major cities. Look for a friendly someone who doesn't mind you sitting alongside and watching him or her cruise cyberspace. And as I mentioned earlier, find out if there's a "Freenet" in your community. The Seattle Library's cadre of homeless Internauts has received wide press coverage.

*Blunder on in.* Just try dialing up, signing on, and following the menu options. Some people learn fine this way—but they probably wouldn't be reading a chapter called "Overcoming the Fear Factor." (Hint: If you get stuck, try typing "off," "hangup," "exit," "bye," "help," "?," "control-Z," or "control-B." And though I'm told this may not shut off the money-clock right away, you can always start over again by rebooting your computer.)

Remember, once you successfully log in to any of the online services, seek out the appropriate "help" areas when you have questions, and listen in on discussions of getting onto the Internet when you're ready to take that step. And by the way, I now know all the answers to my original questions. Here they are:

1. Yes, messages get posted on forums, bulletin boards, roundtables, special interest groups (SIGs), conferences, clubs, and newsgroups. Messages may remain up for several days only, or permanently. It's not a good idea to repost unless or until the message disappears from the system.

2. "Full Internet access" does not include access to any commercial online service, which each levy separate monthly fees.

3. Read about "Schmooze-compatible announcements" in Chapter 8.

4. On the Internet, it's customary to include complete contact information in your "signature" (see Chapter 6). Some online areas also allow it, some don't. Respect the natives' customs!

5. Only on CompuServe, which charges a small fee for each incoming Internet message, might you have to pay anything at all for a flood of E-mail responses.

# PART II

# Online Marketing Tactics

# 5 | Choosing Your Pond and Personality

"My father, a pianist, used to hang out at the musicians' union building and get hired for gigs that way," says New York City new-venture consultant and deal-maker Lee Kaplan, whose current projects for his company, Genesis Venture Development, include electronically originated ones in Las Vegas, Albany, Boston, and San Francisco. "When I use the Internet as a meeting ground, it's similar. I try to figure out the best place to go to get good exposure, and then always keep in mind that there are live people on the other end reading my messages."

Hanging around a certain place online doesn't lead to business unless those are the appropriate people with whom to hang out. "When you have so much access to situations and people that you don't normally have, it's tempting to scan the whole universe for things to pursue," Kaplan says. "For instance, I kept seeing all these deals on the international trade forum on CompuServe and spent time looking into them. But sugar, oil, coffee beans—that's a different world of business from what I know. I realized it's better to stick to your niche." Kaplan didn't want to tell me exactly where he found the best opportunities, because it took a lot of searching to find his hangouts. I do know that for him, the right group wouldn't be skateboarders, police officers, weather experts, or soap opera fans.

Like Kaplan, you will probably need to wander here and there for a while until you find the best ponds in which to fish. Here are some criteria to think about as you explore, and some guidelines to help you make a good business impression when you cast your fly there.

## Is It a Puddle or a Well-Stocked Lake?

The top question to think about as you tour cyberspace is, Who goes there? Are those posting messages mainly veterans in their area of interest, or looking to get started? Do they appear willing to spend money, or are they complaining about prices and looking for freebies and bargains? Do the same names appear again and again, so that it appears to be like a club? Or do names never reappear, so that it's merely a message board, not a community? Do people stay focused on the subject matter or flit from politics to personal chitchat to car problems, as at a cocktail party? It's hard to pin down factors like age, disposable income, and how much people spend per year on office equipment, but you should be able to find clues if you examine a large enough message base. The overall demographics of a paying service may or may not replicate in a given topic area. If GEnie has 23 percent women, for instance, its Investors' Roundtable might tend to have 53 percent women participants—or 3 percent. And on the wide-open Internet, of course, looking through a sampling of postings is the *only* way to investigate the characteristics of participants.

Remember, though, that no matter how hard and long you look at messages, you'll never be able to spot the so-called lurkers, people who read and may respond privately, or pass information on to colleagues, but never themselves post. Experienced board watchers estimate their numbers at anywhere from equal to to double or more the number of those who actively take part. People may lurk out of bashfulness, because they're intimidated by the expertise or articulateness of the participants, because they're more interested in learning than offering opinions, because they feel they're too important or famous to go public, or because they prefer making behind-the-scenes connections.

Normally it's best to try to find out where your prospects congregate online, not where your compatriots go for shoptalk on professional matters. Suppose, for instance, you're an accountant looking for chaotic companies to straighten out. The best pond for business might not be one with the word *accounting* in its title, but one focused on management issues. If you sell skis by mail, you want to schmooze with skiers, not other ski suppliers. But "Head toward your prospects, not your peers" isn't a hard-and-fast rule. Harry Dreier, a lawyer in Bridgewater, New Jersey, estimates that from 60 to 75 percent of those participating in CompuServe's Lawsig forum are lawyers, the remainder being people either generally interested in legal issues or coming in to find information on a specific legal problem. After a year of participating in the Lawsig, business began trickling in to him from other lawyers, not from the nonlawyers looking for help. "Referrals came from lawyers outside of New Jersey whose clients had matters that needed to be taken care of in my state," he says. "I never went looking for this kind of thing. But other lawyers got to know me, and it happened."

Online guide and enthusiast Mike Holman of Queens, New York, gravitated to the areas where he felt he could make the greatest contribution. He offers help and advice on the online world within the topic "Black Enterprise" on Prodigy's Black Experience Bulletin Board, in the Afro forum on CompuServe and in the Usenet newsgroup "soc.culture.african.american," as well as through his own BBS, hooked in to the fifty-plus-member network Afro-Net. For you a more operative question might be places you can frequent that enable you to bypass your competition. For instance, if you're a Novell network consultant, you'll be one of many cruising barracudas in a pond devoted to Novell software or network problems. But if you regularly visit someplace focused on desktop publishing or one on viruses and security, you might be the only save-the-day consultant within hailing distance when problems arise concerning desktop publishing over networks or viruses on networks.

When exploring different online environments, take note of traffic patterns as well as who hangs out where. Messages are always dated, so that you should easily be able to tell whether an area is buzzing with constant activity or rarely visited at all. On your second visit, set your specifications for new messages only, and you may find either a torrent of discussion or almost nothing. Try to figure out too how long messages tend to remain accessible. On GEnie, America Online, and The Well, messages can stay posted for years, while on CompuServe, Prodigy, and Internet newsgroups, they predictably drop off the stage after a number of days or weeks. Each system has its advantages: The long-lasting setting fits announcements and free offers where they're allowed, while the transient context provides a suitable home for fast-moving debate and ephemeral questions and answers. You may also have a preference for whether the information comes to you or you go to it. Subscribe to Internet mailing lists and postings pile up in your mailbox without your having to go look around anywhere. I prefer the "go-looking" mode, however, of forums, bulletin boards, and newsgroups.

Also listen in on the tone to determine if it's a group you'll feel comfortable joining. I quit one board because it seemed populated by pros who seemed quick to criticize and find fault. Other places I seldom visit because the meaty requests and discussions are sandwiched here and there among seemingly endless small talk. On the other hand, one online spot I like a lot is the "Cyberbusiness" topic in CompuServe's Smallbiz forum, where people discuss the electronic marketing tactics they've tried and observed, in a noncompetitive spirit. And of course, since your purpose is promotional, notice how far each environment lets people go in describing what they sell. Bill LaSalle, owner of Craft King in Lakeland, Florida, finds Prodigy the friendliest to business of the commercial online services where crafts suppliers like himself are concerned. "On the Prodigy Crafts Bulletin Board there's a sales and services section where I can leave an offer for a free catalog of craft supplies. They also allow me to answer a question and add that I'd be glad to send along a free catalog. The CompuServe Crafts forum won't let anyone present their business like that. I can offer advice, but then I can only refer people to a file in the forum library where they can find information about our catalog. It's circuitous."

LaSalle is active on "most" of the major online services as well as in two crafts-oriented Internet newsgroups. He also maintains a page on the Internet Arts & Crafts Center, where visitors can request a Craft King catalog. Although I interviewed numerous other people who frequent a similar number of online groups, you can easily sink if you commit yourself to too many swimming holes. Keep your head above water by becoming a regular in just one, two, or three to begin with. Professional organizer Lisa Kanarek found that she could only handle belonging to two services—CompuServe and Prodigy—and dropped the third. Freelance writer Nancy Tamosaitis mentioned at the end of one of her articles that she has almost 100 different online addresses, but when I wrote to her at one of them, she never replied.

And of course you can't overlook the price and ease of access of different electronic ponds. If you live far from a major metropolitan area, you may have local access numbers for some options and not others. A GEnie member described that service to me as a "little CompuServe," but unlike CompuServe, it carries a whopping prime-time surcharge, along with a 9600-baud surcharge, which put me off. If I'm going to commit time and energy to a community, I'd like to be able to quickly post and collect messages midday without opening myself to (at this writing) $15.50 per hour on top of the monthly membership fee.

## The Influence of Personality

Some years back, a fellow National Writers Union member called me at a busy moment and asked me if I had the address for *Cosmopolitan* magazine, which I had written for. I set down the phone on its side and started expostulating audibly about how stupid and annoying I thought the question was. "Geez, if you're not #%&*!@ smart enough to find their address, you shouldn't be #%&*!@ writing for them! Here, here it is. . . ." I'm still embarrassed that I let myself go like that, especially since I could not afterwards recall the name of the person at the other end of the phone. Somewhere there's a person who either has or could spread a tarnish on my otherwise sterling local reputation. Fortunately, I've never done anything like that online. Thousands of people might remember—to my detriment, since in the world of electronic communication, business opportunities blossom or wilt because of the imprint in readers' minds left behind by words on a screen. Sales and marketing consultant Ralph Katz of Newton, Massachusetts, remembers a time when he was about to explore business opportunities with another consultant when that person's conduct stopped him short. "Someone had asked that consultant a straightforward question, like 'What do you recommend?' and what came back was a totally unprovoked slam at the person who had asked the question. I was aghast and completely lost interest in any sort of communication with him."

"From what people say and how they express themselves, you can get a good feel for their personality," reflects Paula Berinstein, an independent researcher in Los Angeles. "People who get really sarcastic, for instance, and don't seem to care what their audience thinks are probably hard to deal with. Other people seem to become argumentative for no reason. And I don't like to see people putting others down. Once a writer wanted to fire his agent, and asked seemingly endless questions after getting some advice. The other person came back on and said, 'Look, I was just giving you a suggestion. Take it or leave it.' I didn't think that was called for." On the other hand, Berinstein gets a positive impression of people who contribute witty, eloquent, or insightful comments on an issue. Even typing style can have an influence, she says—to her, typos show carelessness.

To understand how the way you express yourself and interact with people affects your business prospects, consider this data from a survey taken by public relations consultant Mike Bayer. Of 71 small to midsized business owners with minimum revenues of $1 million a year, 93 percent identified their main reason for hiring a particular lawyer as their "inner feeling about the attorney"; 91 percent said that how well the attorney showed an understanding of their problem was a "major factor" in their hiring decision. "The overwhelming conclusion is that business owners do not hire attorneys that they don't feel good about," Bayer wrote. Another indication of the pertinence of personality comes from a very different realm of business: software. With so-called shareware, software authors distribute copies of a program as widely as they can and request that satisfied users send in a stated registration fee. Several surveys have shown that a measurable number of those who register do so because they "like the author." Unless users call the shareware author by phone with a question, their impression of the author's personality derives completely from their writing voice in the instructions for the program, in the trust they've shown by releasing it as shareware, and in the wording of the invitation to register the product.

"It's comparable to the reason my wife shops at the supermarket where she does," explains Bob Schenot, author of *How to Sell Your Software*. "Because the store is active in the community, hires disabled workers, and has a reputation for being generally nice people. With a shareware product, this kind of likability is terribly important because you're asking people to send you money when they've already received most of the value they'll receive." Dallas investment banker Fred Richards told me about an agricultural expert in Nebraska he developed an interest in doing business with because of the way the man answered questions. "He was forthright, talked down-home common sense, always said his opinion was based on his experience of the last forty years, and tried to steer people away from trying to make a quick buck every time."

Since how you come across online will influence whether people will want to do business with you, think about the image you'd prefer prospects to have of you. I don't recommend that you choose a persona at odds with the way you normally are—you'd probably find such a pretense difficult to keep up over time. Rather, you might resolve to be more patient or friendly than is your wont, or try harder than you would among chums to stay on your best behavior. "For me, being online is serious business," says magazine writer Jack Germain. "If I were to make an offhanded snotty remark it would reflect not only on me, but also on the magazines that run my columns." According to Howard Rheingold, author of *The Virtual Community: Homesteading on the Electronic Frontier*, the intermingling of chitchat and commerce in electronic communication has precedents almost as old as civilization. "The agora— the ancient Athenian market where the citizens of the first democracy gathered to buy and sell—was more than the site of transactions; it was also a place where people met and sized up one another. It's where the word got around about those who transgress norms, break contracts. In a virtual community, idle talk—where people learn what kind of person you are, why you should be trusted or mistrusted, what interests you—is context-setting." In the online marketplace, *how* you are speaks just as loudly as what you say.

# 6 | Schmoozing: Making Connections Without Soliciting Business

NEWS FLASH: SAVE YOUR TIME, SAVE YOUR MONEY
The forum is being flooded with messages and library submissions from people *trying* to use the forum to sell something or develop business. If this is your primary purpose in using the forum, save your time. Nineteen sets of eyes of forum staff members see your ads and remove them from view. Repeat offenders are subject to losing forum privileges.
—Paul and Sarah Edwards,
Forum Administrators (SysOps)

If you had entered the Working from Home forum on CompuServe on February 12, 1995, the notice above would have greeted you. (I condensed it slightly.) It reminds me of those signs, hand-lettered and askew, that a cartoon hero encounters at the foot of the long climb to the moated castle: *Turn back now!* Just as the intrepid hero gathers courage and proceeds, however, after reading this chapter you too will be equipped to forge on ahead safely. Armed with the knowledge of what will arouse the wrath of forum guardians, and what earns their blessing, you can blend right in with all the schmoozing *and* develop business.

## Schmoozing Wins, Soliciting Loses

If the Yiddish word *schmooze* is foreign to you, don't worry. It denotes a cozy kind of conversation that people of any ethnic background or nationality can enter into and enjoy. Unlike some cold-blooded versions of networking that became popular in the late 1980s, its object is not collecting as many business cards or E-mail addresses as you can. Nor is electronic schmoozing aimed at making distant friends (though that often comes about as a by-product). Rather, it's an interactive tool for building remote—but otherwise real and beneficial—business relationships.

I doubt very much the Edwardses will mind my explaining to you the spirit and mechanics of schmoozing, because for this method to prove rewarding, you must in your heart and soul actually value person-to-person business relationships—which come pretty close to the official purpose of a forum like theirs. Phoniness eventually rings as hollow on a computer screen as it does in a used-car showroom. And you'll quickly get bored if you cynically go through the motions of schmoozing with your arm ready to stretch out and grab the golden ring. So I'm assuming that you want to meet people who share your business interests and are prepared to spend time at your computer participating in discussion. And after pondering Chapter 5, you have an idea of where you wish to fish and how you'd like to come across. You still need to understand how to avoid committing the grand transgression of soliciting, because it's very easy to step over barely visible, rarely pointed out lines without realizing it. Let's begin by looking at two clearly acceptable examples of schmoozing and two examples of soliciting that would be decidedly unacceptable in most online discussion areas.

*Schmooze #1*

To: all
From: Ron Tyler
Re: Etiquette?
Does anyone know the appropriate way to address a

supreme court justice? Is it just "your honor" or
something else? We got a reservation at my bed &
breakfast inn from one, and I don't want to make a fool
of myself! Thanks, Ron.

*Schmooze #2*

To: Geri Burkhardt
From: Bruce Han
Re: ADA
I disagree with what you wrote about the disabilities act
being a terrible burden on small businesses. In my
seventeen-person accounting firm, we installed a ramp
before we ran public seminars in our conference room,
and bought a TDD machine for an employee who lost his
hearing suddenly. Total cost for both: $5,500. The
former gives us community good will (and one or two
extra registrations) when we write on our brochures
and ads "Wheelchair accessible." And the latter saved
us the cost of recruiting and training someone new.
Bruce Han

*Solicitation #1*

To: all
From: Ron Tyler
Re: Vacation ideas
With the incredibly frigid weather in many parts of the
country these days, your thoughts may be turning
south. If so, there's no friendlier, more interesting
destination in Florida than Key West, and no friendlier,
more interesting place to stay there than the
Buccaneer Bed & Breakfast. E-mail me for complete
details on a special weekend package deal in Key West!

*Solicitation #2*

To: Geri Burkhardt
From: Bruce Han

Re: ADA
Geri: Did you know that the cost of compliance with the
ADA is a legitimate business expense, and therefore
fully deductible? Our full-service accounting firm
specializes in helping small businesses like yours keep
your hard-earned profits legally out of the hands of
Uncle Sam. We're friendly, experienced and affordable.
Let me know if you'd like to set up a no-obligation
appointment.

Did you notice significant differences? Schmoozing is purpose-
ful chitchat likely to be of interest to others, while solicitation involves a blatant invitation to do business. Schmooze #1 consists of
one of the most common forms of appropriate discussion, a
business-related question. Note, though, that Ron's question sets his
business in a highly favorable light likely to make others curious to
know more. If a curious someone does ask, "Where are you located?" and then, "Geez, Key West—I was thinking of going there
in April. Tell me about your B&B," he's allowed to present the selling points of his business to his heart's content. Schmooze #2 consists of another common form of participation, contributing views
on an issue. Here Bruce responded substantively to a comment by
Geri and subtly injected the description, "my seventeen-person accounting firm." Over time, if Bruce continues to post reasoned, so-
cially enlightened arguments and experiences linked to his name
and a phrase like "my seventeen-person accounting firm," regulars
needing accounting services are going to turn to him.

Solicitation #1, addressed to "all," has no purpose or context
other than conveying Ron's marketing information. It also has no
discussion value or informative content—you wouldn't learn anything by reading it. Note too that it ends, like any good advertisement or direct-mail piece, with a call to action. Although schmoozy
in tone, it comes across unmistakably as a sales pitch. It would
therefore be removed from or provoke criticism in every area that
enforces a "No commercials" rule. Solicitation #2 reminds me of
classic ambulance chasing—as in lawyers going to the funerals of
accident victims and tucking their business cards in the suit pockets
of the family members. Here Bruce joins an ongoing discussion but

instead of furthering the interchange, he injects his selling agenda where it's beside the point. As in Solicitation #1, Bruce recites his selling points and concludes with an invitation to call him. In addition, several phrases crop up in his note that one rarely encounters outside of marketing pieces, such as "small businesses like yours," "hard-earned profits," "the hands of Uncle Sam," "affordable," and "no-obligation appointment." Bruce does offer some helpful information about the deductibility of ADA compliance expenses, but he then switches unnecessarily to selling mode.

"People who haven't been working for themselves don't know that there's any other way to market besides advertising," says Alice Bredin, who has been a home-business expert on Prodigy and writes a column on home business for *Newsday*. "They assume that marketing means setting up a billboard somewhere by running big ads on radio, TV, or in a magazine, and if you can't afford that, well, at least on online services you can slap your message up in front of people's eyes and they are going to buy from you. Actually, the reverse is true. Being online is like being at a party, and the other people there aren't likely to buy from you if you just come up and tell them what you do. But after you talk a while about where you're from, ask them about their business, you exchange information, maybe then you've made a business connection." It's foolish to think that one note you wrote in half an hour is going to perform magic for you, says Bredin. "Instead, when someone posts a note, take off your salesperson's hat, or at least tilt it to the side, and give that person some help. Get a little relationship going, and they'll get a trial run with you that might get them wanting more."

If I've convinced you of the value of sticking to schmoozing and avoiding flagrant selling, here are some guidelines for promoting yourself unobtrusively and staying out of trouble:

*Do ask questions that enable you to describe what you do.* It's fine not to know everything. Just make sure your questions aren't too elementary and don't cast doubt on your ethics. Investment banker Fred Richards says he sometimes sees questions "so basic that it's obvious the person asking has no experience whatsoever, like 'is it cheaper to send things by mail or by UPS?' Just call and ask!" Another time, someone in mail order was asking about having to pay sales tax to other states: "Can I get around this?" Rich-

ards remembers giving the person a stern warning about the
consequences of not going by the book.

*Do answer questions from others you're qualified to address.*
Even when the topic isn't smack on target with your service or
product, your reputation with the group rises whenever you demonstrate that you know your stuff. Generosity makes a good impression too. Paradoxically, in this medium, selfless sharing of
information sells.

*Do contribute to discussions that put you or your business in a
favorable light.* Taking a strong stand is fine so long as you can
back up your position with facts or experiences and stay in control
of your responses.

*Do be constructive in tone.* Avoid sarcasm, put-downs, and personal attacks—even if someone throws verbal digs your way. See
Chapter 19 on ways to avoid reputation-damaging conflagrations.

*Do stay focused on the announced topic.* "Nothing is more irri-
tating than to go into a thread marked FREELANCE WRITERS NEEDED
and find a discussion about restaurants in Omaha," says
CompuServe member Kathy Sena, who adds that the problem has
a name: thread corruption.

*Do offer valuable information.* Ron could have turned his "Vacation ideas" solicitation into a solid discussion starter by continuing
after "there's no friendlier, more interesting destination in Florida
than Key West" with a description of its attractions: the Heming-
way connection, its typical February temperatures, the tolerant life-
style, its accessibility by car and air, etcetera. By setting himself up
as someone knowledgeable about Key West, he's more likely to
make a memorable impression in this medium than by pushing his
B&B directly.

*Do slip in offhand curiosity provokers.* One of my first posts on
Prodigy succeeded in this category when I posted a message that
mentioned the fact that my book *Smart Speaking* was going to be
featured on the Oprah Winfrey show that Wednesday. Barb Tomlin,
president of Westward Connections in Albuquerque, New Mexico,
and at that time board leader of the Home Office Board, became
curious enough to watch the show, ask me to tell her more about
myself, and then invite me to become a special contributor (see
Chapter 12) on the topic of media and publishing.

*Do balance getting with giving and showing off with humility.* Although author Charlotte Libov spends a good deal of energy online sniffing out publicity opportunities, she says she deliberately tries to give back as much help as she's received. "I share my contacts with people who have similar interests, and I take part in nonpromotional discussions," she says. "If I feel I've been promoting myself a lot lately, I'll hold back, or approach someone privately, by E-mail."

*Do check messages frequently.* Glassblower Strat McCloskey of Newcastle, Delaware, got the opportunity to present a seminar when someone else couldn't make it at the last minute because he was the first out of fifty people to respond to the online appeal for a replacement.

*Don't expect results from vague questions or answers.* "Nobody is going to respond helpfully to a question like, 'I need some help with taxes.' It looks lazy, as if you haven't put any energy into it yet at all," says Alice Bredin. "But if you make your question more specific—as specific as you can—people will respect that and put energy back toward you." Likewise, the more examples and details you can offer as advice, the more you showcase your expertise.

*Don't use all capital letters, even in your headline.* Online, people consider that overexcited, the equivalent of shouting, and it makes them want to cover their ears—oops, their eyes. An extended patch of uppercase letters also slows down reading.

*Don't irritate discussion participants with advertising stunts.* Don't use gratuitous exclamation marks, empty superlatives, self-serving exaggerations, unsubstantiated boasts, and other symptoms of hype, such as words like *amazing, revolutionary, breakthrough, unique, fabulous* or *extraordinary.* Avoid any sort of promise or offer, so that you keep a safe distance from the verboten territory of advertising.

*Don't post the same message repeatedly.* Charlotte Libov recalls getting her knuckles rapped when she posted announcements about the appearance in paperback of her book, *The Woman's Heart Book,* in several sections of the same forum. The forum guardian objected not to the content of the message, but to its repetition. While Libov is correct that some people have automated software set up so that they read only certain sections, it is also true that some folks would encounter her note over and over. A solution: Stagger the timing of multiple posts and vary the wording appropriately for each site.

*Don't carry out "bombing runs."* Several CompuServe veterans used some variation on this term to denote the practice of scattering one message almost indiscriminately throughout the service and then ending with, "If you want to know more, please E-mail me rather than reply here." The impersonality implied in your scatterfire is offensive enough. It's also insulting to the regulars to say you're too busy or not interested enough to hang around their neighborhood for responses.

*Don't expect instant results.* "I've seen people come on a board, introduce themselves as a hotshot, and two weeks later they're gone. A week after that someone has a question for them, and they're not there," says Peggie Hall, owner of Peal Products in Atlanta, which sells marine-sanitation products. "After I first went on the Sailing forum on CompuServe, introduced myself and started answering questions, it was three or four months before someone requested a catalog. In a year, though, we've done more than enough business to justify the expense of being online."

*Don't mention fees or prices unless your are asked.* Even then, you might be better off providing them privately. A reasonable rule of thumb: If you don't normally include fees or prices in ads or a brochure, don't quote them publicly even when you're asked. One exception I can think of is a response to a discussion concerning prices. For example, no one will object if someone has asked, "Anyone know where I can get quality bulk three-and-a-half-inch disks for less than fifty cents each?" and you respond, "We sell name-brand disks, guaranteed, in lots of one hundred for thirty-two cents each."

*Don't ask for the order.* Lawrence Seldin, author/publisher of *Power Tips for the Apple Newton,* got reprimanded several places online for using the words *to order.* Complaints vanished when he said, "For more information, please contact me by E-mail." Instead of asking for the order, slip in some information that would catch the interest of someone in your target market, and let them approach you if they wish more information. If Ron Tyler added just a little to Schmooze #1 above as follows, he'd probably inspire someone to respond, "You're in Key West? We were just talking the other day about going there. Can you send me a brochure?":

> Does anyone know the appropriate way to address a supreme court justice? Is it just "your honor" or something else? We got a reservation at my bed & breakfast inn from one, and I don't want to make a fool of myself out here on the sands of Key West! Thanks. Ron Tyler, owner, Buccaneer Bed & Breakfast

Finally, accept the fact that what gets perceived as a solicitation will vary from group to group. In borderline cases, the overall spirit of a note may determine whether it attracts criticism or not. For instance, in the following message Perry Smit let readers know that he's available to be hired, but he did it in such a charming way, tucked into an irresistibly friendly invitation, that none of the patrol officers on CompuServe pulled him over for it.

> I LOVE MY AMSTERDAM
> Hello everybody,
> I have seen a lot of cities: Sydney, Paris, Munchen, Brussels, Antwerpen, Frankfurt, etc. Beautiful cities but you never feel what you feel when you are in Amsterdam.
> From the smell of the dogshit to the smell of the Heineken bier coming out of the cafes, it really got something.
> From busy businesspeople to the junks on the street. In one day you can see all kind of people from all over the world.
> From the jingle bells of the trams to the chattering of people on the leidseplein. When you have never heard that noise, then you never been really in Amsterdam. Amsterdam, you have to feel it.
> When you have plans to come over, then let me know. If it is for business I can bring you in contact with the right prospect that you are looking for. When you want to

come for a visit then let me know and I tell you more
nice things that you have to see, hear, smell and to feel.
What are the nice things that I have to see, hear, smell
and to feel when I come in your city?
Kind regards,
Perry Smit
International Business Services (Holland, Amsterdam)

Two hot prospects, planning a trip to Holland, responded, along
with three people wishing to set up a similar service in their city
and three people sending back humorous portraits of their beloved
hometowns, Smit told me. I wasn't surprised.

# 7 | Schmoozing: Understanding the Medium

"The medium is the message," wrote Marshall McLuhan in his 1964 book, *Understanding Media,* meaning that the same material won't have the same impact on the cover of a magazine as on a flashing neon sign. Not only does every communication medium affect our sensibilities in subtle ways, it also imposes an invisible grid of possibilities and pitfalls on participants and onlookers. McLuhan's perspective explains why people who listened to the 1959 U.S. presidential campaign debates on radio thought Nixon had won, while those who watched on TV hailed Kennedy as the winner—and why I got clobbered on CompuServe by what I thought was an utterly safe, carefully reasoned, constructive post.

Puzzled by the way several people were using the word *scam,* I looked it up in several dictionaries and presented a logical dissection of its meaning. To illustrate a point, I made the kind of argument I used to offer in college classrooms: "If you use the word *scam* in this sense, then it would allow you to label a scam my course where I teach people how to get published, since in fact very few people do go on to get published, percentage-wise, after taking the course. Obviously, I don't believe my course is a scam and no one has ever made any such complaint." What happened next mortified me. Within a matter of hours, the thread evolved into a debate assuming that my course *was* a scam. Like the hapless Sorcerer's Apprentice who only made a disaster worse, the more I tried to mop up the damage, the more people spun off on their own, disconnected from my original post, discussing me in the same breath as bona fide scammers.

The lesson couldn't have been more dramatic: A discussion group is not a lecture hall. I had no power to set the ground rules or the context, or to control what my audience did with the thoughts I shared. Their agenda could and did differ from mine, and while I could watch my comments being taken out of context and distorted, any protest I made about a misreading had no special claim to attention. As this example shows, the bulletin-board medium can trip you up if you don't appreciate its peculiarities. Here are the fruits of my observation and experts' analyses, along with ways to up the chances that you become the beneficiary and not the victim of your efforts to schmooze.

## Joining the Stream of Pieces

To exploit the potential of the medium, you must understand the following characteristics:

*Participants choose which discussion threads to read by their headings.* Unlike newspaper headlines, which appear immediately atop their articles, online headings almost always appear separately first in a list detached from the content of messages. The more your heading points to the specific subject of your post and to your intention, the more likely you are to snag the audience you want. Consider, for example, these vague or lifeless headings and their improvements:

Research Question (murky)
Do You Read Fine Print? (clearer)

Choosing a DTP Program (weak)
Pagemaker vs. Ventura: Help! (stronger)

Q about "Who's Who" (bland)
What's What about Who's Who (snazzier)

What adman David Ogilvy wrote about ads in newspapers and magazines applies even more online, I believe: "On the average, five times as many people read the headlines as read the body copy." A limit of sixteen to twenty-four characters in headings may force you either to use standard space-savings devices, such as "Q" for "question" and "DTP" for "desktop publishing," or to make some up. Whenever you respond publicly to someone else's message, of course, your reply bears their heading—unless you deliberately create an offshoot with a related heading.

*In an environment of ever-looming information overload, brevity is at a premium.* Not only will you provoke irritation when readers wade through screen after screen of something that could have been stated in two sentences, but many of those readers will have paid incrementally more to look at or download your bloated time-waster. State your piece simply and clearly and sign off, preferably within twenty lines or less. If you have much more than that to say, either apologize at the beginning of your message or summarize it and invite those interested to ask for more. Avoid the temptation, if your software makes this easy for you, to include the entire message you are replying to before you add your comment. Pare your quote of the previous note to the bone, so that it sets the context, then get to your point.

*Newcomers to the medium and to your discussion can and will look in on an exchange at any moment.* This implies two imperatives if you're online to build your business. First, resist the temptation to become too clubby with others who post regularly. Abbreviations and obscure in-group references are fine when you really are hanging out only with each other, or when you only wish to socialize. A public response like "ROTFL—doesn't it remind you of Saratoga?—H.H." may make its recipient smile, but it sends the message to others that you're online for fun and relaxation, not for business. I'm going to take a strong position on this and recommend that you *never* use special online slang like "ROTFL" for "rolling on the floor laughing" or "<BG>" for "big grin," no matter how prevalently you believe they are understood. Be inclusive rather than exclusionary, and you'll reap the rewards of a welcoming attitude.

Second, try to restate your business identity or business message in every follow-up post. You have tossed away a valuable opportunity when people come across a message from you like "Sure, I'll be glad to send you a copy. What's your address?" or "It costs only $20 a month for as much time as you want." Compare the effect of rewording those replies as "Sure, I'll be glad to send you a copy of our free report on keeping your tropical fish healthy. What's your address?" or "The Internet access provided by our company in 75 major metropolitan areas costs only $20 a month for as much time as you want." And unless your online area discourages the practice (see below, Local Differences), sign every post with at least your whole name and your business name, business slogan, or a revealing occupational title. For example: "Norris Kruntz, Financing for 'Unfinanceable' Upstart Businesses."

Never assume the entire audience knows what you do just because the regulars do. Take a cue from skilled radio talk-show guests who know that listeners are continually leaving and joining them; they always toss in phrases like "As I'm always careful to tell my therapy clients" or "As I explain in Chapter Two of my book, *MegaBusiness Secrets. . .*" Sandwiched amidst substantive information, this slides by as a clarification rather than as huckstering. Recognize that even the regulars may have only a shady understanding of your scope of business. Over the space of a month or two, I interacted with a fellow named Dan Veaner, from Lansing, New York. Although I connected him with the product he had created, called "Catalog-on-a-Disk," until we exchanged E-mail messages for some reason, nothing he said led me to understand that this was a program for creating a catalog on disk rather than a singular disk-based catalog for specific products. It's a good idea to develop and test a brief spiel that truly communicates what your company does and then insert it as appropriate. For instance: "As you may know, we have created a program that anyone can use to place their catalog, complete with interactive order form, attractively on an IBM-compatible disk."

*Anyone can comment or criticize.* Unlike online conferences (see Chapter 11), which may have a host, a guest, and ordinary participants, in a forum or newsgroup all contributions appear, at least initially, equal to each other. That means that until people stop and ponder it, an uninformed or misinformed response carries the same weight as an informed response. Don't depend on any authority you may have outside of the group to add clout to your message. Instead, count on your online readers to be skeptical and irreverent. Only two factors make your contribution believed more than an opponent's: (1) how well your argument is reasoned or documented; and (2) your reputation for reliability *within the group*. In the latter case, other members of the group may urge others to pay attention to you because you have previously demonstrated your trustworthiness. Still, credibility online is short-lived; you'll never be able to coast for a long while without pedaling in additional displays of know-how.

In some ways, cyberspace is a radically egalitarian environment. You have the right to mount a soapbox, but everyone else also has the right either to shout you down or ignore your brilliance. Other media upgrade you at least to a podium and a microphone. For example, if you share your information in a newspaper article, people can disagree in a letter to the editor, but not all of those get printed, and you usually get the privilege of the last word. Implicitly the article carries a greater claim to attention than the reply, unlike the free-for-all melee in a forum or newsgroup. Similarly, most promotions you send out into the world lack any sort of talk-back feature. With online schmoozing you can't stop someone from tagging onto your message, "Hey, aren't you the one I sent $30 to last year and wouldn't refund my money?" All you can do is shout back "No!" According to Bryan Pfaffenberger, author of *The Usenet Book,* Intel CEO Andy Grove stubbed his toes against the participatory nature of Usenet when he posted a message in newsgroups downplaying the flaw in its Pentium microchips. That message got sent around everywhere with comments attached like, "Can you believe this?" Grove's response might have had a different effect in another medium, Pfaffenberger says.

E-mail, more than snail-mail, voice-mail, or any other kind of communication, seems to place everyone at the same level. That's great when people respond with interest in how you can help them, not so great when people bombard you—or your suppliers and customers—with complaints for having somehow offended them. I believe this great leveling effect accounts for humorist Dave Barry's comment that he never receives letters through the mail that start off, "Are you the real Dave Barry?" as many E-mail messages that reach him do. If you prefer the role of distant, lofty authority, disconnect your modem immediately.

*Any message is fragmentable, and any discussion can get away from you.* The ability to take your words out of context is almost built into the technology, where someone can select any portion of a previous message to include in theirs. It's usually more difficult and sometimes impossible for a reader to go back and see those words in context. And since many people follow online discussions on an irregular basis, you can't assume that any rejoinder or correction will get seen by everyone who saw the unfair response. "Usenet in particular is like a yard full of snakes—at any time a snake can come up out of the grass and bite you," says Pfaffenberger.

John Glenn, publisher of a guide to translation agencies, heard those snakes hissing after he posted a very casual comment in CompuServe's Foreign Language forum, his prime pond for prospects. In a thread titled "Pornography," someone asked a question about Japanese pornography that commonly appears in that country on CD-ROM. "I chimed in to say that they had them in the U.S. as well, I'd seen them in a CD store the other day. I didn't add, 'Glenn's Guide to Translation Agencies' after my name as I usually did, but I'd joined the forum as 'John Glenn/Glenn's Guide,' and CompuServe added that automatically in the header of my reply." Of the droves of people reading that thread out of curiosity, one asked, "What is 'Glenn's Guide'?" and suddenly everyone drawn there was learning about his product in the puzzling context of pornography. "I got about twenty inquiries from that thread, but it was uncomfortable for me. Someone even suggested it was a good idea to get attention with the word *pornography,* and I had to keep explaining that I hadn't done that."

*Contributions can and do show up twenty-four hours a day.* You're courting disaster if you expect the online world to have any consideration for a nine-to-five, Monday-through-Friday, two-weeks-off-in-summer schedule. One of the most dramatic examples of this I've seen occurred when Sheridan, Indiana–based CBSI agreed to participate in a dialogue on Prodigy about its high-priced business start-up packages. The kick-off announcement went up as mutually agreed upon on a Friday at noon, and it wasn't till almost forty-eight hours later that the CBSI representative showed up online. In the meantime, some extremely damaging claims about the company and numerous "Where are they?" notices remained visible to every Prodigy member without any company response. Where participation is international, those sorts of allegations could build to crisis proportions even overnight. I'm not saying not to sleep, just to be aware that rumors, inquiries, and complaints take no account of your convenience.

As a corollary to this, if you're soliciting business online, respondents will be getting in touch 24 hours a day, 365 days a year. Since telephone calls and faxes will come in day and night, weekday and weekend, be prepared. Turning off your company's fax machine when you go home for the night or the holiday is unacceptable—people in Europe who don't know that it's Thanksgiving or in Nova Scotia who don't realize you're in Hawaii may simply conclude you've gone out of business. The same goes for companies that allow phones to ring forever outside of office hours. Yet if you're a home-based business and allow your business line to ring in your bedroom, the impression you give could be even worse. Before breakfast one morning I called an 800 number for a sample copy of a newsletter I'd seen discussed on America Online. From the sleepiness of the "hello?" it was obvious I'd woken up the publisher. I wondered about the viability of a publication whose creator had either no money or no business sense.

*A public question requires a public answer.* When CBSI finally did show up on Prodigy, the owner of the company, George Douglass, responded again and again to specific, pointed questions with "Call our 800 number and get our tapes." Frustrated participants rejected that answer and repeated their questions, to more frustration. Whatever the rationale, this kind of behavior appears evasive, shady, and manipulative to onlookers. Maintain your credibility by providing as much information as you can, along with appropriate qualifiers, such as: "Our literature contains full details, but basically with the XYZZ program a purchaser receives a 486 computer, a modem, five proprietary software programs, a 453-page manual, and unlimited telephone support for $10,329." Or: "According to the ground rules of this forum I cannot give you specific legal advice. However, I can say that in several jurisdictions petitioners have gotten the courts to overturn prohibitions against giving tarot and astrology readings for pay in one's home."

*Where you can delete messages, be aware that they may never entirely vanish.* They may already have found their way into the archives of the system or of individuals, and system administrators may have easy ways of restoring deleted material, as we learned in the case of Lt. Col. Oliver North in the Iran-Contra affair. Just how hard it can be to recall or correct misinformation online we know from the Federal Communications Commission, which is still dealing with protests stemming from an unfounded 1986 "modem tax" rumor. "Some days we get dozens of messages about the tax, sometimes just a few," sighs an FCC spokesperson. The best policy here: Think before you post!

## Local Differences

At a chamber of commerce luncheon, people may be visibly impressed when you refer to your little law firm as a $4 million business, while at the bar assocation dinner, any mention of dollar figures may provoke raised eyebrows and significant glances. Similarly, the online medium is not monolithic, so that figuring out one outpost's ground rules doesn't mean you've scoped out all of cyberspace. A method of schmoozing that works perfectly well in one locale may violate the norms in another province. The members of the group may be different, or distinctive traditions may be involved. You have to remain observant. Online, Bryan Pfaffenberger illustrates this principle with the example of the newsgroup "rec.backcountry" for avid mountain climbers: "If someone dies climbing, a friend is supposed to post an obituary of a certain type, because in this group death while climbing is noble, a kind of victory," he says. "If you didn't understand this and said how terrible the death was, you'd find yourself at the wrong end of flames."

Be especially sensitive to expectations about so-called signature files. Sometimes nicknamed ".sigs" on the Internet, these function as the electronic equivalent of a business letterhead. Once set up by the user, they get inserted automatically at the foot of all of his or her postings. For example:

```
***********************************************************
*                                                         *
*  Publicity/Publishing Coach        Marketing Makeovers  *
*  Marcia Yudkin, P.O. Box 1310, Boston, MA 02117, U.S.A. *
*  Phone: 1-617-266-1613            Fax: 1-617-871-1728   *
*                                                         *
*  letscreate@aol.com        75200.1163@compuserve.com    *
***********************************************************
```

Since professors and researchers started this tradition, on the Internet this format doesn't usually count as commercial promotion, unless you take it too far. How far is too far? Even the most staid newsgroups and mailing lists seem to tolerate four-line signatures and regard eight lines as too much, and accept a simple description of your line of business but not necessarily a brazen sales pitch like "Call IDP for the best desktop publishing in Iowa!"

However, on the commercial online services you'll have to tone down a signature like the above, or leave off everything but your name and a minimal identifier. "We had to make a rule against the Internet kind of signatures, because they were abused," says Janet Attard, a sysop on GEnie and America Online. "People were posting one-line messages and ten-line signatures." I was severely chastised on a Prodigy bulletin board for mentioning one of my book titles along with my name, although on CompuServe this was not usually considered overly promotional. When in Rome, you might say, it's safest to observe what the Romans do and follow their example, being perhaps a teensy weensy bit more daring than the norm, if you like.

Another issue on which expectations differ is the extent to which people will put up with the same old questions. Participants in newsgroups and mailing lists are supposed to familiarize themselves with the FAQs—Frequently Asked Questions, available in standard places like "news.answers"—and not to bother the regulars with them. By contrast, on the commercial online services a question that has come up a thousand times before will almost always receive an informative, courteous reply, although possibly a "canned" one. This difference makes sense when you consider that in contrast to the no-one-in-charge, no-one-collecting-fees-for-participation Internet, services like America Online and Delphi make money by catering to newcomers and making sure they feel comfortable spending their time exchanging messages.

Before joining in on discussions, you may want to know how long contributions remain accessible in that online region. Some newsgroups and mailing lists maintain archives of all messages, while others don't. On America Online, GEnie, and The Well, your messages stay visible indefinitely, which feels spooky to me for off-the-cuff conversations. I prefer the way postings disappear sooner or later from CompuServe and Prodigy—but you may have the opposite predilection. You may also wish to investigate the extent to which postings are screened, sifted, and possibly rejected or edited. Prodigy maintains its status as a family-oriented service by filtering out messages containing profanity, the sort of thing that I've heard has created problems for some men named Dick. Some moderated groups simply include or exclude offerings, while others may trim an offering in ways objectionable to the one whose name is on it.

Marshall McLuhan coined the phrase *the global village* to describe the effect of electronically linking people all over the world. Jay Linden, an Internet provider and consultant in Toronto, calls the Internet "the world's largest, most diverse small town." Perhaps we just need to change that to "villages" and "small towns" to remind us to check out the local customs before we hang out our shingle and walk up and down Main Street shaking hands.

# 8 | Schmoozing: Advanced Tactics

One week, two people showed up in the PR and Marketing forum on CompuServe looking for me. "Where's Marcia Yudkin?" one wrote. "She wrote me a message and I accidentally deleted it." The other headed her search, "Seeking Yudkin . . . Anyone know how to find Marcia Yudkin? She's the author of a book called *Six Steps to Free Publicity* and she's not listed in the member directory." I rather enjoyed the ring of "Where is she?" and "Oh, here's where she is" from others, and pondered whether it might be clever to keep my member number unlisted. I decided a listing would be smarter and here's why and how, along with other advanced and creative moves in schmoozing that I would recommend.

## Being Findable Online

Although posting regularly in your chosen pond helps people find you, formal mechanisms exist for helping people connect with you. On CompuServe and Prodigy, for instance, anyone can hunt for you by name in the member directory. If you're cursed with a common name—CompuServe has almost two dozen Jane or Janet Smiths listed, for instance—people can narrow the possibilities by tossing in your home state or city. Try to make sure your moniker in the listings matches the way people you do business with know you, which might not be the case if on your credit card you're "James S. Polsky," while everyone besides banks and the IRS knows you as "Skip Polsky." I took the option of staying out of the member directory when I joined CompuServe because they would have listed me by the town of my street address, rather than Boston, my official business location. Once I ascertained that I could switch to my Boston PO box address in their records, I did so.

The member directory of America Online serves several functions. As on CompuServe and Prodigy, people can find your online identification name or number by your name, city, and state. If you go to the trouble of filling out a "member profile," anyone who runs across you online can press a button or two and read what you've chosen to say about yourself. You'll also turn up when clients and peers hunt for members by subject words. For example, typing in "consult*" yielded 250 members, most of whom, I had to conclude, must belong to the service for fun. Almost none of these consultants appeared to have thought of using the profile as an online marketing tool. Although everyone had plenty of space available, most described their specialty with a generic phrase and no elaboration, like "computer consultant." Several listed no personal name, only their so-called screen name, and only one or two included a full business address or phone number. In numerous cases, the business information presented was overpowered by the personal data, like marital status, birthdate, favorite quotes, and hobbies. One man went so far as to list his height, weight, chest and waist measurements, and hair color! A born-yesterday woman listed her birthdate as "8/26/94" and a poor speller called himself a "Personnell/Marketing Consultant." Most astonishing to me were the cynical quotes chosen. Try to imagine any of these impressing a potential client:

"A consultant is someone who eats your lunch to tell you if you were hungry."

"Those of you who think that you know everything are annoying to those of us who do."

"Ask a consultant what time it is—he'll charge you a large fee, borrow your watch, and ask you what time you'd like it to be."

"There are more horses' asses than horses."

"The difference between consultants and prostitutes is: There are some things a prostitute won't do for money."

"If it ain't broke, don't call me."

Such confidence-killing slogans don't belong anywhere near your business identity—even if you do belong to a service for fun. If you wouldn't include something in your professional Yellow Pages ad, don't put it in your member profile!

If you think of this tool as a cross between a business card and a minibrochure, as providing a link for people between learning about your services and taking the step of contacting you, you'll be on the right track. For instance, here's the sort of profile you might put together if you were a literary agent:

| | |
|---|---|
| Screen Name: | Yrlitagent |
| Member Name: | Jennifer Jenns |
| Location: | 555 East West Street, Suite 1101, Gotham, NY 11099 |
| Occupation: | Literary agent, 35 clients, 8 years experience, 100+ sales |
| Hobbies: | Trying to find the next John Grisham or Sue Grafton |
| Quote: | Especially interested in mysteries, thrillers, and romantic suspense. Query first by mail with a synopsis, bio, market analysis, and comparison of your work with the competition. |

An equivalent to such a profile exists on the Internet. Someone who gets intrigued by a comment you made in a newsgroup can "finger" your ID and discover your real name, when you last logged in to the system, and any other information you chose to put on file. Since no one sees this file unless they look for it, it can safely be as promotional as you like. Ask your service provider how to upload your ".plan" file for such access.

Of course, you also make yourself accessible online to the extent that you publicize your E-mail address offline. I hear from readers of my books who spot my E-mail address somewhere who probably wouldn't trouble to write a formal fan letter. Remember that E-mail feels easier than a letter or phone call to many online regulars. Include your electronic address wherever you'd give out your phone number or postal address: on your letterhead, your business card, bio notes for your books and articles, magazine ads, press releases, and the like. Then send copies to your online service. GEnie gives you a usage credit for spreading your E-mail address around publicly.

And don't overlook the cachet of the ultimate guessable Internet address: your own domain name. That is, if you're "PKI Associates," Internauts might try you first at "pki.com" instead of looking you up. That's also infinitely easier to remember than "pki2578.com." If you suspect you might ever wish to use a certain domain name, register it now. Names are going fast, and like 800 numbers, each can only be assigned once. If you were "PKI Training Tools" and "PKI Associates" had already registered themselves as "pki.com," you'd be plain out of luck. Direct marketer Sheila Danzig of Fort Lauderdale, Florida, hurried to register "danzig.com" when she learned that 5,000 applications were backlogged at InterNIC, the Internet registration agency, and that one could reserve a name and use it with any Internet provider, anywhere. Why did she choose "danzig.com" and not her company acronym, "nsmi.com"? " 'Danzig.com' makes our company look bigger and more prestigious," she said, "and this way the name is reserved for my children and grandchildren and great-grandchildren, forever. Each of us can be 'someone@danzig.com.' "

## Feeding a Fan Club

If you already have some standing as a Somebody, you can create a stir of interest in interacting with you merely by announcing your availability to answer questions. Washington, D.C., literary agent Bill Adler arranges what he calls an "online publicity tour" for his clients. After selecting appropriate electronic ponds, his firm posts a notice saying that so-and-so, the author of such-and-such, will be around from when to when to answer questions on the subject of X. During the appointed time frame, the author responds online to the posted questions. Because his firm keeps a computerized master list of Internet newsgroups and mailing lists and of forums and bulletin boards on the commercial services, finding appropriate venues for the tour is a simple matter of searching the list by keyword. "There's been only minor backlash," Adler says. "Everyone likes to have access to an expert."

You don't have to be an author to try this, of course, just have solid, authoritative experience ready to dispense through your fingertips. And if you offer to answer questions on an ongoing basis rather than for a limited time, you have the opportunity to watch an amazing dynamic take shape. Assuming you're at least moderately personable, patient, and credible, other fish in your pond begin to refer questions and point customers toward you along with priceless word-of-mouth praise. If you stick around and treat members of your "fan club" well, they will continue to do valuable marketing for you. Tarry Shebesta, president of Automobile Consumer Services, Inc., in Cincinnati, Ohio, a nationwide new-vehicle buying service, joined CompuServe's Cars forum in 1992 and began answering questions from people looking for specific cars. He always made sure to offer facts about cars and car buying as well as, where appropriate, information about his company's quote sheets for bargaining and its full buying service. After six or seven months, he says, he no longer had to say anything about his company aside from signing his posts, "Tarry Shebesta/ACS." "Someone would show up looking for a car, and a half dozen people would say, 'Call Tarry at ACS.' Just in the CompuServe Cars forum, there are now fifty to one hundred people who have directly done business with us. The rapport we've built—you can't buy it," Shebesta says. "Besides, it feels good to be helping people."

To build and sustain a loyal following, advises Shebesta, consistency and dependability count, not only in the online information you give out but also in the way you treat customers when they contact you to do business. "Your customer service has to be top-notch. We're honest and we do what we say we do." Every morning and evening Shebesta looks through the messages on the Cars forum and answers those for him or on automotive issues he knows a lot about, unless the tone of discussion seems too argumentative. "When someone shows up and attacks buying services in general I don't get involved. Others do it."

Jan Melnik's fan club on America Online took only one month to emerge. "I was the only highly experienced secretarial services business owner around who was also an author," she explains. Orders for her books on running a secretarial or résumé business, or for her newsletter, arrive every day not only from America Online members but from nonmembers who heard about her from her fans. "People are so hungry for information that this is less than soft-sell—it's no-sell," she says. "And I imagine it would happen for anyone who has professional advice to offer that's not readily available elsewhere." With a typing speed of 130 words a minute, Melnik finds it a cinch to blast off lengthy replies to public questions. The E-mail poses a bit of a burden, though, with people sending two- to-three-page letters "pouring out their background. I answer every one and try to keep it personal, but I don't have time to write more than a paragraph or two back to them."

Like Melnik, Bob Coleman, who for a time wrote an official "Great American Ideas" column for Prodigy, tried to reply courteously and briefly to the average of six E-mails a day he received from fans seeking advice. Although it might have saved him time with certain questions that he got again and again, he avoided prepackaged responses both privately and publicly on the Business Board because "when I first trolled around the service, the canned responses really stuck out." Coleman laughs that the two most common notes he got were variations on either "Dear Bob, No lawyer is going to sucker me into paying for him to draw up a contract" or "Dear Bob, I didn't use a contract and someone shafted me." He says it takes good interpersonal skills and flexibility to deal with questioners at all levels of sophistication, courtesy, self-discipline, and initiative. For him the payback included a unique kind of market research, "not structured or analytical, so that you get a good sense of what people really want to know." The second edition of Coleman's *The Great American Idea Book* included a new section on financing ideas because that proved one of the top three concerns of his online questioners.

Besides cultivating fans, who tend to be less experienced than you in your field, you can nourish relationships with peers online. Because I appreciate it so much when others do this for me, I make a point of putting in a good word where appropriate for other experts whom I feel I can vouch for. I can't prove this, but I'd guess that an aura of thoughtfulness associated with your name would help encourage valuable peer-to-peer referrals.

## Schmooze-Compatible Announcements

I don't recommend trying to post a formal press release in an online area designed for discussion. Although less pushy than an ad, it's still "canned," and thus violates the flow and purpose of a forum, mailing list, or newsgroup. But that doesn't mean you need to renounce notifying your market of relevant events, products, and opportunities. Just personalize your announcements, keep them short, and couch them in the buddy-buddy idiom of schmoozing. I've seen appropriately phrased contest announcements, seminar notices, requests for writers, new-product introductions, and offers of survey results get by without complaints. Stress that you're letting people know something they've been trying to find out, not that you have something to sell. Public relations pro Marty Winston used this approach in 1989 after convincing his client, Palindrome, to sell its superior tape backup software separately from the hardware with which it had initially been integrated. "I went into one of the Netwire forums on CompuServe and wrote, "Hey, I just spoke with Palindrome (my client) about the Network Archivist, and they agreed to unbundle the software.' A couple of guys tried it and loved it and started talking it up as a solution. One of them was a reseller and put together a package of Palindrome together with someone else's hardware. I successfully launched the product without any advertisements."

Another way to tone down the "salesiness" of an announcement is to preface it with "People have been asking me . . ." as in "People have been asking me when my PR seminar would be available on audiotape." Naturally this helps only if you've already been hanging around that area and the regulars would believe that you *have* been asked! If you're loath to appear even that self-promotional, you can ask one of your online pals to send you public congratulations. Self-deprecatory or tentative preambles like "I hope I'm not out of line to . . ." and "Is this the proper place to . . . ?" also take the edge off your announcements.

Paradoxically, you come off as less offensively aggressive when you present something new of yours with an outright brag. In this quintessentially personal medium, it must be a distinctly human brag, though, not a hyped one. You want to come across as charming, disarming, or merely understandably excited about something wonderful that has happened. If many people know you, for example, you could post:

> Guess what, friends, we're spreading! Accountability, Inc., just opened our third branch office, in Colorado Springs, in addition to our Denver and Santa Fe offices. As many of you know, our niche is small businesses needing tax-return preparation, financial planning, and bookkeeping. We're thinking of starting to sell franchises next year. Watch out, H & R Block!

Or try a more modest brag:

> A friend suggested the other day I tend to hide my light under a bushel. "When you achieve something wonderful you've got to tell people," he said. OK—gulp—I want to tell you guys that the 1.2 release of my human-resources management software program, Workworks, is selling unbelievably. We've made sales to 240 of the Fortune 500 already, with more getting checked off our wall chart every day. We're having a one-year celebration tomorrow.

Instead of waiting till you have an actual achievement to brag about, you can also attract customers by floating an idea. This worked for me unintentionally when I said I was thinking of putting together a flat-fee package of services and wondered how that approach had worked for others. Questions prompted me to explain what was different about my idea, and I picked up a customer for a $395 consulting package that was still in the testing phase. Don't forget, though, that if you reveal a hot idea publicly you're revealing it to competitors who could snatch it right off their computer screen.

A variation of the float involves asking people for feedback, not on a business concept itself, but something related to it. For example, when you post a draft of a press release and invite helpful comments, people get exposed to what's new and newsworthy about your business. Once a guy working on the final edit of a video asked publicly for advice on whether or not it should be indexed on-screen and for help on whether he had left anything crucial out. "I'm not trying to sell you anything," he emphasized, and I agreed to offer my two cents on his outline. I was slightly annoyed to receive a gargantuan sales letter from him two or three months later, when the editing was finished and he was definitely looking for buyers. Be true to your word if you want to keep the goodwill of those you schmooze with.

## Running a Column

When I was a philosophy graduate student at Cornell University in the 1970s, I had an idea I wanted to get across to the all-male faculty. Instead of making a speech to them—all champion debaters—or issuing a memo that they could glance at and crumple into the wastebasket, I commandeered a section of the chalkboard that took up an entire wall of the departmental lounge. In big letters I printed, *SEXIST QUOTE OF THE WEEK,* and below that a quote from Aristotle. Every week for the rest of the year, I'd post a new quote from one of the greats, like Immanuel Kant, John Locke, or Jean-Paul Sartre. No one ever erased my messages or added graffiti. I didn't sign my name, but word got around that I was the one responsible, and once in a while in the lounge a professor would clear his throat and make a few nervous comments about the interpretation of a particular quote.

Cumulatively my efforts helped remind faculty of one of the more subtle ways in which women students were experiencing a hostile learning environment. My guerrilla communication tactic has an analogy for electronic bulletin boards and newsgroups where you're hoping to convert regular readers into customers. Issue periodic communiqués that challenge or inform group members, and you'll solidify a corresponding reputation.

I call this tactic running a column, because as with pieces appearing regularly under a byline in a newspaper or magazine, you build an audience by expressing a consistent point of view in a specific topic area. Columns should be short to very short, be spaced in predictable intervals, and include material you don't need to burden with a copyright notice. Compared with self-sufficient postings designed for permanent availability (see Chapter 9), columns are more ephemeral and provocative. If they generate dialogue and mostly positive discussion, over time they will probably generate business for you too. Just make sure they're not blatantly self-serving or explicitly promotional.

A CompuServe member from England who wished to remain nameless called his series of conversation starters in the "International Business" section of the Working from Home forum the "International Business Quiz." Under the heading of "Int Biz Quiz ? #111," for example, was this:

111 In a program I saw, John Naisbitt (the Megatrend guy) lives up in some place in the mountains in a 1300-soul town. Nice, expensive houses. Everyone is on an InfoZone network. The British TV commentator seemed worried about this view of paradise. Seeing it as a form of escapism. In fact the whole program was expressing concern at the American approach to teleworking and the destruction of former societal structures. Naisbitt described himself as a "globalist"; some might see him as a little-towner. Your opinion please?

On Prodigy, a video producer launched a series with a note on how to produce low-budget infomercials—but then didn't keep it up. Perhaps he concluded that a lack of immediate response meant no one was reading and paying attention, which wasn't so.

Mike Holman of Queens, New York, sees his column, called "Info Highway Lessons," as more of an educational service than a provocation. A banker by day, Holman is working toward venturing out on his own by posting his weekly column on Prodigy's Black Experience Bulletin Board (under "Black Enterprise"), on

CompuServe's Afro forum, on his own BBS, and in the Usenet group "soc.culture.african.american." "I'd had to learn on my own," he says, "with a high frustration level, and this is my way to give back to the online community. Some people feel that they can't obtain technological skills, and this helps make technology accessible to them. But I also believe it will benefit my business. Your business progresses when people know what you're contributing."

Whether you assume the role of educator or provocateur, an online column offers a continuing opportunity to win name recognition and respect among prospects. Suppose, for example, you're a commercial real estate broker. Once you find a group that contains a lot of prospects for your services, you could provide a paragraph or two of commentary on how the week's economic news might affect the buying, selling, and leasing of real estate. Or you could highlight a sale of the week (not necessarily yours) and what it shows about trends in the market. Or set up a series of myths about real estate to expose one by one.

Let's say, on the other hand, that you're an editor who helps small-business owners improve their sales letters, brochures, and ads. Once a week you could analyze (disguised, perhaps) a specimen that landed on your desk that badly needs your tinkering and polishing. You could reprint, as *The New Yorker* has for years, bloopers in newspapers or press releases. You could offer an educational series on punctuation—one week a light disquisition on the semicolon, another week dos and don'ts for hyphens. Short and informal notes win the day here.

You generally won't need anyone's permission to run the kind of column I'm talking about. Make it seem casual but consistent, and respond promptly to any objections, praise, and inquiries sparked by your messages. Like Miss Manners or Dear Abby, use the same header every time, and then below the heading, write, "Second (or twelfth) in a series." You'll know you've piqued the right kind of interest when people ask you how they can get ahold of previous installments, or the whole series. If there's constant turnover in the group, you could even rerun the series after you run out of ideas, explaining in the first message of the reprise that you'd been asked to do so. For example, novelist Harry Arnston posts his fifty-three-part "Novels 101" lessons all at once on Prodigy's Books & Writing Bulletin Board several times per year.

In most active groups, you'll get maximum effect if you space the installments at intervals of a week. You could run a column at your World Wide Web site (see Chapter 13) as well. There it offers a powerful answer to the question, How do I get all those sightseers to come back? If you resist the urge to make all of your past sallies accessible right there, those you hook won't have any other way to keep up besides adding you to their regular Net-surfing route.

# 9 | Posting Free Information

"I wrote a piece of Windows code that solves a common problem, and posted it in a forum library," says Terry Richards, a computer consultant in New Brunswick, New Jersey. "From there it spread to several Internet sites, America Online, at least two shareware CDs, and a number of BBSs. The code is free for private use, but I charge for inclusion in a commercial product. The real benefit, though, comes from people who have seen my work and want to hire me to have other things done. After I posted the code, customers from all over the world got in touch. I was able to quit my regular job, now work from home and travel at their expense. The really great thing is that they call me—I never have to make a cold call! It has completely automated my marketing."

If you have a friend or relative who ties up their phone line for hours downloading software, you may have thought that the obsessive pursuit of files was limited to the computer field. Not so. Twenty-four hours a day, people hunt online for free tips on everything from recovery from bankruptcy to vegetarian nourishment for kids. Hence almost any business can benefit from making reports and articles available for free to hungry information seekers. Direct-mail specialist Susanna Hutchinson of Wichita, Kansas, posts one article a month in a dozen forum libraries on CompuServe and on three Internet newsgroups. In an average week, these bring her three to five faxes, five phone calls, and up to twenty E-mail inquiries. "These are *very* serious prospects," she says, "especially those who pick up the phone. Some of them have read all of my articles and not only know I'm competent, but feel they know me." Around five percent sign on as clients, willing to pay her fairly high writing fees.

Unlike the intensive time commitment necessary for effective schmoozing, file posting involves doing something once and then passively reaping the benefits. If you've already written various things for different purposes, it's a cinch to adapt them for posting. Here's how to take full advantage of the power of the online environment to put evidence of your talents in front of those who need you precisely when they are searching for help.

## Pulling Treasures from Your Drawers

To give you an idea of the sorts of goodies out there for the taking, on GEnie, looking up "bonsai" on the Gardening Roundtable yielded two articles by someone named Karl Van Sycle of New Horizons in Bonsai in Washington, D.C. On the BBS of my local writers' organization, I was able to browse articles about tax problems specific to writers, uploaded by Peter Desmond, who both prepares taxes and writes. On the Internet, I found articles from back issues of *Wired* magazine that I found so interesting that it encouraged me to give the publication a closer look. In hooking electronic treasure hunters, the first step is to dredge up or create something they'll be overjoyed to find. You include an invitation to readers to contact you to buy something, hire you, or at least talk business. Finally you post the file and describe it so serious prospects for your business will want to peruse it. Just remember that your information will be posted outside of a sales environment, so that people will be expecting the file to have a ratio of at least 95 percent valuable information to 5 percent marketing or sales talk.

You may have something you've already done that can serve as a lure for customers or clients online. Think about these categories of temptation:

*Samples or excerpts.* With software the sample might be a demo version that motivates users to buy the full-featured edition or a clever solution that inspires those needing programming to call, as with Terry Richards. You can edit and post for permanence a message thread from a newsgroup or forum where you helped someone solve a problem. If you publish any sort of newsletter, or have authored a book, make tantalizing portions available.

*Adaptations.* If you've ever presented a seminar, your handouts may serve as a perfect skeleton for a piece worth posting. Or perhaps you wrote a client proposal that you can turn into a "white paper" on your industry. Maybe you already have a fact sheet such as "Myths and Realities about Pawnshops" or a customer briefing like "How to Choose a Printer"—just transform it into the format recommended below. Even a list you've compiled, like bookstores that welcome self-publishers or famous quotes on procrastination, can qualify if it relates to your area of specialization. I converted four press releases from my files into an article format, posted them, and received not only orders for my booklets but in the first three months seven or eight requests to print them in business magazines.

*Original articles.* If you can't find hidden wealth in your file cabinet, write something. Seven hundred to fifteen hundred words—the length of a magazine column—is ideal. "Short enough to prevent boredom, long enough to be substantive," suggests Susanna Hutchinson. For best results, keep the focus practical and reader-oriented, as in:

- 12 Ways to Keep Your Aquarium Fish Happy
- How to Be Your Own Private Investigator
- What You Should Know about Home Inspections and Why
- Eight Investment Mistakes You May Be Making
- Backcountry Camping without Deprivation
- Dos and Don'ts When Upgrading to OS/2

In-depth reviews of books or other resources may also give you a chance to show off what you know. Blatant sales letters and catalogs are unwelcome almost everywhere online, so just keep them in your office ready for the follow-up stage.

## Where and How to Share

BBSs and all of the online services except Prodigy accept uploads of informative files, with a fairly standard set of procedures and rules. I'll cover these before I discuss your more complicated set of options on the Internet. Although throughout this chapter I'm emphasizing providing substantive information online, a related strategy involves creating a free booklet on paper and announcing its availability via "snail-mail" during schmoozing in forums or newsgroups. Whenever she spots relevant questions in CompuServe's Sailing forum, for instance, Peggie Hall of Peal Products in Atlanta responds, "We've written a piece that's not sales literature called 'Marine Sanitation: Fact vs. Fiction.' We'd be happy to send it to you if you E-mail us your address." During winter, the off-season, Hall says she receives about twenty requests a week for it, "and it's led to more than enough sales to make it worthwhile." Though many have asked her to upload the piece to the forum library, she doesn't think that would work as well for her. "I want people's addresses, and the opportunity to send my sales literature along with the 'Fact vs. Fiction' piece. I want people to discuss it with me, and that wouldn't happen as much if they just downloaded it." Keep in mind, though, that some people search forum libraries who lack the patience to follow the discussions.

If you do decide to place valuable information online, begin by finding the appropriate locations for your file. Library postings always get screened by a human being, and can be rejected for irrelevant subject matter. The bonsai pieces I found in GEnie's Gardening Roundtable, for instance, wouldn't make it into GEnie's Astrology or Scuba Roundtable libraries, even though a few astrologists and scuba enthusiasts undoubtedly have an interest in miniature tree growing. Similarly, a BBS that specializes in customer service will be more receptive to your article on service-training programs than a board devoted to games. However, it's worthwhile to poke around an online service for multiple appropriate locations. For example, on CompuServe the Hong Kong, Netherlands, Crafts, and Desktop Publishing forums, among numerous others, have a section devoted to business or marketing.

Except for software programs, prepare your file with the following components:

*Title.* A confusing or vague title decimates your chances for getting read. Compare, for example, "How Does Your Client Want to ..." with "Sales Letters Without Fear!!!" The latter, posted in America Online's Small Business Center, had been downloaded 1,525 times in three months, compared to the former's 601 downloads in an entire year. Remember that your article title, like the header for a forum or newsgroup message, will compete in a list of other titles for readers' attention.

*Byline.* Under the title, the words "by Yvonne You" (your name goes there) visually emphasize your role in creating and offering the information. For best response, don't leave out the byline.

*Copyright and distribution terms.* Optional. To prevent your piece from becoming misappropriated, it's wise to insert a copyright notice here and a statement of the extent to which you wish to encourage, control, or forbid reprinting and distribution. For example: "Copyright 1995, Jim Author. Not to be reprinted, resold, or redistributed for profit, except with written permission, but may be freely distributed electronically provided that the entire file, including this notice, remains intact."

*Your text.* Follow the instructions in Chapter 14 for greatest readability. Use short paragraphs, subheads, an extra Return between paragraphs, and a line length of sixty characters or less. Make sure it's straight text (so-called ASCII) without any formatting codes.

*Tactful marketing pitch.* Here's your chance to motivate people to call or write you. If you provide a service, describe what you do, specifically and interestingly. This is much more important than providing biographical information such as where you went to school or what your previous career was. If you sell products, describe at least one of them in this space. If the area you plan to upload to allows it, include the price. On CompuServe, for example, the general rule is that you may mention either price *or* your address and phone and fax numbers, but not both. Since the price won't do folks much good by itself, that means to omit the price and include contact information. Keep this section to seven lines or less.

Wait—there are two more components to prepare before you're ready to upload:

*Description of the file.* Most of the time people have the choice to look at descriptions before choosing which files they want to have in full. In five to seven lines, then, motivate someone hooked by your title to want to read and keep your work. I always include my name and either a book title or my telephone number in this section, since people may see it who don't take the next step of downloading the file. When you upload, you'll be asked for this description.

*Keywords.* Except on America Online, the uploading process will also prompt you for words by which the file can be indexed. The more relevant categories you include, the more likely it is that the right people will stumble across your magnificent offering. I always include "Yudkin" along with the subject headers so that someone who finds my work and likes it can easily retrieve it all. For instance, here are the title, keywords, and description for one of my uploads:

Get Your Press Release Read and Used
[Keywords] PRESS RELEASE PUBLICITY MARKETING
NEWS MEDIA YUDKIN
Get your media message out of the trash can and onto
the front page or the evening news by avoiding the four
most common mistakes in press releases.
Tips from Marcia Yudkin, author of *Six Steps to Free
Publicity* (Plume Books).

Since you've already expended most of the labor involved in preparing a library posting, why not spread it around as much as you can? I was surprised to observe that people who post a lot of files on a particular online service tend to have nothing anywhere else. All the services give away a free trial month, so you can use that to increase your marketing reach with just a small amount of additional work. Similarly, placing your files on specialized BBSs costs you only the time it takes to research them and upload, plus perhaps a one-time long-distance phone charge. Posting widely doesn't commit you to spending your time everywhere, since you can direct readers to your phone, fax, and E-mail address at your "home pond."

## Options on the Internet

However many millions of people worldwide have access to the Internet, no method of placing information on the Net places it in front of them all. Experts estimate that in mid-1995, the current darling of the hypemasters, the World Wide Web, was fully accessible to less than 10 percent of those online. Gopher, another Internet storage and retrieval tool, requires no advanced setup and very little technical sophistication for access, but many Internet newcomers simply don't bother with it. Overall, the Internet is such a dispersed, massive information network that the passive approach possible with the commercial online services—simply post your file and wait—doesn't work as well. That is, on the Internet you generally have to post your file *and* do your utmost to motivate people to go find and take the information that you've left there for them. Here are my comments on the possibilities:

*Newsgroups and mailing lists.* Since these are not designed as permanent repositories of information, they offer distribution more comparable to publishing in one issue of a newsletter than placing it in an electronic library. However, I've included them in this chapter because in a few cases you'll be able to adapt a library file for these media. Be very, very careful, though, since you could quickly get overwhelmed with flames if the regulars perceive your offering as inappropriate, irrelevant, or too commercial. Make sure the file is very short—750 words or less—very high in hard-to-find information pertinent to that specific group, and includes a signature file or a no-sell signoff with how to get in touch. See the section on columns in Chapter 8 for more suggestions.

A much longer file will be welcomed in newsgroups if you call it a "FAQ"—Frequently Asked Questions—and design it in that spirit and format. FAQs are highly appreciated throughout the Internet, often archived, and widely read and recommended. They lend their creators worldwide visibility and name recognition among Internet aficionados. Terry Carroll, a law student when he created his FAQ on copyright law, mentioned in the FAQ that he was looking for a job and listed the FAQ as a credit on the résumé that landed him a position. "Its big value," Carroll says, "was that on the CNI-Copyright mailing list, where I'm well known in part because of the FAQ, when I announced I was looking for a job, I got a number of recommendations of firms that were looking. A partner in an Oregon firm who read the FAQ invited me to send a résumé. Later, someone from a major legal publisher wrote, inviting me to send a résumé, but by then I already had a job." Similarly Claire Walters, a writer and computer consultant in East Windsor, New Jersey, spent a few hours a day over several months creating the BBS FAQ and reflects, "Since I'm trying to get the FAQ published, this is a valuable form of prepublicity. It's given me an idea of what the public wants, how long a shelf life the book might have, the demand for something like this, and more. No one has sent me any money (yet), but I received a handmade glass ornament, and someone in Ireland offered to send me good Irish whiskey." Follow the format and approach of other FAQs and suggestions in the official FAQ guidelines, available on the World Wide Web (see Resources).

*Gopher.* This menu-based method of accessing files allows shoppers and information seekers to find your stuff both accidentally and intentionally. Some businesses have invested in full-fledged Gopher "storefronts," where they describe their wares, declare their prices, and automatically take credit-card orders right there. Or they post a catalog and ask customers to order by telephone, fax, E-mail, or mail. SBR, a small-business reengineering consulting firm in Swampscott, Massachusetts, has a series of menus about its services, the background of the principals, and four articles about its philosophical approach on the Gopher server of Software Tool and Die, an Internet provider in Brookline, Massachusetts. The "Gopher mall" approach can range wildly in price, from being included along with your Internet service to $1,000 or more a year. If you have valuable nonsales information that just includes your contact information at the end, you might be able to persuade someone with extra space on a Gopher server to provide your files as either a community service or a personal favor.

*Ftp.* Otherwise known as "file transfer protocol," this tool allows Internauts anywhere to fetch a file you've placed on a computer open to the public. Ftp is so user-unfriendly, though, that only gearheads and Internet veterans seem to know how to use it. I suggest you make files available by ftp only if your target market is highly skilled computer users. And in that case, you undoubtedly already know everything you need to know about ftp!

*The World Wide Web.* Part of your World Wide Web strategy (see Chapter 13) might involve making documents available at your site for free reading and retrieval. If you decide to do this, be polite enough to offer files in a plain-text (ASCII) version that anyone who finds their way there can read. Some business-school professors offered a paper of theirs at their Web site coded in Postscript, setting me off on a several days quest in search of information on how to read the file. After I finally learned the procedures for printing the file on my laser printer, I was able to print out pages 1 and 2 only. Most people in my position would already have given up.

*E-mail.* You can take advantage of E-mail, the closest thing to a lowest-common-denominator tool on the Internet, by offering a free document to anyone who sends a message to a certain E-mail address. A program called a "mailbot" or an "autoresponder," set up by your Internet provider, robotically shoots back your information to any and all who write there. The Internet equivalent to a fax-on-demand system, this saves you the trouble of dealing with every inquiry individually. While most people use this technique for straight catalogs or sales letters, there's no reason you can't set up a mailbot to offer a bait piece that inspires prospects to hire you, or that delivers excerpts from your newsletter (see Chapter 17 for more on mailbots). Note that you'll have to use publicity, ads or notes in forums, mailing lists, and newsgroups to let people know about your offer.

## The Shareware Route

Software developers who release their creations so that users try before they buy have accumulated a wealth of effective methods for spreading their wares and persuading users to send them money. Some shareware distribution methods can apply to information vendors selling something besides software if the material is packaged to resemble a program—in the format of an electronic book. Instead of paper pages to turn between durable covers, an E-book offers a disk that can be loaded into a computer disk drive to reveal on-screen a title page and menu of chapters. The reader chooses a chapter by pressing a key, scrolls through the chapter on-screen, and returns to the table of contents to select another chapter. Because of the format, which usually includes attractive colors and boxes and, optionally, sound effects, an electronic book seems more inviting and substantive—more like a product—than regular old text files. Like software, an electronic book can either be distributed on a tangible disk or compressed into a single file that can be uploaded to the online services, sent by E-mail, or retrieved by ftp on the Internet, then uncompressed. In contrast to original software, however, a technological klutz can create an original E-book. Simple shareware programs (see *Paperless Publishing* by Colin Haynes in Resources) enable virtually anyone to convert text files into an electronic book designed specifically for a DOS, Windows, or Macintosh platform.

In late 1994, I felt a mental lightbulb go off when I was looking through a highly recommended E-book creation program for IBM-compatibles, Writer's Dream, and read, "You can put a commercial in your disk which inspires some of the readers to send you money. For instance, your commercial could introduce another disk-based book you have also written, called Dogs. Dogs is not shareware. The only way the readers can get your excellent dog disk is to send you $19.95. No doubt you see the potential!" I became even more excited about the potential when I tried following the Writer's Dream directions to put together a sample product out of random files. In less than ten minutes I had finished it. It took longer than that, of course, to plan my strategy and write and polish an electronic book called "Get Priceless Media Coverage for Pennies" that included six chapters, an introduction, a bio, and a sales pitch with an order form. I read more about shareware and learned of a venture that distributed shareware through the 20,000-plus member FidoNet BBS network in exchange for a voluntary donation.

Just after New Year's 1995 I received my first product order even before I received a self-addressed stamped envelope back from the Shareware Distribution Network saying that my E-book had been launched on BBSS worldwide. Two months later I learned from another buyer that my E-book had been taken off a BBS and included in a CD-ROM of business shareware. I also persuaded several direct marketers to distribute "Get Priceless Media Coverage for Pennies" to their customers at no cost to me. (One of them pegged its value at $49.95.) In addition, I plan to test online and print ads that would give the E-book away for $2 to cover my postage and duplication costs. I may also do a test mailing to shareware distribution catalogs, and a version will be posted on the World Wide Web. Note that I designed "Get Priceless Media Coverage for Pennies" to have serious educational value in itself and to serve as publicity for my book, *Six Steps to Free Publicity,* and other products. If you want to try this route, consult the Resources section in this book for E-book software and strategies, and upload your creation to as many online arenas as you can.

## Fear of Freeness

A popular saying on the Internet proclaims, "Information wants to be free." Deciphered, this means, "Many people believe all information should be free because so much of it already is." If you sell information in some form—software or books, say—this aphorism may give you the willies. Relax. Yes, cyberspace has more than its share of bootleggers, cheapskates, and pirates, but with intelligent marketing you can get back one hundredfold what you give out for free. Several factors motivate people to pull out their credit card or sign a contract with you when they received something gratis:

*1) They liked what they saw and want more, which they can't get without paying.* Compare a test drive at a car dealer or coming attractions at a movie theater. Or you can provide information free for a while before you announce a membership, sales, or subscription fee. PR pro Dan Janal calls this the "heroin marketing strategy"—give it away until they're hooked.

*2) They want convenient packaging or delivery.* Although we can read the newspaper for free at the library, we'd rather pick it up from our doorstep and read it at breakfast. Similarly, we may prefer to have each issue of a magazine arrive in the mail without our having to go navigating around cyberspace to download it. Laura Fillmore, president of the Online Bookstore, points to what hap-

pened when her company posted the complete text of Tracy
LaQuey's *The Internet Companion* on the Internet in 1992.
"Counterintuitive as it may seem, giving the ASCII files away by
anonymous ftp spurred the print sales of the book. Who wants to
read hundreds of pages in ASCII?"

*3) They want customization of the information.* No matter how
detailed your advice, it can't cover every nook and cranny of someone's individual situation. With almost any subject, if you know
enough and can communicate and apply your expertise, people will
pay high fees to have you help them understand and put into practice what you know. Your consulting business will boom as you disseminate free information. I was happy to learn that a large number
of public libraries in the Boston area carry my books, even though
for each person who checks one out, I receive no money. Nevertheless, those readers can and do sign up for my seminars, recommend
my books to others, and call me to arrange to pay for guidance on
their unique project. The same thing occurs with files I've made
public in cyberspace. John Perry Barlow, lyricist for the rock band
the Grateful Dead and a theorist on intellectual property, has a
point when he asks, "Who needs copyright when you're on
retainer?"

I need to add a caveat here: Your consulting business will boom
so long as you disseminate free information *to those with the
means and the need* to hire you. That's why I'm sold on the commercial online services, especially those with a minimum of teenagers working on term papers and grown-ups grabbing what they
can on someone else's dime.

*4) They want it before it's released to the masses.* Some magazines that post the complete contents of each issue online appear to
keep a one-issue lag, so that just about the only way to read the
current issue is to buy it. Quoting Barlow again, "Most information
is like farm produce. Its quality degrades rapidly both over time
and in distance from the source of production." Many who truly
value the information don't want to wait, just as some folks will
pay to call a 900 number to find out if they won the day's lottery,
rather than suffer the suspense until the winning number appears in
the next morning's newspaper or on the wall board of the convenience store.

Still skeptical that the giveaway approach works? By spending just $415 in online fees in all of 1994, Susanna Hutchinson got 20 percent of her business from online classifieds, 10 percent from her activities on the Internet, and *70 percent* from her articles posted on CompuServe. "I did a lot of experimenting," Hutchinson says, "and fortunately what worked was the cheapest. It has also picked up momentum. My latest article was downloaded 625 times in the first three weeks. I expect to spend even less money on marketing next year because I've found my focus and it works."

# 10 | Answering Reporters' and Authors' Appeals

To: all
From: Tracy Touchstone
Re: article sources needed
Hi everyone! I'm a freelance writer working on a story for a major business magazine on people who have been dragging their feet on getting wired up by modem but have finally jumped on into using online services or the Internet. If this applies to you, please E-mail me at the address above. Thanks . . .

Don't pass over notes like the above. Feeding your story to a journalist may seem a far-fetched, elusive way of wooing clients, but for many it proves more lucrative than, say, E-mailing one prospect who needs immediate help. In this chapter I'll describe the route between appeals like the above and the warm, rewarding glow of media attention. I'll also describe more active tactics people have used to get their tale across to online members of the press. If you're thinking, "Not me! I'm not *People* magazine or *Wall Street Journal* material," hang on a minute. Even a humble Boonesville operation can deserve and reap the benefits of entering into the public eye.

# Publicity 101

Most of all, media coverage bestows credibility. When you tout your own product or service, people discount your pitch—after all, that's you praising yourself. But when you're featured in a newspaper, magazine, radio show, or TV program, it implies objective worth, even when you initiated the contact. People presume that experienced reporters know how to see through flimsy self-promoters. Kimberly Sheasby of Santa Fe, New Mexico, who bills herself as The Secretary Different, responded when a writer for *The Los Angeles Daily News* posted a note seeking people to interview about using America Online to enhance their businesses. Not only did she appear in that newspaper, but also in *The Tampa Tribune* and other papers subscribing to the New York Times Syndication Service. "Without the online connection, my little one-person operation would have been hard put to get such national publicity. My local customers now look at me with awe," says Sheasby.

When the media features you, your message reaches thousands, hundreds of thousands, or even millions of potential customers at no cost to you. Michael Burlingame, a history professor at Connecticut College, casually sent a copy of his biography of Abraham Lincoln to a reporter in Springfield, Illinois, who had helped him with his research. The reporter wrote a story about the book that went out on the Associated Press newswire and ended up in dozens of newspapers across the country, and even in David Letterman's nightly monologue. All those column inches and sound bites undoubtedly spurred the sales of his book. Boston consultant Marcia Layton doesn't need to guess at the effect of national press coverage. When *USA Weekend,* a Sunday supplement with a circulation of 39 million, mentioned her as a specialist in writing business plans, her phone started ringing at 5:30 in the morning and didn't stop until she had received forty calls. "At least three clients came out of that," she recalls.

And when you're trying to build a name for yourself, each time your public reads or hears about you, you come closer to—or cross—their threshold of recognition. Since more only brings more in this arena, I'm always delighted when someone sends me a public message on CompuServe congratulating me for appearing in the pages of, say, *Entrepreneur* or *Home Office Computing.* Invisibly and inexorably the meter of reputation goes up.

But these rewards aren't automatic upon any reply to an appeal like the one at the beginning of the chapter. You must be quick, informative, responsive, and confident to earn your turn in the media spotlight. Let's look at each of these guidelines in more detail.

**Be quick.** "To take advantage of publicity opportunities, you have to check messages frequently and carefully," says Layton. "A notice may only be up once." Cathryn Conroy, a senior writer for *CompuServe Magazine,* says that with a highly specialized request, such as in the RV forum for families who are living full time in a recreational vehicle, she may only receive a few responses. "But for small-business stories, I usually have to take down my message after twenty-four hours because I've gotten fifty responses. That's too much."

**Be informative.** In your response, provide enough information for the reporter to determine whether or not your story is relevant for the article or chapter at hand. "Don't say, 'Hi, this is Bill from Montana,'" urges medical writer Kathy Sena of Manhattan Beach, California, who really has received such responses from doctors. "Give your full name and affiliation and how I can reach you. Recognize that writers are confronting a deadline." Since some reporters will conduct their information gathering through E-mail and others by telephone, provide as many ways as possible for them to get through to you quickly, including after-hours phone numbers. And when it comes to the substance of the requested information, "Be quotable and not too dry," says Sena. "For instance, for a story on indoor pollution, the head of an emergency room referred to the image of the canary in the mine and said, 'It's the asthmatics who will let us know the planet's in trouble.' The artist used his quote as the basis for an illustration. I just keep coming back to this guy again and again as a source."

**Be responsive.** Stay focused on the questions and needs of the reporter rather than your private publicity agenda. When I contacted the director of a media institute for this book, for instance, he seemed more interested in convincing me that the authority the institute was named after had been maligned in his lifetime than in finding out how he could be helpful to me. And the materials he offered to send me never arrived, not even after my second reminder. In responding, it's usually far better to offer too many facts, examples, explanations, and leads to other sources than to hold back. Indeed, the more information you provide that's relevant to the story, the more likely you'll be consulted at a later time on a related topic.

**Be confident.** When reporters put out the word for examples, they aren't seeking businesses whose foibles and faults they plan to investigate and expose. Almost always, they'll cast you in a good light. Remember that sharing your successes with a journalist is just an extension of the kind of communication you're online for to begin with, says Jack Germain, a Barnegat, New Jersey, writer who uses almost all the commercial online services for research. "I'm never overwhelmed with responses when I ask for interviewees. The typical person online is leery of being quoted, just as someone who stands up at a public meeting to speak may get timid when a reporter comes over to them afterwards. People are unnecessarily intimidated by writers." Cathryn Conroy says that many of those she interviews are reluctant to toot their own horn to her. "You have to brag to me, though, so I have something to write. And when I do write it, it goes in in third person, not as a brag. So don't worry, and don't hold back."

## Publicity 707—Taking the Initiative

During a year on CompuServe, I probably saw at least a hundred direct appeals from writers and responded to perhaps fifteen. As you might guess, that response rate doesn't reflect shyness but the fact that I had little of relevance to contribute on many of the announced topics. At least seven of those fifteen times, my response led to a significant mention in a national magazine or another writer's book. Yet you don't have merely to keep your hunter's eye open and then pounce. So long as you're careful how you do it, you can also hunt for media personnel and contact them on their electronic turf.

Charlotte Libov of Bethlehem, Connecticut, for instance, is constantly thinking about opportunities to promote her book, *The Woman's Heart Book.* On numerous forays into CompuServe's Journalism and Broadcast Professionals' forums, she has sought and found people eager to interview her. "I've met about fifteen other health authors online, who will think of me when they're writing about heart disease, someone from *The Los Angeles Times,* and a reporter from the New Orleans *Times-Picayune,* who wrote a piece about my book. I've gotten the most 'hits' among broadcasters, though, since they're so hungry for information—something like eight to ten radio interviews, including the Jim Bohannon Show, which goes out to hundreds of stations and where I went on right after Dan Rather." Libov emphasizes that when she finds someone who identifies himself or herself as a talk-show host or a reporter, her approach is always low key. "My E-mail messages are very self-effacing, something like, 'I don't want to disturb your privacy; I was just wondering if you would be interested . . .' Most people are receptive, and the broadcast people especially have steered me in the direction of appropriate health shows and said I could use their name."

Similarly, Marcia Layton ended up in *USA Weekend* through an enterprising electronic communication. She sent a note to the publicity director at CompuServe saying something like "I just wanted to introduce myself and make you aware of the fact that I'm benefiting a lot from my membership in CompuServe, and if you ever have inquiries from journalists or writers, here's my story. . . ." Not long afterwards, the publicity director thought of Layton when a *USA Weekend* reporter asked for leads.

Over on America Online, Jerry Harmon of South Lyon, Michigan, noticed that an area called "Newsstand" included the E-mail addresses of numerous editors at newspapers. He E-mailed an editor at *The New York Times* a chatty pitch letter describing how and why his wife, who uses a cane due to multiple sclerosis, patented a line of colorful fashion-accessory covers for canes. Harmon received a courteous reply suggesting that he try his local paper. E-mailing the feature editor at *The Ann Arbor News,* fifteen miles from South Lyon, produced a nice article, as did a similar letter mailed to his hometown paper, which ran an article in the section that goes to six different communities. "Some local people cut the article out and sent it to friends and relatives elsewhere who have MS, and orders came in." Kathy Sena, the medical writer, says she's seen doctors approach journalists along the lines of "Hi, I'm so-and-so, I do such-and-such, and if you ever need someone in my specialty . . ." Sena always files their information carefully. "They're a valuable resource, because these are people who want to talk to the media."

If you do decide to put your story forward to a reporter, contact him or her in the form of a brief, personable note—ten lines at most—rather than a formal press release. Beginning with an apologetic phrase like "I know you must be busy, but . . ." or "I hope it's all right to use E-mail to let you know about . . ." starts you off on the right foot for this sort of intrusion. Someone who wants to know more will contact you for additional details. You want to avoid annoying those in a position to give your business publicity, and a simple, informative note that can be scanned in twenty seconds will rarely impose a burden on the recipient. Of more than 2,000 journalists who write about the computer industry who were surveyed by publicist Marty Winston, all but fifty said they objected to receiving full-length press releases via E-mail.

But regular mail is still a viable medium for distributing news about your online activities to reporters, editors, and producers. My book *Six Steps to Free Publicity* (see Resources) contains samples and advice concerning traditional press releases. Don't overlook the trade press in your field—narrowly focused business magazines and tabloids such as *Coin-Op Industry News* or *The Gourmet Retailer*—when you've launched a specialized bulletin board, become a sysop, or published a new Web page. The media's hunger for information on trends and new developments in cyberspace has shown few signs of abating, so that almost anything new and different online can catch a reporter's fancy. Laura Fillmore, president of the Online Bookstore in Rockport, Massachusetts, showed me a full-page article about her company's Internet presence in *Forbes ASAP,* a high-tech offshoot of *Forbes* magazine. She observed, "Yes, they mention that we lost one hundred thousand dollars last year, but if we were a shoe store losing one hundred thousand dollars would that get us into *Forbes?"* If you have your own online site, investigate free print listings. Mike Holman of Queens, New

York, publicizes his multicultural BBS by following the specified procedures to get listed periodically in *Computer Shopper, Online Access,* and *Bulletin Board Systems* magazines.

## The Press Are Not Your Pals

An incident that took place during my research for this book reminded me to end this chapter with a warning. Never let down your guard with a journalist and reveal information that would damage your company if it were broadcast to the world! Here's how the scenario goes: A writer calls to get your story and the two of you quickly build up some rapport. Twenty minutes later you're speaking as frankly as you would with a trusted colleague. But unless you're willing to see your dirty underwear hung out in public, watch your tongue. Many writers will feel more loyalty to their readers than to you. I don't see my role as pulling off exposés, so that when a source for this book confessed unethical behavior, I asked, "Are you sure you want that story connected to your company?" He said, "Yeah, that's okay." After thinking it over, though, I decided not to be the agent of his destruction and sent him back a note explaining why he shouldn't spill those kind of beans with reporters, and why I personally disapproved of what he was doing.

Don't commit any of these potentially devastating mistakes:

*Assuming that a "nice" reporter couldn't possibly do you wrong.* If Mike Wallace of *Sixty Minutes* fame showed up on your doorstep, you'd be on your guard. Yet a heart-to-heart confession is never appropriate during an interview, no matter how well intentioned a representative of the press seems. Remember this basic rule: If you don't want your mother, clients, or competitors to know about it, don't mention it to the reporter.

*Asking a journalist not to print something—in the same breath as saying it.* This still amazes me after more than a decade as a freelance writer. So many people say, "Don't put this in your article, but . . ." The reporter has no obligation after the fact to honor your request. If you don't want it in the article, don't say it.

*Trying to avoid trouble with a pompous "No comment."* This phrase became notorious during the Watergate years and will convey the impression that you're engaged in a coverup. Instead, explain why you can't answer the question, as in, "I'm sorry, that's proprietary information" or "We don't release our sales figures."

*Equating the end of note-taking or tape-recording with going "off the record."* Someone who has tucked away her notebook or turned off the tape recorder hasn't shucked her job. Remember: If you don't want it transmitted to millions, don't say it, even while you're walking her to the elevator!

Finally, prevent errors in media publicity by emphasizing details that matter to you. Writer Lary Crews told me, "Make sure you write a note to your copy editor that my first name really does have only one *r*. Otherwise they'll 'correct' it for you." By taking this kind of responsibility, you up the chances that you'll be proud, not apologetic or angry, about your turn in the media spotlight.

# 11 | Making a Guest Appearance or Hosting a Live Conference

"When I talk about marketing electronically," writes Studio City, California, consultant Bob Serling, "I mean actually placing an ad, getting a response, and attempting to close a sale. I don't mean customer support or long hours giving advice on 'chat' forums." This statement, part of a column titled, "Marketing on the Information Superhighway: Truth vs. Hype," put me in mind of Humpty Dumpty, who in *Through the Looking Glass* said, "When I use a word it means just what I choose it to mean—neither more nor less." By narrowing the term *marketing* to include only one method of attracting customers, Serling casts aspersions on the power of talk to lure prospects closer and closer to the point of money changing hands. But don't be fooled. All the king's horses and all the king's men can't stamp out the effect of online tête-à-têtes.

Up to now we've been discussing asynchronous communication, where ideas go back and forth and around with breaks in time. Whereas electronic messaging resembles public letters, cybertalk is the closest equivalent to face-to-face or telephone conversation. Whether relatively formal and structured or so relaxed that you can endlessly interrupt each other, talk occurs in "real time." That is, the parties involved are all logged on and simultaneously present in some online location. Although your fingers do the talking, and you can't see or hear the people involved in the session, online conferencing and chatting have a cozy "getting-to-know-you" flavor. They help you spread the word about what you do and help build business relationships. Let's consider three roles in electronic talk that might become part of your marketing mix: honored guest, host, and participant.

## Being an Honored Online Guest

Very much like radio and television talk shows, the online services offer guest appearances of celebrities, experts, and specialists. Even more so than with radio and television, appearing as an online guest puts you in front of many more people than those who actually show up at the appointed time in the designated electronic space. This publicity option often puts your name in front of tens or hundreds of thousands, even millions, of members who see announcements of upcoming guest sessions. Guest appearances often show up on the special events banner that greets members of the online service or forum upon signing in. During the appearance itself, those attending have the opportunity to interact with you and get to know you better without your having to leave your office, worry about what to wear, or get concerned about controlling your nervous voice. Afterwards, an edited transcript of the session may become available indefinitely to anyone who did not attend the session. "A lot of freelance writers see the transcripts," notes Lisa Kanarek, author of *Organizing Your Office for Success,* who has appeared on both Prodigy and America Online. "It's a good resource for them." Don't take for granted the "before" and "after" segments of publicity, however; it never hurts to prompt your sponsor about pre-event promotion and whether or not a transcript will be generated for later public posting.

Although authors and luminaries of various sorts predominate among online guests, you don't have to be published or famous to make a guest appearance. A reputation helps, but all you really need is expertise or experience and willingness to share what you know with what may be a very specialized audience—like backpackers, Windows programmers, or people interested in Italy. For instance, if you're an intellectual-property attorney, you might appear to answer questions about copyright on GEnie's Writers' Ink Roundtable or CompuServe's Shareware forum. If you've achieved something noteworthy, like some sort of rags-to-riches entrepreneurial journey, folks on Prodigy's Business Bulletin Board or America Online's Small Business Center might be eager to hear about your story firsthand. Don't be shy about volunteering to be a guest, since if you have something valuable to offer, the service and your sponsor make money from the extra time people spend online to be with you.

Most of the services call the event organized around your presence a "conference," but it resembles a radio or TV call-in show more than any other sort of guest-audience interaction. Basically, you answer questions during the conference from those assembled. Although you'll have a host or a moderator, you'll interact mostly with the participants. Unlike the radio or TV host, who lends his or her personality to the proceedings and shares the spotlight with the guest, online the host's role is mainly to keep the conference rolling along smoothly. Best-selling mystery writer Sue Grafton says she gets the same sorts of questions online as elsewhere—no better, no worse—"but it's an interesting way to reach people you might not reach otherwise. Lots of folks are plugged into the computer world, and they're a different breed of people." The major skill you need for appearing online that you don't need for radio or TV is fairly quick typing. The pace will be quick and relentless for the hour or two that you've agreed to be "on." For that reason Terri Lonier, author of *Working Solo,* calls an online appearance being a "guest typist."

Besides inquiring about pre-event publicity and a transcript being made of the event, here are some tips to ensure that your conference goes smoothly:

*Get a telephone number or two to call in case something goes wrong.* You do not want people showing up and spending money only to find a discussion like, "Where's Rhonda? Gee, something must have happened to Rhonda. Well, folks, sorry, let's call it a night." If your modem happened to choose that evening to retire, at least you'd be able to call the moderator to pass on your explanation to the assembled multitude. Bob Coleman and Deborah Neville, authors of *The Great American Idea Book,* suffered an electrical blackout that made it impossible for them to turn up at their guest appearance on Prodigy, but at least they knew someone to call who let the audience know the circumstances of the no-show.

*Visit the conference space beforehand if possible, so you know how to get there and how to participate.* Graphic designer Heidi Waldman once agreed to moderate a desktop publishing conference on America Online and found herself wandering through rooms devoted to wife-swapping and worse, trying to find the right place. "I had 'Aldus volunteer' on my ID. It was embarrassing!" Following the precept that it's better to be safe than sorry, you might ask your host to meet you there at a certain time the week or day before to practice. Or attend someone else's conference, which would also provide a taste of the degree of interactivity you should expect at yours. Prodigy has the most structured kind of conferences, with an audience member asking a question, the guest simply answering it, and on and on with no interchange or cross talk. Lisa Kanarek told me that she saw the questions for her Prodigy conference ahead of time and got to choose the ones she wanted to answer. Indeed, one novelist confessed to me that he wasn't even anywhere near his computer the night he supposedly appeared on Prodigy—he had received the questions from the coordinator and responded, whereupon the coordinator posted the Q&A session as if it were happening right then. On the other services it's easier to ask the questioner a question and maintain a dialogue—although "polylogue" might also be more accurate when there are five different conversations zipping around, some completely independent of the honored guest.

*Get directions and arrive early.* On America Online, if you don't know the name of a conference room that was created as a "private room," you'll never find it. And if you arrive after the room is already full, you may have trouble entering. You avoid putting your host in an awkward spot and making the audience restless by being there prior to the announced starting time.

*Make sure you double-check the time.* If someone tells you you're on at the Crystal Theater at 7 P.M. in Minneapolis, you know that means Minneapolis time. But if someone in Minneapolis tells you, who live in San Francisco, that the online conference starts at 7 P.M., is that 7 P.M. Minneapolis time, San Francisco time, or, according to a convention on that online service, Eastern Standard

Time? Also, the conference host usually has the power to give you a "free flag" or a credit for the time you spend online during your conference. When this isn't mentioned, ask.

*Be prepared to give brief answers.* On the air, they call these short takes "sound bites." The online medium also prefers dialogue to monologue, and constant momentum. Keep your responses to three sentences at a time, tops.

*Motivate participants to want to do business with you.* There's more than one style of turning an online appearance to your advantage. Harvard law professor Alan Dershowitz, who literally wrote the book on "chutzpah" (nerve), used a heavy-handed approach in his appearance on Prodigy in late November 1994. Notice in this selection from the transcript how he repeatedly turned questions about his career or his profession into opportunities to plug his new novel:

**Q. Mr. Dershowitz, if you find out your client is guilty during the trial, what do you do?**
*A. That is precisely the theme of* The Advocate's Devil. *You can't leave the case. You can't blow the whistle on the client. And you can't defend him as if he didn't do it. It's one of the most difficult dilemmas an ethical lawyer faces. Read* The Advocate's Devil *for the answer.*

**Q. What made you decide to get on the O.J. case?**
*A. It's a case that will educate a generation of Americans about our legal system. I'm a teacher, and I want to be part of that educational process. I wrote* The Advocate's Devil *for the same reason: to teach a wide audience about how our legal system really operates and the complexities of the defense attorney's role.*

**Q. To what particular event, person, or experience do you attribute your success?**
*A. My childhood primarily. I grew up in a wonderful neighborhood in Brooklyn where my parents always encouraged me to defend the underdog. My character in* The Advocate's Devil *has a background very similar to my own.*

Although those attending may not have learned as much as they'd hoped about Alan Dershowitz, he probably did succeed in making them at least curious about his novel and familiar with its title. Jay Levinson, creator of the "guerrilla marketing" books, used a more subtle, give-the-readers-value approach when he appeared as a guest on America Online. Levinson began by summarizing the nine differences between guerrilla marketing and standard textbook marketing, each in one snappy sentence. When people began firing questions at him, he offered pithy, substantive answers, as in:

**Q. What is the best tool for the cash poor young firm?**
*A. Phone, letters, brochure, convenient hours, networking, free any-thing. Other tools for cash poor businesses: flexibility, referral pro-gram, testimonials, barter, fusion!!! Follow-up is the best tool of all, and hardly anyone does it right. To prospects and customers.*

When Levinson slipped in references to his newsletter and books, he was less obtrusive about it than Dershowitz. I certainly don't recommend making *no* mention at all about what you do or what you have to sell—after all, it's a publicity appearance. With practice, you'll learn your most comfortable and effective mix of references to your wares and services and useful information.

*Tell participants how to buy or get in touch.* A considerate host will every once in a while feed you lines like, "Marcia, please tell everyone how they can order your book, *Six Steps to Free Public-ity."* But if that doesn't happen, give out your ordering or contact information every twenty minutes or so, since your audience will be constantly changing as people enter and leave the conference. You can say, "By the way, if your local bookstore doesn't have *Six Steps to Free Publicity,* you can order it by calling 1-800-8YU-DKIN" or "Feel free to E-mail me at 'Letscreate' if you'd like more information about how I can help make over your company's mar-keting materials." When Alfred Glossbrenner makes promotional appearances online in connection with one of his many how-to-use computers titles, he invites people to send a message to his E-mail autoresponder at books@infomat.com for more information.

## Playing Host Online

The official conferences described in the previous section aren't the only "real-time" colloquies taking place online. Some individuals sponsor their own live schmoozing or professional exchange sessions. For example, Wally Bock, publisher of *Cyberpower Alert!* newsletter, hosts a get-together for professional speakers, trainers, and consultants every Monday night on America Online. Most, although not all, of those who attend are fellow National Speakers Association members. "I wanted a place for people to go online regularly," he says. "It started off as a semi-NSA event, but it's mainly my thing now." Bock E-mails announcements of the weekly meetings to a list that grew from 12 to 140 people in less than a year. At times attendance strains against the America Online capacity of 23 people per conference room. The sessions remind me of the monthly networking meetings run for years by my chapter of the National Writers Union in a Cambridge, Massachusetts, bar: People talked shop, greeted old friends, met new colleagues, and exchanged news about opportunities and problems in the profession. As host, Bock subtly but regularly reinforces his position in the vanguard of online developments.

Similarly, Nikki Sweet, a member of the public speaking organization Toastmasters International and a partner in the consulting firm Up Your Business! Inc. in Jupiter, Florida, took the initiative to organize networking meetings for other Toastmasters every Wednesday evening on America Online. Sweet got started by searching America Online's member directory for the word *Toastmaster* and sending E-mail invitations to each of the more than 200 members she found. From posting notes on the Internet in the newsgroup "alt.org.toastmasters" she receives 30 inquiries a week, not counting the E-mail messages from people who've heard about the sessions from attendees. "For me, business is all about creating relationships, and with live conferencing, it's as if you're really there and can express yourself to others spontaneously," Sweet says. "One of my ground rules is that everyone must introduce themself, so that it's good visibility. Someone who finds out what I do might ask, 'Hey Nikki, I want to start a business but I don't know how to do a business plan,' and everyone in the room sees my answer." Sweet has applied to turn what she calls "Toastmasters Online" into an official area on America Online, with all the added exposure that such a status would bring.

A more structured model for online conferencing comes from Jeff Senné, a consultant in Fairfax, California, who specializes in sales leadership, team building, and strategic planning. Senné's vision involves an international community of consultants who use cyberspace to create strategic alliances so that teams of consultants can successfully compete against "the big guys." As part of that effort, Senné hosts two educational meetings a month on America Online, one of them with a guest speaker who submits a five- to ten-page handout before the meeting to those on his list. Senné collects questions from those who show up at the meeting and passes them along to the speaker, saves the proceedings, and E-mails them afterwards to everyone in the network. In the works is a Consultants Online Directory to be posted on the World Wide Web as a sort of virtual mall of consultants. Asked how he expects this whole venture to benefit him, Senné says, "Someone has to stand up and say, 'I know this and this and I'm willing to share it.' I'm an educator and want to educate people about what these new tools offer the business community. I'm doing all this as a volunteer, but it will give me personally an enormous resource pool to draw from."

## Simply Chatting

A final variety of online talk that can benefit your business involves settings where you're neither host nor guest and there's no agenda, just a designated special-interest space. For instance, Dick Sine of Fort Mill, South Carolina, a stamps journalist and entrepreneur, logs on just about every night around 10:20 to attend a drop-in gathering in a conference room on CompuServe's Collectibles forum devoted to stamp collecting. Informally he fields questions about stamps from the ten to twenty folks assembled—"dealers, collectors, journalists, some regulars, some newcomers, ranging in age from twelve to retirement, some from outside the

United States. Conversation is wide ranging, fellowship is excellent," he says. He participates so religiously because he's found it useful in collecting information for his writing projects and developing new product ideas. "CompuServe offers contact with participants who don't necessarily know the stamp establishment," Sine explains. "If you want to have a market-driven approach, where else to get information than from the market? Also, I make friends this way. Later, when people want to buy, they prefer to buy from a friend."

Jan Melnik found it just as useful to attend chat sessions for people in the secretarial or desktop publishing business that were organized for a time on America Online by fellow member Deb Matthews every other Thursday evening. Between fifteen and twenty people, mostly beginners and thus potential buyers of Melnik's book, *How to Open and Operate a Home-based Secretarial Services Business,* would show up. Similarly, when writer Lary Crews has a few minutes to spare, he visits the chat room of America Online's Writers' Club, always open and nearly always, day or night, holding writers eager to talk to other writers about their trials and triumphs. "If I see an opportunity, I'll jump in and say, 'You know, I teach an online writing course here,' and then E-mail stuff about the course immediately to them. That's gotten lots of people to sign up," Crews says about his "Writing the Novel" course, offered under the auspices of America Online's Interactive Educational Services. "Also, more than 400 graduates, some of whom might be in the chat room, generate a lot of word of mouth."

If you enjoy talking, ask around online for live chat sessions in your subject area. Some are publicly announced and others, although open to visitors, require that you wangle a space on the invitation list. Behave as you would at any networking event: introduce yourself professionally and show as much interest in what others do and want to know as in any marketing message you weave into your conversation. Don't focus so much on business that you forget to relax and just enjoy being in the presence of others who are as fascinated by, say, Chinese cooking or furniture design as you are. Reach out person to person, come back, and people will remember you.

# 12 | Becoming a Designated Expert or System Operator

"When I went on Prodigy in 1992, I started a subject heading called 'Ask Lary Crews' and posted a variation on my résumé to explain why I had the audacity to offer my advice," mystery writer Crews of Sarasota, Florida, told me. "To my amazement, I got an average of four thousand questions over an eighteen-month period. It was a big hit with the writers, and although I had the support of the Nonfiction pro paid by Prodigy to do similar stuff, the Prodigy brass ignored my contribution. After eighteen months of paying an average of twenty-five dollars a month to volunteer my help, I went through the roof when they announced a rate increase. So I tried America Online in June 1993 and instantly fell in love with the superior graphics, the lack of ads, the easy-to-navigate system. Again I opened my 'Ask Lary Crews' folder and started doing my volunteer work. Two months later, the leader of the Writer's Club asked if I'd be willing to be a writing consultant for the Writer's Club in exchange for some free hours. I said, 'You bet.'"

Crews's official position on America Online has counterparts on every commercial online service. If you have decent communication skills and expertise in a profession, hobby, or technical area, you might be able to wangle an exchange of your time and energy for free online access and a title. Paid arrangements where you become a contractor with an online service exist as well. Chapter 13 covers situations where you're king of your own online castle, but here you function more like a big shot or a chief within someone else's empire.

## Recognition, Free Online Time, and Fulfillment

Except for the Prodigy detour, Lary Crews's story about how he got invited to become an official part of the Writer's Club is typical. Different services have different names for their leading members, but just about everyone I spoke with who held a position comparable to his had been invited. As with the Nobel Prize, it doesn't seem to help if you "apply" for the honor. Instead, you earn someone's attention, you get scrutinized, and you are chosen. That was certainly how I came to serve as a special contributor on the Business Board on Prodigy. As a Prodigy manager explained it in my official welcome letter: "We recognize that there are certain Prodigy members who significantly enhance and energize the bulletin boards, members who ensure that the boards remain interesting and enjoyable for fellow participants. These members may have specific expertise to contribute, making them invaluable to others on the board. Or perhaps they attract other members because of their unique outlook or knowledge. Maybe he or she is just one of those members you always look for when you are on the boards, the kind of member you are always interested in hearing from—a bulletin board community leader. To recognize the valuable role these members play on the boards, we've designed the Special Contributor program."

If you do receive such an invitation, you'll have responsibilities ahead of you, not only a lower online bill and a title. Special contributors on Prodigy are supposed to stimulate discussion in their topic area, answer members' questions where they can, and help keep wayward members in line with the service's ground rules. No significant technical duties are involved. On CompuServe, the "sysops," as they are called—short for "system operators"—do have to have greater technical familiarity than the average member with the service and with computer files of various sorts in order to fulfill duties like keeping their section of the forum library in order. Whatever they're called and wherever they serve, these forum experts or assistants need excellent communication skills, a cool head, and diplomacy, since they're counted on to help solve problems, not create them.

Trial lawyer Dan Kohane, who serves CompuServe's Lawsig forum as an assistant sysop, says that one of the rules he helps enforce is "You can provide legal information, but not legal advice." Information provides a legal context for a person's problem and points in several different directions, while advice zeros in on the specifics of the situation. Sometimes those with the problem think that's a cop-out, and Kohane then explains the reason for the policy. Discussions on issues sometimes get quite heated, but only one message out of 600,000 was ever removed from the forum, he says—a direct racial or ethnic slur. "We don't mind controversy and disagreement. People think as a sysop I have an obligation to be neutral, and I do try to be a calming influence," notes Kohane. He also spends time explaining to people who wrongly believe their messages were removed where they actually went. On CompuServe's PR and Marketing forum, assistant sysop Mike Bayer's housekeeping duties include sweeping the message board of illicit advertising messages, perhaps two or three a day, and letting participants know that they're expected to use their real names, not "handles." Once in a while there's a more delicate situation, such as two people who might or might not be conspiring to promote their product by pretending to be customers. "We'll move a message like that into the sysops-only section and ask them if they have anything to do with the product," Bayer says. "Nine times out of ten, they'll say yes and we tell them they're welcome to post a description of the product in Library Fifteen and that's the end of it."

Bayer credits PRSIG, as the forum is known by regulars, as having contributed more to his public relations career than any other one thing he's been involved with. Similarly, Merry Schiff, who sells a registered business opportunity for medical billing, says she gets "a big credibility boost from being a sysop on CompuServe's Working from Home forum. People have specifically told us that this impressed them." On the other hand, when computer consultant Gary Ellenbogen was answering questions on CompuServe about ECCO software for fun, he picked up clients almost effortlessly as people E-mailed him for additional help. "That fell off dramatically after I became a forum sysop. People assumed I'm employed by

NetManage, the maker of ECCO, or paid by CompuServe, when in fact I just get unlimited free time in the forum. People recognize me as an ECCO guru. But now they don't realize they can hire my consulting services." My experience on Prodigy is that having any sort of special status does constrain your self-promotional efforts more than if you're a private citizen, so to speak. You have more visibility but fewer chances to connect your presence publicly with your business offerings. For me, the most valuable part of being a Prodigy special contributor was schmoozing as a colleague with the other designated experts.

Because it may or may not help in marketing, I don't recommend becoming a designated expert or assistant for that reason. It makes sense mainly as a way to subsidize what you enjoy doing and would be doing anyway. Perhaps the "Don't call us, we'll select you" method of getting such a position shows recognition that the ideal forum helpers carry out their responsibilities as a mission or a semisacred trust. Gary Ellenbogen, for instance, told me that the spiritual guidebook *How Can I Help?* by Ram Dass and Paul Gorman has been a guiding force in the way he helps people stymied by their software. "You need to recognize that when people go into a forum to ask a question, they make themselves vulnerable. They can be in a fragile or frustrated mood, or even angry, lashing out at the product. Instead of telling them what to do, you need to have the humble attitude, 'How can I help?' and give them what they need rather than what you happen to be good at. I also try to be a host rather than an authority figure, and to keep a sense of humor, especially when I don't know the answer. I get a big kick out of service, but you have to be able to do it selflessly."

So far I've been talking about opportunities for helping positions on the major commercial services. On a smaller service, The Well, Boston-based freelance writer Fawn Fitter saw her online bill drop dramatically after she created and began co-hosting a public conference, or message board, called Byline. "I had to persuade what's called the 'conference team' that there was a niche for it," Fitter says. "Although there was a writers' conference it was more oriented toward fiction writers and the process of writing. Byline focuses on marketing your work. I spend even more time online than before, but they now waive my fifteen-dollar-a-month membership fee and I get ten free hours a month." Over on the all-volunteer Internet, so-called net.gods attain legendary status without anyone appointing them. In fact, on your own anywhere in cyberspace you can become a resident expert whom people look up to, without any formal responsibilities—you just won't get your online access bill wiped clean.

## Becoming a Big Cheese Contractor

What Fawn Fitter did on The Well represents a moneymaking opportunity at the major commercial services. In 1992, for example, real estate journalist Peter Miller pointed out to the then 120,000-member America Online that they had nothing on the service covering real estate. Since virtually everyone lives in some sort of housing and since Miller had written numerous books on the topic, America Online readily agreed that this was an important topic to cover and that Miller was an appropriate person to set up and run a section of the service devoted to that topic. As host of the real estate area on America Online, Miller serves as, and gets compensated as, an independent contractor. From scratch, he created the message boards, began stocking libraries, set policies, and recruited assistants to help run the area. As membership has boomed, Miller has been able to add new features, like regular live conferences on different aspects of real estate. Although he says it represents a "huge investment" of time and energy on his part, he explains, "It's another way to promote who I am and what I do, to make sure my books don't disappear from bookstore shelves after sixty days. When I started, fellow journalists asked me, 'Why are you bothering?' Now they ask, 'How can I get in on the action?' "

Although no one who does what Miller does on America Online will divulge their contractual terms, it's generally known that they get paid according to the amount of member activity in their section of the service. Nigel Peacock of Tunbridge Wells in Kent, England, cofounded CompuServe's International Trade forum in 1993 and says that what he receives for the two hours a day, 365 days a year he spends on forum business "would never pay the bills!" His other income streams are trading and accounting for small busi-

nesses. Besides performing forum housekeeping chores and answering users' questions—some of them the same ones that crop
up again and again—Peacock must promote the forum on the
CompuServe service, through its "What's New" banner and in its
magazine. He also promotes the forum on the Internet, on his
World Wide Web home page (see Chapter 13). Perhaps the greatest
headache for Peacock and other forum operators is dealing with
troublemakers, such as what he calls a "confirmed con man," whom
he locked out of his forum. What constitutes disruptive or inappropriate behavior varies from area to area, with forum operators having considerable latitude to define and handle violations.

Peter Miller calls his real estate area a "conservative" area in
that "we don't accept everything that's uploaded to us. We only accept submissions that work, are relevant and valuable for our members, don't infringe any copyrights, and are up to date." Any
solicitations or commercial messages with company names and
phone numbers get taken down, including any notices seeking investors or seemingly selfless offers of help where a referral fee
might ultimately be involved. When someone asks about or de-
scribes software, even if it's about real estate, "we send them elsewhere on America Online," he says. People do protest such
decisions occasionally, and Miller explains that "no library or
bookstore is required to put everything on its shelves, and we're not
the place for something about, say, auto parts. On the other hand,
we do allow messages saying that the area is lousy and the host is
an awful person. Those we don't take down."

Janet Attard, who hosts forums on America Online, GEnie, and
the Microsoft Network, likewise carries out policies to which some
members object. "When someone uploads a library file, I look to
see if it might have been written by someone else, and I might ask
for proof of ownership or permission to upload the article," she
says. "I also look to see if it's an advertorial—one paragraph of text
followed by a catalog of products and services. Several people who
apparently bought 'reprint rights' to certain material have tried to
upload the same article with different contact information at the
end, and I don't allow that." On eWorld, the small but growing service owned by Apple Computers, entrepreneurship expert Terri
Lonier does her best to keep what she calls "multilevel-marketing-

type messages" in just one section of the area she runs called Working Solo (named after her acclaimed series of books).

Problems with network marketing messages also take up a lot of the energy of Bob Osgoodby, who leads the Business Board on Prodigy. "They're a volatile, active group of people," he says. "Every six weeks or so I knock off an electronic chain letter, and members alert me to other scams. One woman showed up to hawk a lottery program that other members told her was illegal. Things got very heated, and essentially she got driven off the board. About a month after that operation got shut down by the feds, she showed up again with another scheme, and people jumped on her mercilessly. Personal jibes started going around, which I always monitor carefully. If it's 'bashing'—personal attacks—I warn them privately to cease and desist. If they don't they lose their board privileges." Osgoodby, who owns an appliance store in Asbury Park, New Jersey, was the one forum operator I spoke with whose other business interests don't really benefit from his online position. "I enjoy it," he says of the six hours every day he spends on his Prodigy responsibilities.

Although all of these system operators have considerable elbow room for setting their own policies, they have to operate within the guidelines of their host service. Because of the overall stricture against solicitations on CompuServe, Nigel Peacock negotiated the opening of a second trading forum called ProTrade that would be accessible on CompuServe only to those who paid an additional monthly fee and on which international traders could solicit to their hearts' content. "The original forum continues," he says, "but it's become more of a discussion forum, with all the actual trading in ProTrade."

Since new online services still seem to be sprouting and growing, there are still plenty of opportunities to persuade their powers-that-be of an online need that you can fulfill. If you already have a fan club, a reputation, a flair for publicity, or all of the above, so much the better. Or when an established service is expanding into a new territory where you speak the native language, that represents another prime opening. Computer trade magazines and general business publications often cover relevant deals and developments.

# 13 | Creating Your Own Bulletin Board, Mailing List, or World Wide Web Site

Control. Exposure. Responsibility. These represent the rewards and costs of creating your own online world, where you are completely in charge. You set the policies, determine the focus, assemble or invite the content. If you want to flatout sell, you can. If you want to outlaw mention of a competitor's name, that's up to you. Just don't believe that if you build it, visitors will automatically come. You'll need to promote it and solve technical and customer-related problems to keep callers coming back. Here are three options to think about, along with the unique benefits and pitfalls of each.

## Your Own BBS

With all the excitement about "getting on the Internet," it's easy to overlook a low-priced method of making your company accessible online to customers and prospects who don't subscribe to any online service. All they need to dial you up is a modem and a simple communications program (often free with the modem). Once their call goes through, they're in your online world, which you are free to structure and fill as you like. Reasonably priced new BBS software provides an interface that will seem fairly intuitive to new, nontechie users. You can establish the bulletin board system as a customer service or a marketing cog in your ongoing business or develop it as a business venture in itself. Here are only a few of the purposes a privately sponsored BBS can serve:

*Deliver ever-changing information when the customer or prospect needs it.* "Traditionally, mortgage rates are disseminated to real estate agents by mass faxing, which is expensive," says Pat Pisarski, president of ExpresSearch, Inc., a company in Lake Zurich, Illinois, that designs, customizes, and operates BBSs for other businesses. "But when you post rates on a BBS, the agents only call in when they need the information, and *they* pay for the phone call. Most real estate agents perceive the BBS as a convenience, because instead of having to go into the office to pick up a fax, they can plug in their laptop and get the up-to-the-minute rate from wherever they are."

*Facilitate communication with clients in very different time zones.* Agnew Tech-II, a translation firm in Westlake Village, California, makes it convenient for European clients to send or pick up messages and files by operating a twenty-four-hour BBS. "The fact that clients don't have to go through any online provider makes the communication quicker and more personal," says company president Irene Agnew. Since modems transmit faster than faxing, the clients save money, too.

*Expedite product orders or disseminate scheduling, reservation, or inventory information.* According to Pat Pisarski, a Chicago-based food-store chain runs a BBS that allows customers to order groceries online from work, to be delivered when they are home. A band or professional speaker could offer booking bureaus the chance to dial in and match a potential engagement against the already set itinerary. Any sort of business that involves reservations, like a golf club, a beachfront motel, or restaurant, could use a BBS to post available dates and times as well as soft-sell promotional messages like "What's New." Pisarski says that a company that used to fax its inventory to 300 distributors in the United States and Canada every day now has a system set up so that the distributors only need to call in, type their name and password, and what they need gets downloaded automatically.

*Make answers to frequently asked questions accessible.* According to Mustang Software, manufacturer of the popular Wildcat! BSS software, "a BBS is the ultimate self-service information provider, and it's a perfect way to help those customers who already know what they're looking for." It's also a perfect marketing vehicle to establish yourself as *the* resource on cat health, if that's your specialty as a veterinarian, or on estate planning if that's your bailiwick in the law. Via the BBS you can provide a message board, file libraries, and live conferencing, just like an online service.

Bill Koch of Baltimore, Maryland, runs a bulletin board that started out as an information center for an alternative bookstore in Baltimore called Atomic Books, specializing in underground topics like UFOs, hacking, drug culture, and comics. The BBS has evolved into an independent entity still partially supported by Atomic Books but slowly developing into a business. "The BBS generates some sales for the store, but it's more like an extra service for its die-hard customers," says Koch, who holds down an unrelated full-time job as a computer support professional. He is pursuing sponsorship by other small companies with a compatible orientation, such as a maker of "weird videos" and a shop called the Baltimore Hemporium. By designing and selling T-shirts with a logo of the BBS, he thinks he can bring in more income than from user donations. Another idea is producing and marketing a CD-ROM compilation of hard-to-find files from the BBS, gathered through around eight to ten hours of cyberspace hunting per week. "It's easy to run a BBS as a hobby, but getting paid subscribers is a challenge," says Koch. "Either you have to carve out a niche or go the 'adult' BBS route [sexually oriented content], which is a proven draw but risky given the possibility of a crackdown."

Kevin King of Sacramento, California, who has run My Favorite BBS since 1989, agrees that a specialty is essential, "especially if you have limited storage space on your hard disk." In the beginning King tried to offer a little bit of everything, but now he focuses on business topics and uses the BBS as one marketing and ordering vehicle for his major mail-order product, a source directory for computer resellers called "The Resellers Source Kit." "If you run a public board, as I do, you can force people to read your bulletins before they get to the file areas. It's a good promotional tool," King says. He devotes a considerable amount of time, money, and energy to securing up-to-date software to lure callers. Like Koch, he holds down a full-time outside job.

Both Koch and King say that setting up and running a BBS does not demand an inordinate amount of technical expertise. "It's a lot easier than navigating the Internet," suggests King. "I once helped a twelve-year-old do it." Koch adds that even the highly customizable BBS software he's now using could be up and running in a weekend with the default settings "if you follow the instructions exactly." The customizing options allow him to design a unique graphical look and feel for the BBS. "That helps you keep up with the competition. The content plus the 'cover'—the look—are what count for success," says Koch. The most popular BBS software can run on an old machine and costs about $130. Besides the dedicated telephone line or lines you need, plus Internet access, which has become de rigueur for a public board, the rest of the expense is upkeep time.

Probably the wisest combination of attractions is distinctive content with an attitude and membership in a wider BBS specialty network, which gives your callers access to a relevant national or international message base. For instance, ordained elder and banker Mike Holman offers a scriptural quote of the day on his BBS, Holman's World Ministries, along with information from the fifty-plus member BBS network Afro-Net. "I want it to be a board where I can minister to people educationally and culturally," says Holman, who has about 300 regular callers. Kevin King hooks his BBS up with BizyNet, a fifty-two-member business network, and Bill Koch with NirvanaNet, a twenty-plus-member network of free, anonymous-access, underground-topics BBSs.

Publicly accessible BBSs spread the word about their focus and features through listings in *Boardwatch Magazine* and *Computer Shopper,* through publicity in nonelectronic media reaching their target market, through non-BBS online postings, and through cooperative lists maintained on certain BBSs either geographically or by topic. For example, Mike Labbe in Warwick, Rhode Island, maintains a list of BBSs in his state on his board, The Eagle's Nest, while Dennis Hauser of Saginaw, Michigan, keeps track of business and professional BBSs on his Delight the Customer board.

If you can't spare the time or energy to run a BBS but think it might benefit your business, you can hire a BBS service bureau, like Pat Pisarski's ExpresSearch, to do it for you. But whether you're aiming to make it a customer service tool, a marketing vehicle, or a profit center of its own, make sure you're well informed about your special legal exposure as a BBS operator. Lance Rose's *Netlaw* (see Resources) contains plenty of ominous examples of pirate and adult boards that have landed in legal hot water as well as perfectly innocent boards shut down by authorities or jeopardized by the illegal activity of a user. Find out the policies and procedures that will protect you.

## Emperor of a Mailing List

The accepted terminology for starting and managing an Internet E-mail discussion list is "owning" the list, but I like the imperial metaphor because by creating an online environment, you get the right to say, "Here's what this is and isn't, and if you don't like it, join another list or start your own." Quilting artist Melissa Bishop of Coram, New York, had exactly that motive in mind when she launched Interquilt, one of three mailing lists she has started, in 1993. "Quiltnet, a very large list, goes through periodic upheavals with people getting very intolerant of off-topic discussions or beginners making posting mistakes. I didn't like its unfriendliness," Bishop says. "Quilting is a very social activity, and I saw the need for a list that welcomed newcomers and allowed the warm, chatty talk that goes along with quilting." Making clear that she wasn't intending to replace the established list, she posted an announcement of her new group to relevant newsgroups and America Online and sent it to members of Quiltnet. Within three days she had 250 members. Her other lists are the Pfaff Sewing Club and Ragdolls, a cloth-dolls club.

Most lists are programmed to run automatically on large computer systems using either Listserv or Majordomo software, both available free on the Internet, so that subscriptions get processed and messages sent to the list address go out to all list members without any human intervention. Bishop, by contrast, keeps her lists only partially automated—to give her more control, she says. Anyone who writes to her asking to be put on the list has to read a statement about the purpose and ground rules of the list and send back an application acknowledging that they understand its spirit and expectations. Once she has placed an applicant on the member list, her software automatically sends any properly addressed message from a member out to the entire list. A message from a nonmember goes just to Bishop, however. She fine-tuned the programming by using friends for guinea pigs. "I drove them crazy for a couple of weeks until I got all the bugs out," she says.

Because her lists run from a server at the university where her domestic partner works, Bishop cannot allow any commercial messages. Nevertheless, she considers the lists a business venture—without profit. Probably the closest nonelectronic equivalents are organizing a business or professional organization and publishing a participatory newsletter, both of which likewise bestow credibility and visibility among members of a target group. For Glenn Fleishman, president of an Internet services company called Point of Presence, the opportunity to stand out among peers and spread one's point of view is a clear benefit of the work he invests in the Internet Marketing discussion list, with 1,000-plus members. His work on the list attracted interviews from *Forbes, The New York Times, The Wall Street Journal,* and *Internet World,* which marked him as a leader in the industry and gave him another chance to evangelize for his cause, the soft sell. "The list gives me an opportunity to sell my company, but also to sell my worldview," Fleishman says.

Instead of distributing all submitted messages automatically to members of the list, Fleishman moderates the discussion, rejecting about half of the fifty to sixty posts that come in daily, many of them for being repetitive, some for being inappropriate sales pitches. For better or worse, his filtering makes him more of a personage than the owner of an unmoderated list. Fleishman says he spends about ten hours a week on the list, down from twenty to twenty-five when he first started. Bishop calls her lists moderated to a slight extent in that she will explain after the fact to someone who had sent in an inappropriate posting what she was doing wrong—although the person who sent a chain letter to one of the lists got summarily kicked off. "Chain letters are illegal and drag down computer resources across the globe," Bishop says. "There were thousands of headers at the foot of the message from everywhere it had been, and it clogged the mail queue of the whole university system, designed to serve more than twenty-thousand students, staff, and faculty."

Serious technical glitches bedeviled the launch of Stefan Gruenwald's Bio-tech mailing list in February 1995. Four hundred subscription orders arrived the very first day, causing the system to crash three times. "I had to keep doing backups, and even so some subscriptions got lost. For the first two weeks, it was a mess," Gruenwald recalls. During the launch, his job as director of molecular biology for a San Diego biotechnology firm took him out of town and he had to try to straighten things out on his portable computer in his hotel room every night. Although work on the list still takes him about two hours a day, he feels good about his effort, having signed up 1,500 or so subscribers and having received more than 200 thank-you notes from people grateful for the existence of the list. "I thought we needed a way for academics to tell biotechnology professionals about their discoveries and things they want to license. Otherwise we wouldn't know what they have in the academic pipeline." Gruenwald adds that heading the list gives him a powerful vantage point on what's happening in his field and has made him much better known in the biotech community. He is looking forward to archiving back messages from the list on the World Wide Web and posting current messages there as well in an easier-to-scan hierarchy of topics, similar to an arrangement Fleishman's Internet Marketing list has already made.

Another list owner, Terry Oakes, says that he just manages to eke out the necessary list-maintenance time for his six lists, given his full-time job as production coordinator of the printing shop at the University of New Brunswick in Canada. Daily maintenance includes dealing with messages that bounce back to him when the recipient's mailbox is full, forcing him to guess whether the recipient has left school for the summer, has allowed messages to pile up temporarily for some reason, or is the victim of a systemwide computer breakdown. But he has been giving short shrift to another pressing need: trying to keep flaming to a minimum. "Since I'm very busy at work, it's hard to find the time to write properly diplomatic and constructive letters to intervene and give direction to Litho-L, the most active list, on desktop publishing and printing," he says. One of the other lists, on letterpress printing for people who own vintage printing presses, has more than 200 members worldwide, all so gentlemanly, he says, that that list pretty much runs itself. "I'm an Internet fanatic," he explained when I asked why he started so many lists. "When I get involved in a hobby I tend to dive headlong into it." Like Fleishman and Gruenwald, Oakes says that his lists give him high visibility in his field of expertise, printing and publishing. "People write to me with questions, saying they see my name everywhere," he says. Although he acknowledges that commercial lists aren't common, Oakes is mulling over the possibility of charging a subscription fee for a list that involves bids and tenders for printing.

One bit of advice emerging from these stories for those aspiring to become emperor of a list is to be sure you're ready technically and equipped to handle anything that might go wrong with the software or system you're using. Oakes suggests enlisting the help of a co-owner or two to make the work manageable. Gruenwald says it's hard to find a helpful service provider because a commercial provider company doesn't make much money from housing a list and a university system won't allow commercial postings. Like Melissa Bishop, you should carefully think through your list guidelines before getting started. It helps too to know your audience. For instance, would they tend to view commercial messages as a service or a plague? Bishop caters to an expectation specific to the quilting world by offering subscribers to her list who send in an unusual fabric swatch a membership card that earns them discounts at quilting shops. If you've targeted a niche that perceives a need for your list, you'll get subscribers at once by notifying the grand old list of lists and posting schmooze-compatible announcements (see Chapter 8) in appropriate newsgroups and related mailing lists. Everyone I spoke with said that after the initial surge of subscribers, word of mouth made it unnecessary to keep publicizing the existence of the group.

## Home, Home on the World Wide Web

In 1995, the World Wide Web proved to be the fastest growing sector of the Internet. Companies huge and tiny, organizations like the city of Cambridge, Massachusetts, and students or technology lovers with nothing to sell rushed to post home pages on the Web. The excitement had to do with three valid factors, I believe. First, businesses operating with the paradigm of getting business through advertising became overjoyed that now here was a legitimate way to set up company billboards on the Internet. Second, technologically the World Wide Web can be exceptionally easy to use, with its one-click navigation system instead of arcane commands. And third, to visually oriented folks frustrated with word-based communication, the colorful images and style possible on the Web came as a revelatory breakthrough. Some commentators went so far as to dub the Web the Internet's "killer app"—the application that would make it imperative for all organizations to go online or risk becoming has-beens.

Reports of the World Wide Web's success in stimulating sales are decidedly mixed, however. The owner of an art-posters shop showed up on CompuServe to complain that he had gotten 2,000 "hits"—visits—his first week without a single sale. A PR person told me in confidence about a client whose Web page was clocking *16,000* visits a week, which in three months had translated into zero sales. On the other hand, Bill Koch told me that Atomic Books' World Wide Web site, which he had peripherally helped to set up, was bringing in "a couple of hundred dollars of sales a week. For a small business, that's like being open a few extra days a month, and it's extremely cost-effective," he said. Glenn Fleishman's comment: "I think the near-term marketing potential [of the Web] has been oversold. I'd be surprised if there's been more than a million dollars of direct sales."

Why have those expecting the Internet cash registers to be ringing like crazy been disappointed? First, most of those cruising the attractions of the Net at this stage of its development do so primarily as sightseers, not as imminent buyers performing the electronic equivalent of flipping through the Yellow Pages. Web advertisers therefore face the challenge of breaking through the haze of the cruising experience and sharpening a viewer's sudden desire to have something that is being pictured and described. Then there's the problem that the sightseers may not have the need for the product. If they don't belong to the target market, trying to put them into buying mode won't help you much. Perhaps you sell get-away-from-it-all vacations in Tahiti, for instance; college students and twenty-something technicians who enjoy your pictures of the Pacific paradise wouldn't necessarily E-mail reservations for a trip. You must also overcome suspicions of even supposedly secure methods of ordering online, if that's how you're set up to sell, though you should always offer offline methods of buying too. Overwhelmed by the millions estimated to be on the Internet, many companies that have leaped onto the Net overlooked the fact that only 30 percent of Americans own a computer and only 4 percent have cruised the World Wide Web even once.

All in all, it's best to consider the Web a marketing vehicle no more magical than the others in this book. Used wisely, it can earn visibility for your business and attract opportunities and leads. Here are some guiding principles for your Web strategy:

*Make your content the draw.* Focus on the informational needs and interests of your target market, not your ego. Too many Web sites consist of a computerized company brochure: The headline presents the name of the firm, and then its capabilities, as if to a hushed, darkened audience with their hands poised for applause. Think about it, though—unless you were already thinking of hiring them, or perhaps hoping to be hired by them, would you go out of your way to go take a look at a collective electronic résumé for Chief, Cook, and Bottlewasher, Inc.? Compare this to the approach taken by Dr. Jim Humphries, a veterinarian who answers callers' questions on syndicated radio and cable TV shows. He heads his home page "Welcome to Dr. Jim's Virtual Veterinary Clinic." The table of contents just below that has four headings: "It's our grand opening!—Who the heck is Dr. Jim?"; "Dr. Jim's Animal Clinic for Cats"—three questions and answers; "Dr. Jim's Animal Clinic for Dogs"—three questions and answers; and "Read My Disclaimer." I hadn't ever heard of Dr. Jim, but the whole setup presents such a wonderful introduction to his expertise that I might E-mail him to find out if my local area carries his radio show and eventually buy his book and video. Other effective sites provide a compendium of valuable resources, like Advantage Solutions, Inc.'s home page, which includes a free business-to-business directory you can browse through or join. Think "How can I show, not tell? How can I *serve* my market in some way?" and you'll be on the right track.

*Wherever possible, give visitors a reason to return regularly.* I'm sure many cat and dog owners will be coming back to Dr. Jim to see whether he has tackled their pets' problems yet. For your consulting prospects, perhaps a new editorial every week would do the trick. For antique auto buffs, maybe you could highlight a different old Porsche or Bentley for sale every month. For folks interested in tracing missing friends or business associates, you could periodically post a new set of tips for finding people. But if you announce a schedule of changing content, keep to it. I couldn't help noticing that the Advantage Solutions site claimed it was updated weekly, yet I visited on May 1 and the last update was listed as April 6.

*Go easy on the pictures.* Currently most of those whose Internet setups gives them access to the images on the World Wide Web have to wait a minute or more for your images to compose themselves on their screen. Since they are sightseers, not captive viewers, they get annoyed when they wait and the image isn't worth it. Or they just don't wait. Dan Janal removed all the photos on the home page for his high-tech public relations firm in Danville, California, after he asked himself, Now would *I* stick around and wait for a few minutes for these pictures to draw?

*Structure your information in levels.* The Web is a hypertext medium, where visitors expect to be able to choose which information they want to access, rather than having it all set out in one fixed sequence. Typically you'll present the main headings on the first screen so that people can click to read the first, the second, or the last topic as they prefer—or go away if they're not interested in any of them.

*Establish links with other sites.* You can make it possible for someone visiting your page to jump to related ones just by listing their Web address on your page together with the code that creates a "hotspot." To get your page listed on others', contact those responsible for sites related to your own and explain why what you have created would be valuable for their viewers to know about. I've heard that some people are demanding money for links from their pages, but in my opinion that's information highway robbery and rather stupid from both ends. If your site is good and relevant to theirs, it enhances theirs that you're listed, while if your site is lousy, a link to you from theirs degrades theirs, whether or not you paid them for it. Think of it as guilt and honor by association. If no one wants to include links to you, that probably means your site needs a complete overhaul. In any case, regularly test the hotlinks on your page, because if they lead to dead ends, that puts a dent in the value of your information.

*Seed cyberspace with pointers to your site.* Post substantive messages on newsgroups, mailing lists, and bulletin boards and list your URL (Web address) within the message or in your signature. Your service provider should be able to give you an up-to-date list of all the official and semi-official "What's New on the Web" sites for you to notify about your new home page. Some providers do those notifications for you. A smart schmooze-compatible way (see Chapter 8) to announce your home page among colleagues and friends without seeming commercial is to ask online buddies for feedback. Ask specific questions like, Is it too detailed or not enough? Does everything work the way it's supposed to? Was it worth the visit?

# PART III

# Problems and Solutions

# 14 | Producing Readable Electronic Text

When desktop publishing boomed in popularity, people who had never taken the slightest interest in fonts, leading, or point sizes developed new habits. They learned how to select an effective typeface, emphasize points with boldface, italics, or spacing, and how to create a formal, "official" look by justifying the right-hand margins. Progress doesn't always march forward in a straight line, however. If you have become skilled at producing a sophisticated layout, you'll have to abandon just about all of your new tools and generate readable electronic text with nothing more than the kind of mechanisms available on an old-fashioned manual typewriter.

## ASCII, the Digital Lowest Common Denominator

When you're posting files online, E-mailing an unknown party, or placing messages on electronic bulletin boards, you have no idea what kind of computer or software people will be using to retrieve and read your contribution. Your brilliant ideas become accessible to all when you incorporate them in a standard, limited set of characters and symbols called ASCII, pronounced "Askee" and short for "American Standard Code for Information Interchange." So-called pure ASCII or straight text includes all the everyday letters and numbers on a computer keyboard, plus a few extra symbols that you probably have no reason to bother with. It lacks any formatting codes for particular word-processing programs or other software applications, and it lacks any font choices or any layout or placement tools besides the Return key and the Space bar. "Boring, boring," you say? I admit it's a limited palette, but just as a skilled designer can create an elegant impact in black and white, you can learn to keep people reading and help them absorb your message using these universal, low-tech tools.

I should add that the following tips apply especially when you are creating a document or message to be sent by E-mail, to be uploaded to an online service or the Internet for downloading by interested parties, or written offline for uploading to a message board. You might be tempted to provide information in the format that's easiest for you, or which you believe presents your message most attractively. For instance, three people whom I interviewed for this book sent me a résumé or biographical statement as a so-called binary file that I had to "unzip" or "unencode" in order to read. But in most cases that's unnecessary, unproductive, and rude. It would have required a lot of extra effort on my part to shuffle the file around among hard disk directories, apply a decoding program, and then open it up to read from within still another program. To me, that's equivalent to saying, "Here's my résumé, in invisible ink. To read it all you have to do is soak it in a pan of lemon juice and then blow air on it with a hair dryer for two minutes." Why should I go to so much trouble when you could have sent it as regular text? One exception: If you are preparing text to be read *on* the World Wide Web, you must do so using a special set of codes called HTML—hypertext markup language. But if you are preparing text to be accessed *from* the Web and read offline, ASCII is the choice that lets everyone in on your wisdom.

One of the biggest frustrations for some people online is that although you can send a message from Seattle to Saint Petersburg in a flash, you can't emphasize important points *with italics,* **with boldface,** or even <u>with underlining</u>. That last makes ASCII even more primitive than a typewriter. Here are three alternative means of emphasis, demonstrated with a signature line I often use on CompuServe:

Marcia Yudkin, Author, *Six Steps to Free Publicity* and six
other books
Marcia Yudkin, Author, _Six Steps to Free Publicity_ and
six other books
Marcia Yudkin, Author, SIX STEPS TO FREE PUBLICITY and
six other books

The first, my favorite method, consists of surrounding the text you
wish to stress with asterisks. In the second, you surround it with
single underlining signs, and in the third, you type it in all capitals.
Caution: DON'T EVER USE LONG STRETCHES OF CAPITAL
LETTERS. NOT ONLY ARE THEY VERY HARD TO READ,
BUT PEOPLE EXPERIENCE IT AS THE EQUIVALENT OF
SHOUTING—WHICH IS AS ILL-MANNERED ONLINE AS IT
IS OFF. (Isn't it a relief now to be looking at normal type again?)
it's almost as bad to use all lowercase letters, as i am doing now—
for different reasons. "One guy who types all in small letters, I
wonder if he is drunk," says Paula Berinstein, an independent researcher in Los Angeles, California. "Another person I can tell is
trying to type fast and spend as little time online as possible to save
money." Using standard capitalization conventions with an occa-
sional very short stretch of all-capitals helps to keep the reader's attention on the message rather than on the sobriety, frugality, or
manners of the messenger.

Although you can't include a graphic logo in text messaging, I
have seen a text version that fulfills a similar function—letting the
reader know in a split second who the message is from. Bob
Coleman, formerly an official expert on Prodigy, is the only person
I know of who opened every message with "Howdy!" In the same
way, certain people who always indent their name and other iden-
tifying information distinctively create a subtly recognizable electronic look. Can you come up with your own text-based trademark,
the equivalent of always showing up in a certain color or having an
inimitable voice?

## Formatting for Readability

When it comes to setting up a file or E-mail message to be readable, you have a number of tools available that can help, including the Space bar and the Return key, which can make an enormous difference if you use them appropriately.

*Use the Space bar instead of the Tab key.* Indented paragraphs are easier to read than nonindented paragraphs, but avoid creating indentations with the Tab key. Similarly, if you want to arrange text on the screen or the page, always use the Space bar. Tabs can cause visual mayhem because they are interpreted differently on different computer systems. If you have your tabs set to every three spaces and I have mine set every eight spaces, a file segment that looks like this to you:

Here are the three biggest fears of those shopping for a used car, along with some remedies:

1. being cheated on price                   statewide price charts
2. being saddled with a "lemon"        30-day guarantee
3. being deceived about car's problems        independent evaluation

will look like this to me:

Here are the three biggest fears of those shopping for a used car, along with some remedies:

    1. being cheated on price
statewide price charts
    2. being saddled with a "lemon"                                    30-
day guarantee
    3. being deceived about car's problems                    independent
evaluation

The damage is equally serious with an Internet signature, which might look like this when you create it:

```
***********************************************************
*                                                         *
*   Marcia Yudkin        Publicity Coach        Writer    *
*   P.O. Box 1310        Boston, MA 02117       U.S.A.    *
*   75200.1163@compuserve.com          (617) 266-1613     *
*                                                         *
*       Helping professionals & entrepreneurs since 1988  *
***********************************************************
```

But if those spaces were marked by tabs, that might come up on
someone else's screen like this:

```
***********************************************************
*              Marcia Yudkin         Publicity Coach
Writer                *
*              P.O. Box 1310            Boston, MA 02117
U.S.A.                *
*              75200.1163@compuserve.com     (617) 266-1613
*
*              Helping professionals & entrepreneurs since 1988
*
***********************************************************
```

Not anywhere as neat, don't you agree?

*Keep your line lengths at a maximum of sixty characters per
line, by using the Return key.* Different systems for writing and
reading messages handle word-wrapping (the system for arranging
text line by line) differently. Some interface programs for online
services and the Internet automatically word-wrap anything you
write within that interface, while others don't. Problems occur
when a paragraph that looked perfect on your screen before you
sent or uploaded it gets crammed into a text reader with a shorter
line length. Instead of this:

The key to success in used-car sales is understanding the
considerable fears prospects bring to the lot, including
most of all getting cheated, stuck, or lied to.

Your recipient might see this:

        The key to success in used-car sales is
    understanding the

considerable fears prospects bring to the lot, including
most of all getting cheated, stuck, or lied to.

One way, although not a foolproof way, to find out if your messages are getting distorted graphically is to send it to yourself and
see how it comes up on your screen. Even better, send it to someone who uses a different kind of computer system (Macintosh
rather than IBM) or online access (Internet rather than America
Online) and ask if the text looks all right to them. Ask your friend
too whether the text looks open and inviting or dense and forbidding. The shorter line length and the next tip help with
reader-friendliness.

*Use shorter paragraphs than you ordinarily do, with an extra
space between them.* Almost always, online text gets read on-screen
single-spaced, which feels crowded and tiring unless you provide
visual relief. Compare this, from an electronic sales letter of mine:

Right now I'm eager to pass along what I've learned
about how to get priceless media coverage dirt-cheap.
Whatever product or service you are offering for sale,
you undoubtedly face the challenge of finding customers
or clients. Sure, advertising is an option, but it usually
costs a fortune even to test the waters. And buyers
these days remain justifiably skeptical of the content of
your ads—after all, it's what you yourself are saying
about your own company!

with this:

Right now I'm eager to pass along what I've learned
about how to get priceless media coverage dirt-cheap.
Whatever product or service you are offering for sale,
you undoubtedly face the challenge of finding customers
or clients.

Sure, advertising is an option, but it usually costs a
fortune even to test the waters. And buyers these days

remain justifiably skeptical of the content of your ads—
after all, it's what you yourself are saying about your own
company!

Doesn't the second version seem more inviting? Shorter, well-spaced paragraphs keep the reader going at a decent clip.

*Use headings, particularly in sales letters and library files.* Any electronic text that goes on longer than a page becomes easier to scan both on-screen and when printed out when it contains subheads. These stand out well all in capitals. You also help the reader keep on going when you organize information into bulleted or numbered lists. Here, as throughout this chapter, your goal becomes easing the effort of reading long stretches of text for someone you hope to gather into your sphere of customers or clients.

## Addressing for Memorability and Legibility

I'd like to add some suggestions for naming E-mail, Gopher, and World Wide Web addresses, where you have a choice. Unlike the postal service, which delivers mail that's misspelled or illegible to the average person, computers can't guess that a comma really should be a period or that "Msra" should really be "mSra." If you've ever tried to read an E-mail address off a handwritten fax or to get someone's Web address over the phone, you know that some addresses are darned hard to communicate accurately. Avoid these elements in addresses if you can, which exacerbate problems for some users:

*Unusual ASCII characters, such as " ~," "^," and " |."* Do you have any idea what to call these characters in words? From my long-ago study of Spanish, I know that the first of these is called a tilde. But the first time I saw it in a printed address I mistook it first for a hyphen and then for a printing blotch. As I was typing up this chapter, I discovered that I can't type a tilde by itself because my word-processing program reserves it for a special function involving hyphenation. It also took me quite a while to locate it on my keyboard. Imagine the trouble a tilde would cause me, then, if I had one in my World Wide Web address and tried to type it into a letter! The second of these obscure characters might be called a caret, but that word denotes a proofreading symbol placed under, not above, a line of type. Or maybe it's called a circumflex, after the accent mark used in French? It was once described to me over the phone as "the wedge that's above the '6' on the keyboard." The third sign I have no idea what to call—"two vertical dashes stacked on one another"? And although that's what it looks like on my keyboard, on paper it comes out from my computer as an unbroken vertical line. Also, the underlining sign is sometimes hard to distinguish from an errant splotch or a hyphen.

*Eccentrically mixed upper- and lowercase characters.* These help a password remain obscure, but in addresses may keep people from connecting electronically with you. They're also very tedious to explain verbally. The safest policy is to stick to lowercase, since that's the general custom on Unix systems. When I hear Tom Brokaw say I can send him an E-mail at "nightly at nbc-dot-com," I don't need to look at the TV screen to know that he means "nightly@nbc.com."

Before committing yourself to an electronic address, make sure it's something you can easily pronounce and convey to someone over the telephone or on the radio, and that it will be easy to pick out and use when someone sees it in print. A good test for the latter is to type it out and handwrite it, then copy the page on your fax machine and see if you can still read it accurately at a glance. If you do get stuck with an address that is easy to get wrong, alert others explicitly to its quirks.

# 15 | Inspiring Trust

Imagine coming home from work one day and finding a simple copied flyer tucked in your porch door: LARRY'S LAWN SERVICE: COMPLETELY TAKEN CARE OF WHILE YOU'RE AT WORK. Since your grass is long and you're out of gas for the lawn mower, you read on. "Larry" (no last name) is offering to mow your lawn whenever it needs it and you're too busy. All you have to do is leave a message on his voice-mail any weekday morning and leave an envelope containing $15 in cash under your front mat. When you come home from work, the lawn will be immaculate.

Hmm, you think. Fifteen dollars is very reasonable. There's a chance he'd pick up the envelope and abscond, of course, but you'd be out just $15. Unless . . . WHILE YOU'RE AT WORK: Could it be a scheme to find out when you won't be home, and then rob the house?

In a nutshell, that's the kind of dilemma into which you put potential customers and clients who encounter you online. They encounter only the messages you've set out for them, which could be mere words and empty promises. From those bits and bytes, they have precious little evidence to judge you by. First, are you for real? That is, are you a genuine businessperson capable of delivering goods or services? And second, will you do what you say without ripping folks off? Your challenge becomes reducing their leap of faith in you from a bound across a chasm to a safe baby-step forward.

## Are You For Real?

Let's think about what Larry could have done to reassure you that he really had a lawn-mowing business.

1. Provided a full name. This should go without saying, but Larry violated this axiom. With his full name, you could at least have looked him up in the telephone book, learned his street address, and driven by to see whether his was a neatly clipped lot or a weedy yard strewn with rusty mufflers. Listing his address along with his name would have saved you a step and implied he had nothing to hide.
2. Made himself available by voice. An answering machine isn't anywhere near as reassuring as a person who picks up the telephone or returns your call. Larry has several options for making himself more trustable here: mentioning on his taped message that he'll return calls during his lunch break or in the evening; mentioning on his flyer the hours when he's more likely to pick up the phone; or best of all, providing on both his flyer and his answering machine the number of a mobile phone where he can be reached at any time. A telephone number doesn't help credibility much when it functions as a dead end. But when it's a route to a live voice you can interact with, it's the next best thing to meeting face to face.
3. Met you in person. Come to think of it, why couldn't Larry have gone through the neighborhoods on a weekend, rung doorbells, and explained his service face to face? "When we meet someone and shake their hand, look them in the eye and talk to them for a while, we tend to feel a higher level of comfort about doing business with them," says Ivan Misner, author of *The World's Best-Known Marketing Secret: Building Your Business with Word of Mouth Marketing.*
4. Given evidence of stability. If Larry could draw your attention to a truck with LARRY'S LAWN SERVICE painted permanently on the side, that would help. During his doorstep visit, it would have loomed behind him. A photo of the truck on

the flyer would imply stability. A slogan like "Serving Yourcity lawn owners since 1990" might have helped as well.

5. Reduced your risk. Larry could have offered to mow the lawn during the day and come back in the evening to make sure you were satisfied and *then* collected payment. Or, taking a lot more risk onto himself, he could offer monthly billing by mail. If Larry mentioned that he was bonded, you probably wouldn't worry as much about him breaking into your house.

6. Offered checkable credentials. Truly suspicious potential customers wouldn't be satisfied with anything less than the names of people they know or know of who can vouch for you. Almost as effective would be stating that you belong to the Better Business Bureau, or that you are a certified lawn technician, second grade, and a member of the National Lawn Care Guild.

I've gone on at length with a hypothetical example because I believe that Larry's case reveals both the challenge of establishing trust in cyberspace and many of the remedies. "We have to work much harder at presenting an image of stability, normality, and integrity than we would if we were, say, an ice cream parlor," says Rob Cosgrove, owner of Precision Data Corporation in Memphis, Tennessee, which markets aggressively on CompuServe, Prodigy, and the Internet its software and business manual for starting a remote computer backup service business. Cosgrove or his staff check their E-mail three times a day and respond immediately with personalized responses, not sheer boilerplate. "The quick response means an awful lot of people," he says. In addition, Cosgrove offers as much information about himself and his company as possible: "phone numbers, BBS numbers, physical address, E-mail addresses, my life story, the works. I'll even talk with people who call if I'm available. Many people tell me that honesty and availability were a deciding factor in their purchase. Some people say 'Thanks for being a real person for a change,' which makes me wonder what other companies are doing." Besides responses to his own online ads, Cosgrove receives about five E-mails a day asking if another aggressive marketer, Sheila Danzig, who lists him as a satisfied customer, is "for real."

Because of its impersonality as a communication vehicle, online advertisers have a hard time engendering trust. World Wide Web sites in particular have less content and more "face," says Kansas State University professor of management John Bunch. "Lots of people have created home pages where it's difficult to find out where the business is located and who the principals are. That sets up legal hurdles for cautious customers, since whenever a business relationship falls apart you can't sue unless you know where the other party is located physically." Schmoozers don't face as great a challenge because the more you respond to textual messages as yourself, the more you gather reality as a distinct individual. Since expertise is awfully hard to fake, whenever you exhibit your knowledge, wisdom, and perceptiveness during an exchange of ideas, you also add to your aura of solidity. Whether you're advertising or schmoozing, however, remember that before people send you any money, they must feel confident that you have an established existence apart from cyberspace.

Don't make Larry's mistake. Exhibit as many of these signs of solidity as you can, and you'll be on your way to credibility.

- Physical address. A street address will seem more reassuring than a post office box.
- Personal names. Cybernauts prefer doing business with "Rob Cosgrove of PDC" rather than with "PDC." Similarly, "Ostrichman" might be a great chat handle, but "Smythe Davies/Ostriches to Go/Houston" works better if you want people to send away for an ostrich farming manual.
- Reachability. Provide as many routes to the real you as you can: phone, fax, E-mail, beeper, etc. Make sure these routes work as they would with highly capitalized businesses—that your five-year-old daughter isn't the deliverer of your answering machine message, and that a fax sent to you in the middle of the night doesn't encounter a sleepy "hello?"
- Responsiveness. Reply as quickly as you can to inquiries—at least within twenty-four hours. Don't slouch around for the FTC-mandated allowance of thirty days before filling mail and telephone orders.
- Indicators of stability. Online these include credit-card pro-

cessing capability, recital of your number of years in business, membership in professional and civic organizations, willingness to provide a client list or references, and so on. When I tested online classified ads, I invited people to check me out in their public library, where at least one of my books was likely to be available. According to John Bunch, when the company D. L. Boone posted a description of its loose-knit confederation of consultants on BBSs and in Usenet groups, it included a list of press mentions people could check.

- Tangibility. Offer to send additional information by mail or fax. To the extent that these materials appear to have been prepared with care—professionally printed rather than a copy of a copy of a copy, or verbally and graphically exact rather than slipshod in spelling and design—you reassure prospects that you're not a twelve-year-old running a computer prank.

## Will You Deliver?

Let's not forget that you could exhibit all the trappings of a thriving business and still be incapable or unwilling to fulfill your claims. So besides the evidence that you exist, you must substantiate your competence and reliability. Although this requirement applies to almost every method of marketing, certain online vehicles enable you to satisfy it almost automatically. That is, people learn of your existence in a way that also demonstrates your professionalism. Regular substantive and constructive participation in a forum, mailing list, or newsgroup can prove that you know how to solve problems, that you have a depth of knowledge and experience, and that you have integrity. Many online communities ruthlessly expose fakers, who offer misinformation, endorse shady business tactics, or lack follow-through. So mere longevity and consistency in an online pond imply you can be counted on. If thoughtful onlookers observe respectful rapport between you and other professionals, they'll conclude you're probably not incompetent or a huckster.

Similarly, a library posting that contains creative ideas or descriptions of previous solutions can show beyond doubt that you're not any old consultant. In effect, file postings get samples of your work onto the computer screens of prospects. Skepticism fades when someone downloads a software patch of yours that works or a dramatic before-and-after editing lesson. A consortium of professors and consultants makes available at their Web site an old transcript of a client session as a credibility-boosting sample of their mentoring.

Beyond opportunities to show off what you've done, be ready to use the trust-building techniques that always work in traditional marketing: fully attributed testimonials, credentials, client lists, and, if appropriate, money-back guarantees.

## On Virtual Business

Ever since I sold my first freelance article, I've been doing business through the mail and by phone, often never meeting in person someone promising to pay me for performing such-and-such a piece of work. Thus I'm used to the idea of making long-distance deals, sealed by signatures exchanged by fax or by mail. But I know from talking about this at how-to-get-published seminars that the suggestion of doing business without face-to-face contact strikes many people as a baffling surprise. A consultant who gets high fees from Fortune 100 corporations didn't believe me when I said I'd interviewed consultants and lawyers who had found work online. Part of it has to do with one's comfort with technology, I think, and the intensity of one's electronic contacts. Debbie Dewey, a special projects manager and private investigator in Fairport, New York, who has been online for about nine years, says she has an excellent business relationship with someone in Switzerland with whom she's done nothing other than exchange E-mail. "I would go into a joint venture with this person, although we've never even spoken on the phone," she says. "I go with my gut instinct, and because of my investigative experience, I'm good at seeing through people." Similarly, Pat Pisarski, whose company ExpresSearch, Inc., sets up BBSs for other businesses, does almost all of her work long distance and says, "We've never encountered a prospect who expressed concern about not having met us in person. This is the wave of the future."

There appears to be a natural progression from electronic communication to telephone or fax and then to in-person meetings, but in some business realms, the prehiring sniffing out does not need to reach the third or even the second stage, while in some other business arenas it does. Bob Schmidt, a freelance copywriter in Orlando, Florida, buys and sells limited-edition ceramic figurines through "collectibles" bulletin boards on several online services. "You describe what you have and either post a price or hold an auction, asking people to submit bids," he explains. Then when the deal concludes, the buyer sends a cashier's check through the mail that might be as large as $1,000. "Most buyers don't even get on the phone," Schmidt says. "They have a precedent of answering classified ads. Once about twenty people were taken in by a guy who collected their money and never delivered the goods, but generally, people online are trustworthy." On the other hand, Stefan Kolle, an Amsterdam-based finance consultant for the entertainment industry, notes that while he has lined up sources of financing for feature film projects online, the finalization has to occur face to face. "No investor will give money to someone he hasn't met," he says.

# 16 | International Considerations

Around the time I first went online, a friend approached me with a proposition: He wanted to help businesses get publicity on the Internet, and he needed a guinea pig. Was I game? Of course. Our experiment would involve announcing the availability of a free sample issue of my creativity newsletter. A librarian working for him drew up a list of about twenty mailing lists and newsgroups that seemed appropriate, and we crafted a note that he would post with his Internet ID: "Would this be the right place to mention a new newsletter called *The Creative Glow: How to Be More Original, Inspired & Productive in Your Work*? You can get a free sample issue by E-mailing your address to Marcia Yudkin at . . ." E-mail responses began showing up the very day of his posting—from the United States, Canada, South Africa, Taiwan, Hong Kong, New Zealand. I gritted my teeth. At around $1.40 each for postage rather than $.29, the foreign requests held the potential of being budget-breakers. Very dumb of me, I thought, not to realize that free exposure on the Internet meant costlier marketing than the media coverage I was used to getting in the States.

If your business has been confined within your national borders, you probably won't instinctively foresee the adjustments in strategy, approach, and arrangements that are necessary in dealing with customers globally. Careful planning is needed whenever you put out the word electronically. So many people are linked up with each other that if you put something valuable even on a local BBS network, you can't expect your news or your offer to stay confined within your area code or your country. Don't skip this chapter! Keep reading, first for the hard-and-fast challenges you need to think about, then for the more subtle ones.

## Open Up to the World

In some cases doing business across national borders isn't much more complicated than dealing with someone far away within your own country. Business plan writer Marcia Layton picked up a client in Saudi Arabia from CompuServe, and says there weren't any problems in the relationship. "We worked with a contract, with one-third of the fee due at the beginning, and he paid in U.S. dollars from a U.S. bank. Faxes were more expensive, but E-mail kept the cost down. And conversing by E-mail was easier than it might have been by phone, since on the computer there wasn't any accent." In an international medium, you don't want to alienate or exclude clients solely because of geography. If you put up signs that amount to "No Foreigners," you could come across as an ill-mannered hick. But you want to be careful because problems with international communication and payment can rear their blazing heads. By learning about pitfalls others have tumbled into, you can avoid putting up unnecessary barriers while appropriately protecting yourself. Here's a checklist to get you started.

*Have you enabled distant prospects to get in touch with you?* In the last decade or two, most Americans have gotten into the habit of always including their telephone area code in business communications, but as Oakland, California, translator Ines Swaney discovered during a European trip, other blunders are possible. "I was particularly proud of my fax number because I'd discovered that the numbers spelled a certain word, so that's how I listed it on my business card: Fax ###-cutewrd—### being the area code and the other seven characters being the word I had discovered. Sure enough, the whole thing fell apart when I handed my card to someone in Hungary who I hoped to do business with in the future. I had assumed that our equivalency between numbers and letters on the telephone keys was universal—and it's not." For Europeans and Asians, you must not only avoid things like "508-CALL-N-US," but 800 numbers without a regular area-code number too, since 800 numbers don't work overseas. So that folks can figure out when to call your office, it's helpful always to include your geographical location along with a telephone number. Within the United States people can look up your area code to learn your time zone, but that may not be possible elsewhere.

*Have you adapted your product, if necessary, to foreign needs?* Tim Bourne, president of Structured Information Analysis Methods Limited in Hemel Hempstead, England, complains that American software manufacturers often neglect to make their parameters customizable for international paper sizes, telephone number formats, postal codes, and date formats (e.g., 31.3.96 instead of 3/31/96). "Products that include spelling checkers without a choice of dictionary are worse than useless here," Bourne adds, "and often you don't find out such things until after you buy."

*Have you investigated and posted appropriate foreign shipping charges?* Bourne cites a magazine subscription offered at $20 in the United States and $80 in Europe, which seems to be way out of line with additional mailing costs. Don't just pluck a foreign shipping charge out of your uninformed head. It's pretty simple, once you think of it, to call United Parcel Service, DHL (a big international air freight company), or the post office to find out how much a parcel of a certain size and weight would cost to send to a sample destination overseas. Shipping across an ocean may not cost as much as you would guess. I was surprised to learn that mailing two of my books "airmail printed matter" to a purchaser in Germany cost less than $6.

*Have you described acceptable payment methods?* For products, the easiest way to pay across borders is via credit card, which eliminates worries on both ends about currency exchange. "The transaction is charged in the currency of the supplier," says Tim Bourne, "and the customer is billed in his own currency. The currency conversion occurs at close to the current commercial rate—in my experience it's a better rate than changing money at a bank. I have credit-card customers in Australia, New Zealand, the U.S., Canada,

Japan, Saudi Arabia, and most countries in Europe." If you can't accept credit cards, or want to put out the welcome mat for foreigners who might not have Visa or MasterCard, you must be very clear and specific about payment methods. Before setting a policy, you might be wise to speak with your bank about its fees for options like checks in foreign currencies from foreign banks, in your own currency but drawn on a foreign bank, and in your own currency drawn on a foreign branch of a bank based in your country.

Bob Schenot, who self-published *The Shareware Book,* thought this through thoroughly before releasing the electronic text of his book on how to market software through the try-before-you-buy method in 1992. Knowing that the electronic text would find its way to many obscure locales, the New Hampshirite quoted prices for the book in French francs, Canadian dollars, English pounds, German marks, and Japanese yen as well as American dollars. "My terms are cash or international postal money orders in those currencies but *not* checks. One-third of international orders arrive in cash," he says, "so round numbers make things easier." Although Schenot's foreign prices use 1992 exchange rates, his profit margin is high enough to cushion any disadvantageous effect. "I am glad I never quoted a price in pesos, though," he adds.

*Have you made your online notes, brochure, catalog, and sales letters understandable to people whose grasp of your language may be shaky?* In particular, watch out for:

- Obscure slang ("scam artists")
- Jargon too recent to be in foreign dictionaries ("outsourcing")
- Nonuniversal measurements (inches, without centimeter equivalent)
- Noninternational acronyms ("IRS"; "VAT")
- Convoluted syntax (sentences only a lawyer would understand)
- Relative terms ("domestic" and "foreign," e.g., would be understood differently in every country)
- National terms ("the Dow Jones average" rather than "stock exchange index")
- Large numbers in words (in Britain, a "billion" is one million million, while in the United States it's a thousand million)
- Humor (rarely travels well)

In most cases, when you make your materials understandable internationally, you improve their readability for natives of your own country too.

According to translation company president Irene Agnew, companies based in the English-speaking world should give serious thought to making their materials available in other languages. "We're just beginning to help others put up multilingual World Wide Web pages," Agnew says. "Consider what it would do for your outreach to post a one-page profile of your company in, say, five languages: Spanish, French, German, Chinese, and Japanese. Companies are missing opportunities by not providing information in target languages. If you're going to export at all, you'll go further against the competition by doing that. Microsoft, for example, was the first to translate its software for Europe and it has the bulk of the market there."

*Have you made sure you're permitted to do business with customers abroad?* The United States government classifies software that produces so-called strong encryption—encoding so secure that even supercomputers can't crack it—as munitions and prohibits its export. The U.S. Customs Service began a campaign of harassment when it learned that Phil Zimmerman had posted his PGP, or Pretty Good Privacy, encryption program on the Internet, where it could be downloaded and, in effect, electronically exported. Similarly, computer consultant Charlie Gallie told me that he was working on bringing the Democratic Party online but facing the problem that federal law prohibits collecting money from foreign nationals. "How are we supposed to prevent this? We're waiting for a ruling from the Federal Elections Commission on applying laws and FEC regulations to this new medium. The problem doesn't occur only on the Internet, but we don't send mail solicitations outside of the country, and borders don't exist on the World Wide Web."

## Be Sensitive and Flexible

For providers of business services, it's probably even more important than for those selling products to keep your radar tuned for intercultural static that may impede your attempt to build a relationship with someone you've encountered online. Don't assume that the buildup to a deal with someone from another culture will look or feel the same as with someone from the same background as you. Alan Weiss, president of the Summit Consulting Group in East Greenwich, Rhode Island, and a consultant for numerous multinational companies, says that the decision-making process differs in different parts of the world. "Americans prefer to make relatively quick decisions, and except for the Germans, Swiss, and Dutch, most other cultures have a much slower process," Weiss says. "You have to be patient and understand that even if the other party isn't ready to act immediately, that doesn't mean they're not interested." You may also have to adjust your style of communication, he says. "Americans are likely to put a subject on the table and say, look, this is a difficulty, we need to discuss it. That could be suicide with other cultures. For example, in Latin America, people can say 'yes, yes, yes' to you forever and not mean it for one minute. It's not that they're dishonest, it's that culturally they don't confront issues that directly. So I would think that online, you need to be very circumspect in how you present things. Instead of asking, 'Do you like this or not?' it might be better to ask, 'What questions do you have about what I've just told you?' "

Several people, both British and German, told me that Europeans are in awe of American marketing savvy, but this has several consequences that may not be obvious. A straightforward chase after business may make some otherwise promising prospects from other countries skitter for cover. Stephan Uhrenbacher, a marketing strategist in Hamburg, Germany, put it this way: "Although I have quite a lot of experience with American marketing, I am still often amazed by the kind of hype that is created by some people online. We here in Europe very often prefer a more low-key approach to new contacts, even when selling our products. On the other hand, sometimes I have found that even when I was seriously interested in an offer, my relatively low-key reaction ('please send more information') led my partners abroad to believe that after all we were not too convinced of their product." Similarly, although Peter Wherritt, a technology consultant based near Oxford, England, was wary of overgeneralizing, he said, "In the U.K. there is not usually the open sharing of personal and company objectives as seems to happen in the U.S., and many American methodologies seem a bit too 'pushy' or even 'embarrassing' for the typical Englishman. I must stress it's only an initial reaction because people are good at accommodating that kind of thing when meeting face to face."

According to Wherritt, these cultural differences very much complicate international E-mail business communication. "E-mail makes it difficult to accommodate these differences. Because E-mail can be so impersonal, the individuals never get a chance to become comfortable with each other. People in the U.K. often need to get to know you, your values, how you work, and only then will they start thinking about how you may be able to help them. When you add the cultural differences to the impersonal aspects of E-mail it gets quite interesting. On the other hand, I have noticed a tendency for U.K. correspondents to open up more via E-mail, so that possibly it gives them a means of 'escaping' from their more restrained normal environment and exploring opportunities that they wouldn't otherwise seek out."

Another area of potential international friction in business relationships concerns the attitude toward rules, agreements, and contracts. From what I can observe, the United States may be the most legalistic country in the world. "Americans love rules, and are very rigid about them," says Edna Aphek, a professor of educational psychology in Jerusalem, Israel. Englishman Tim Bourne agrees: "The legal side of running a business seems to be very important to Americans, but is largely nonexistent in Europe—I've never consulted a lawyer in ten years of running my business. I have an agent in Germany who sells my products there. The deal is good for both of us, so we both want it to succeed. What good could a lawyer do?" I can add that when I worked in mainland China in the early 1980s, I noticed a very different attitude toward agreements from my American assumption that "a deal is a deal." There even formal contracts weren't taken as binding so much as merely summarizing the intentions of the participants, barring any major change of circumstances or heart. Someone who routinely asks all his or her business contacts to sign a formal agreement needs to know that in many other countries, that may not carry the same meaning or effect.

I've only scratched the surface with respect to crosscultural dif-

ficulties that might crop up in your international dealings, which
are probably as various as the countless combinations of back-
grounds of parties engaged in global business. Some general guidelines worth keeping in mind include these:

- Remember that your assumptions about how to carry on
  business might be considered bizarre, obnoxious, or even unethical in another part of the world.
- Whenever possible, seek out information about the culture of
  the other countries from which your clients and customers
  hail.
- Avoid remarks that cast you as the superior or as the party
  who has to educate the other side. Humility works better. Hoo
  Shao Pin, co-founder of Asia Online, an online service business in Singapore, told me that he was getting E-mail from
  Americans who had spent some time in Asia telling him that
  his Internet name, Online Coolie, was derogatory. "But I was
  raised in the vicinity of the Singapore River, where coolies
  would load and unload sacks of goods on and off the bum-
  boats. When I got to know some of the coolies personally,
  they seemed like friendly folks to me and although they had
  a hard life, seemed contented with it. Since then, I have always associated the word *coolie* with the positive meaning of
  hard work and earning an honest living. Hence I called myself
  Online Coolie, first to signify my late nights building the
  server, and secondly because it contains 'cool' if you read it.
  People need to recognize the cultural diversity on the Net and
  realize that I am free to call myself whatever name means
  something to me."
- Actively display your awareness of the international environment. According to Jay Linden, an Internet presence provider
  in Toronto, Ontario, non-Americans almost always name their
  country in their Internet signature, while Americans rarely do.
  "Also, no Canadian, Latin American, European, Asian, or
  Australian would dream of describing part of his country's political process without also naming the country and explaining
  anything which might be vague to 'foreigners.' Yet Americans
  on the net are constantly talking about First Amendment is-

sues and other facts of American life whose effects on the rest of the Net community will be indirect at most." Pause before pressing the Send button to think about how your message will come across in the wider world community.

- Let your foreign business prospects know you are open to learning what you can do to make them more comfortable doing business with you. As you build up mutual trust, this kind of feedback becomes more likely. You might learn not to send faxes or expect an E-mail reply on a certain day of the week—or that a phrase you considered innocuous has a salacious connotation somewhere else.

Most of all, don't let the possibility of knots keep you from tossing out international ropes. I'm happy to follow the advice of Meinrad Mueller, owner of an innovative recycling business in Munich-Grafath, Germany, who urged me, "Encourage your readers to take advantage of the new highway tools to reach out to the entire world!"

# 17 | When and How to Run Paid Online Advertisements

If you picture marketing methods arranged from those that *push* people into taking action to those that *pull* people into your sphere of customers and clients, most of my time in this book has been spent on methods toward the "pull" end of the spectrum. In most online contexts, pushiness backfires; sometimes it opens you up to severe consequences. In April 1994, for instance, two immigration lawyers from Phoenix, Arizona, earned lasting international notoriety for a gargantuan hustle on the Internet. Laurence Canter and Martha Siegel "spammed" Usenet—they placed an advertisement for $95 application assistance for a United States work-permit lottery in more than five thousand newsgroups, including those on totally irrelevant topics, such as "alt.sport.bowling" and "comp.sys.mac.graphics." Outrage from Internet users arrived in such intensity and volume that their service provider became unable to function and disconnected their account. The book they hastened to write, *How to Make a Fortune on the Information Superhighway,* contains the most incredible collection of fallacious reasoning and defenses of boorishness that I have ever seen in print. I definitely do not recommend their tactics if you value a business reputation.

Yet in one online zone—the classifieds on the commercial services and BBSs—you can push away to your heart's content. You can unleash all the carnival-barker tactics I've elsewhere warned you against, make outright offers, urge readers to "Act now!" and freely display your prices. Where the classifieds are concerned,

sales, not visibility, are your goal, and practically all the accumulated wisdom of the advertising/direct-mail world applies. And
those exasperated by the unquantifiability of soft-sell techniques
can get happily to work here, since costs and earnings are very
neat, contained, and easy to compute.

## Do Online Classifieds Work?

CompuServe member Bobby Bhasin gets about two leads a day
from a long-running classified ad on the service for his father's
eighteen-room bed-and-breakfast inn in London. That may not
sound like much of a response, but it has translated into one or two
guests every week that the inn would not otherwise have. "Travel
agents normally don't book small places like ours because they
don't know us," says Bhasin. Similarly, writer Marcia Layton receives from five to twenty inquiries a week from her "Need a Business Plan?" classified on CompuServe. "A very small percentage
has turned into business, but each client represents thousands of
dollars," she notes. San Francisco copywriter Jonathan Mizel could
hardly stop jumping up and down with excitement after he, a self-
described "absolute computer idiot," placed a free classified ad on
America Online for his *Direct-Marketing Firepower* electronic
book and received a paid order within an hour. Over on Prodigy,
Merry Schiff of Medical Management Software in San Mateo, California, had to take a breather from running her ad because the
thirty to fifty responses a day she was getting for her registered
business opportunity were overwhelming.

On the other hand, Chris Brandlon, a marketer based in Portland,
Oregon, tested online ads for several clients and for one of his own
information products, but didn't find it profitable enough to continue pursuing. "When I ran more ads, I didn't get a mathematical
increase in sales," he says. "It's an excellent testing ground for new
concepts, but I'm going back to magazine ads, newspaper classifieds, card-deck mailings, etcetera. Online ads are cheaper, but the
volume is much better offline."

When I talk about profits being easy to calculate with online
ads, I do not mean mathematical exercises like this one, taken from

a sales letter by one Mike Collands of San Diego, California: "Say you create a little report priced at $10. Then you start putting word out in cyberspace. Assume your report isn't real popular. So, only 1 in 10,000 people want it. However, a big commercial online service can easily reach 650,000 people for you. So, you'll still sell 65 reports. At $10 each you'll take in $650. Hang on, you're not finished. The top five services have at least 5 million people online. Selling to just 1 out of every 10,000 people will generate $5,000. Whoa! Not bad for a lousy $10 report?" Using the same premises, Collands goes on to add in an additional $15,000 from the Internet—"an easy, bare-bones minimum—$20,000!"

The problem here is the premise that 1 out of 10,000 will buy. Perhaps it's reasonable to suppose that 1 out of 10,000 *exposed to* your message will buy, but membership numbers do not equal the number of people exposed to a classified ad. A majority of online-service members never go anywhere near the classifieds, and of those who do, many will select only certain categories to browse and never run across your ad. Similarly, the vast majority of folks with access to the Internet only exchange E-mail and do not browse anywhere. So don't be fooled by this all too common kind of rosy-lensed forecast. The only way to predict response is to test, and the only dependable formula for success is this one:

*Profits = Revenue minus (Cost of ad, Fulfillment costs, and, optionally, Cost in time or labor to deal with responses)*

For example, if I decided to place a four-line ad on CompuServe for four weeks, right now that would cost me just $12 (not a misprint!). It would cost me approximately $.12 to send each person who responded a 4-page electronic sales letter. Some people will ask for the information to be sent to them by mail, and those each cost me $.32 postage plus $.14 for the letter and envelope. If my product sells for $50 and costs me $10, and only 1 out of 5 asks for mailed information, then if I can convert 1 out of every 50 inquiries into a sale, my profits equal 50 - (12 + 10 + 4.8 + 4.6), or $18.60 for every 50 inquiries I receive. (I didn't include the CompuServe membership fee because I am on the service anyway.) Now if it took me five hours to deal with fifty inquiries, that's a

very different proposition than if I am able to take care of fifty inquiries and one sale in half an hour. So even if you don't count
your labor into the monetary equation—as I customarily don't, considering marketing an inescapable part of being in business, like
keeping records—be aware of how much or how little time online
ads require versus other methods of selling. Take into account too
the possibility of so-called back-end sales—selling further, perhaps
higher-priced products or services to those who buy initially.

The ability to lower both the cost of ads and the fulfillment costs
explains why many direct-mail veterans have fallen head over heels
in love with online classifieds. In 1993, when Sheila Danzig of Fort
Lauderdale, Florida, retired from the direct-mail business, it was
costing her more than $2 for every person who responded to a print
ad. Finding out that electronic marketing cut that cost by a factor
of ten brought her out of retirement. Jonathan Mizel, who publishes
the *Online Marketing Letter,* lists one more advantage of selling
online versus via snail-mail or print ads: It's incredibly quick. Instead of waiting months until a magazine ad appears and a while
longer as responses build to a peak, you know within twenty-four
hours whether or not an ad is going to work. Then, he points out,
if you can ask people to reply to an Internet "mailbot," which automatically sends back your sales message to anyone who E-mails
it, your rate of converting prospects to sales becomes irrelevant. In
other words, you tell people to send an E-mail message to
"info@yoursite.com" for more information, and then you can go
fishing and at your leisure just check your fax, phone, and regular
E-mail and snail-mail boxes for orders. I've seen mailbot offers for
just $20 a year. However, responses to an ad on the online services,
which have better demographics for many marketers than the
Internet, can't easily be robotized in this way, and CompuServe
members in particular get charged extra for mail to and from an
Internet mailbot.

Because online classifieds cost so little to place, you might want
to perform some tests to see how favorably the profit equation
works for your product or service. Privately sponsored Internet
classifieds, where you rent a paragraph or two on someone else's
World Wide Web site (see Chapter 13) or on their electronic mailing list (see Chapter 13), are beginning to spring up as well. Ac-

cording to Sheila Danzig, anything that you can sell without visuals or over the telephone can sell through online classifieds. Information products, consulting services, and computer-related products and services do best. If you use a mailbot, adds Danzig, use the kind that sends your message back to anyone who writes, not the kind that does so only if a prospect writes a precise combination of words and symbols in the subject heading or the message.

## Classified Copywriting in a Nutshell

In just a few pages I can't turn you into a copywriter par excellence. But I can highlight the most important proven principles that bring you paid orders.

*The clout of headlines.* As with discussion messages, your headline determines how many people choose to look at your classified ad. Before committing yourself to something you like, spend some time scanning others' headlines to see which ones appeal to you. Mizel points out that a good way to scope out the wording and topics that are real grabbers is to search forum libraries for files that have the most downloads. Make sure that the headline tone is compatible with your professional image, though. Direct-mail pro Sheila Danzig can scream out with I MADE $16 MILLION!! but Marcia Layton's much pricier, professional service fits well with the low-key, straightforward NEED A BUSINESS PLAN?

*The old two-step.* Instead of trying to get orders directly from your classified ad, first collect leads that you then convert to sales with a multipage, in-depth letter. That is, keep the text of your ad to four lines or so, ask people to reply for more information, and then get them a detailed sales pitch that they can read when they are mentally out of browsing mode. Pack the letter full of substance as well as sales talk. As Chris Brandlon puts it, "When people ask for more information, give them an education, not just a sales letter." Mere "Buy now! Hurry! Offer expires in forty-eight hours!" does not work in the information-rich online environment.

*Test, test, test.* Intuition, experience, and study do not give *anyone* the ability to forecast what words, what punctuation, what offer will get the greatest response. Would you have guessed, for instance, that the headline HERE'S A STRANGE WAY TO LEARN MUSIC outpulled A FEW MONTHS AGO I COULDN'T PLAY A NOTE by a wide margin? John Caples (see Resources) provides scores of illuminating examples, highlighting the monumental sensitivity of readers to minuscule differences. My favorite is the headline HOW TO REPAIR CARS—QUICKLY, EASILY, RIGHT, which did all right, but changing the single word *Repair* to *Fix* while keeping everything else the same increased orders 18 percent.

*The personal touch.* Since your sales letter will show up in people's electronic mailboxes, use the time-tested format of a letter. That means including a date, salutation, dynamic opening paragraph, closing, and signature line and a "P.S." The one extra ingredient you should add is a selling headline, perhaps the very one used in your ad, at the beginning. When you can, customize your standard reply letter for each recipient with his or her name in the salutation. Lawrence Seldin, author of *Power Tips for the Apple Newton,* did this until he got tired of customizing each reply. Within a week he received his first negative feedback ever, and promptly returned to adding "Dear ————."

*Conversational tone.* Rather than a formal, off-putting brief or a simple but distant list of prices, establish a connection with your respondent by explaining your offerings as if you were telling a friend about them. Alfred and Emily Glossbrenner's mailbot sales piece, for instance, starts off with a spread-out W E L C O M E! and then says, "This file is being brought to you by an autoresponder that lives at books@infomat.com. It will tell you how to get your hands on some truly wonderful computer books, if we do say so ourselves." The letter continues with the same casual voice, distinctive with personality.

*Many contact points, many payment mechanisms.* In your letter, make it possible for people to order by phone, by fax, by E-mail, by mail, and in any other way you can imagine. Insert all your contact information obviously and more than once. An order form that people can print out and fax or send helps, as does your announcement that you accept major credit cards, checks, money orders, and cash. As I explained in Chapter 16, wherever you advertise online, you may attract international attention, so be prepared with overseas shipping prices and a foreign-payment acceptance policy.

*Guarantees.* As I explained in more depth in Chapter 15, online prospects have plenty of reason to be more suspicious than elsewhere. Reassure them with a way to back out of the deal if you let them down. Counterintuitive as it may seem, the stronger and longer your guarantee, the less likely you are to have to deliver on it. "When I first started out in mail order, I offered a three-day guarantee," remembers Sheila Danzig. "This didn't instill confidence in the buyer, and pressured those who did buy it to return it right away, before the deadline passed. With a thirty-day or one-year guarantee, people take their time, and then forget—although if you sell a bad product, you'll get returns even if you don't mention any guarantee."

*Incentives.* Provide an incentive for people to act now. Regardless of how much they need your help, human beings procrastinate and then they fail to act. Special prices if they order in the next ten days, strict expiration dates for offers, and the like, help them break through their inertia. Rob Cosgrove of Precision Data Corporation in Memphis, Tennessee, has found that nonelectronic response methods, such as fax on demand or an 800 number, move people more effectively toward a buying decision than a mere mouse click or R-Return. "When we can get them to stop typing at us, we can sell," says Cosgrove.

*Effective Presentation.* Take care with layout, spelling, and descriptions. All people have to go on is the text in front of them, and if it's verbally, aesthetically, or logically a mess, some will not respond. See Chapter 14 for suggestions on making plain text as easy as possible to read and absorb.

# 18 | When and How to Send E-mail Solicitations

Normally I'm a pleasant person, but I've been known to scold tele-marketers who interrupt my work with smooth pitches I've heard before. When I can figure out who's selling my name and address, I may call to get myself taken off the lists. I even gave the county sheriff a talking-to when he showed up at my door for the third time trying to serve a summons on a previous occupant. Obviously I don't appreciate intrusions—and I'm not alone. Michael Strangelove, author of *How to Advertise on the Internet,* calls mass unsolicited E-mailing "bad PR. Stealing both time and money from the recipient, it is in direct violation of the most emotionally charged community norm in cyberspace—do not put unwanted information in my mailbox." Strangelove also notes that people regularly lose their Internet and online service accounts for disregarding this norm. Yet I don't hesitate to extend a blessing to two varieties of unsolicited E-mail. When done right, E-mail to people who are not expecting it is hardly intrusive or risky at all.

## You Were Asking About . . .

Mike Bayer, an assistant sysop in CompuServe's PR and Marketing forum, explains the well-mannered method of snagging clients online with the example of a coffee dealer who serviced professional offices and showed up asking about a mass mailing he was working on. "About five or six of us asked questions and offered advice. Someone suggested that he hire someone to write the piece, and he shot back, 'Do you know someone?' I sent him an E-mail saying that I could help, and then sent my electronic brochure, receipt requested, when he asked for it. A day later I sent him another message and three days after that he called me. He said I'd been one of five or six who had contacted him, and he picked me because I'd done a lot of work with his target audience—doctors and attorneys." Note that Bayer didn't send his information until the prospect asked for it, a policy Bayer follows "because I don't like it when people promote themselves aggressively to me."

Bayer's procedure is practically guaranteed to keep you in the good graces of its recipient because (1) the offer of help is brief, informal, and related to a need the prospect publicly expressed; and (2) after offering help, it puts the prospect in the driver's seat. The farther you stray from those two guidelines, the greater your risk of annoying a prospect and inviting complaints that, if repeated, could lead to losing your online access. This is not a matter of respecting arbitrary rules but of understanding how communications come across in cyberspace. Someone who asks for help or information does not experience a courteous offer of help or information as intrusive. This holds as true for E-mail as it does in the antipromotional atmosphere of an Internet newsgroup, about which Bryan Pfaffenberger told me, "If I had a company and saw someone ask if anyone knew where to get a certain kind of product, no one would get upset if I posted a response about my product and said where you could find free files about it. Ninety-nine percent of Usenet people would see that as a positive contribution to the discussion, not an ad."

When in doubt, think about appropriate behavior at a social gathering. If someone at a dinner party said, "By the way, everyone, I'm looking for a portrait photographer. Can anyone recommend someone?" would you whip out your briefcase right then and there for a show-and-tell of every item in your portfolio? You'd do far better to pass your business card to that person and say, "Give me a call and I'll be glad to show you my portfolio." In E-mail as well, avoid overwhelming the person. I once asked for some information in a forum and found an enormous file in my E-mail the next day from a consultant with qualification after qualification, credential after credential, testimonial after testimonial. It took more than a minute to page through to the end of the file in order to get rid of it (which I did). What irritated me in this case was the amount of information, not the consultant getting in touch with me per se. I felt helpless in the face of this onslaught of words because I didn't know how to quit the file to go on to the next piece of mail except by scrolling through to the end. Had the very same file arrived at a later stage of my decision-making process, I might have welcomed it and read it carefully. But this fellow won't get a second chance with me. Too much too soon gave me the impression that he's self-centered and overbearing.

Now rewind to the person mentioning at the dinner party that she's looking for a photographer. Would you take that as a cue to stand up and perform a loud television-type commercial message to her? I hope not! It's just as bad to send a "Three for the price of one! Special offer expires December 31st!" ad to someone's mailbox when they have indicated a need. Your offer of help needs to be low-key, conversational, and person to person, not worded like an ad or a promotion. Frederic Wilf, an intellectual property and business law attorney in Media, Pennsylvania, mutes the promotional aspect of an E-mail response by providing an answer to the seeker's question—or as much of an answer as he reasonably can. "Since I am a lawyer and am asked legal questions, I can't provide detailed legal advice without first getting all the information (and without first getting a retainer to cover my services). However, I can respond to a request for legal information by providing general background information, and by pointing the person to resources for more information. This way, the person who asked the question has received helpful information and knows that I am available to provide legal services. Enough of these contacts do mature into paying clients to make the process worthwhile for me."

Some of the people I interviewed who get business by approaching potential clients through E-mail do not wait until a person explicitly asks, "Does anyone know a . . . ?" Instead, they humbly and politely introduce themselves and state how they might be of help with respect to something that person was discussing in public. Computer consultant Gary Ellenbogen, for instance, relies on his intuition to tell him when someone wrestling with a technical problem in a forum might be open to hiring him. "When it's clear that someone is looking for something that they're not getting and that I could help with, I might pop them a note. Usually I get a reply saying, 'You couldn't have done this at a better time. I'm so grateful.' " Numerous unsolicited offers of this sort go unanswered, but Ellenbogen has never received a complaint.

## Here's Our Newsletter or New Offer

There appears to be a prevalent principle online that if you specifically request information from a company or individual, later promotional communications from that source don't count as unsolicited messages. However, this doesn't mean you should cling to the letter of this rule and violate its spirit. The underlying thought is that in the context of a business *relationship,* unexpected, uninitiated contact is perfectly fine. Some companies periodically send broadsides to their E-mail lists of everyone who previously answered one of their ads or wrote them for information. To head off complaints, do your best to create a connection with those on your list that goes beyond mere one-time contact. In addition, tiptoe in to their attention with a careful, low-key reminder of the link. If you show up screaming "Buy! Buy!" in the mailbox of someone who doesn't recognize who you are—even if that person did once request information from you—it feels like a hustle, and will antagonize some of the folks you are trying to sell to. Carefully soothe your recipients' sensitivities, however, and hardly any hackles will go up.

Looking back through several months of my E-mail messages, I can find two examples of companies that did this right. The Online Bookstore sent me an unsolicited notice about its new multilingual, international BookFinder service. It reduced the annoyance factor almost to zero with this preface:

****This message details The Online BookStore's
(OBS) new efforts to expand and customize our
offerings to readers on the Net. You are receiving this

message because at some time since OBS started in
1992, you have expressed interest in hearing about
OBS activities. This is our first mailing to the list; if for
any reason you want your name taken off the OBS list
(which list is strictly confidential, in use only by OBS, and
will not be sold, shown, or leased to any third parties,
and is maintained offline), let us know by simply
returning this message to us with UNSUBSCRIBE in the
subject line and we'll delete your name. If you are
interested in hearing from OBS from time to time, no
response or commitment is necessary, just read on.
Thank you for your interest. * * * *

Similarly, something called the *Net Marketing Newsletter,* which I
had not intentionally subscribed to, arrived with the following mol-
lifying introduction:

You have responded to an ad for an e-book in the last 6
months. That book was Make Money On the Net . . .
The Right Way. This e-book has become the first
WeBestseller and we are sending a FREE newsletter to
everyone who has responded assuming you are
interested in the latest marketing developments on the
Net. Following 'Netiquette you can send an email
message to me at stu@3adata.com and your email
address will be immediately deleted from the database.
We plan to send a quarterly newsletter with 'net news
from the marketing front. Hope this explains!

The paper promotional tools that these electronic dispatches resemble are press releases (for the Online Bookstore piece) and a
marketing newsletter (for the 3adata one). However, they were appropriately modified in form to take account of the E-mail medium.
Done right, these follow-up communications to your own list can
serve numerous purposes. By putting your company's name in front
of people who have previously bought from or written to you, they
build precious familiarity for you. When you use a soft-sell approach, mentioning products and services without pushing them in-

sistently, they can bring in orders. And with a strategic choice of content, you can have a chance to *demonstrate* your talents and capabilities rather than merely *tell*. Do you want to be known as the up-to-the-nanosecond firm? Then issue news flashes about legislative developments or periodical technical updates. Do you want prospects to appreciate your mastery in your field? Then send a quarterly electronic newsletter containing how-to articles and stories of how your clients succeeded.

Stay out of trouble with recipients by keeping the informational content of your missive high. Before sending out anything of this sort, subject your piece to a stringent "What's in it for the customer?" test. Instead of being self-serving, your piece must be reader centered. Ruthlessly slash any hype from it. Tell recipients how they got onto your list and let them know the painless, no-questions-asked way of getting off. And never, never, never trade, sell, or rent your E-mail list if you have any hope of continuing to operate smoothly in cyberspace.

## E-mail Etiquette

While we're discussing E-mail communication, let's review some dos and dont's that apply to any electronic business messages you may send. If you're instinctively considerate on paper, on the telephone, and in person, most of these guidelines will appear obvious, since they have to do with respect for those you communicate with. Don't worry, however, if some take you by surprise. Mannerliness can always improve when you put your mind to it.

**Don't pester people.** Sending E-mail seems so easy that some people overdo it, says Susan RoAne, author of *The Secrets of Savvy Networking.* "If you call someone who's not your friend every three days, that's encumbering, and the same goes for E-mail. Use some decorum, honor people's time. Don't use the technology to excess just because it doesn't take any brains to press Reply."

**Don't be devious.** A best-selling novelist told me that someone had tracked him down through an E-mail account held by his wife. "This person had quizzed anyone and everyone, randomly firing off inquiries until she found my wife. I don't recommend this tactic. It felt like an invasion. And with that kind of sneaky stuff at work, it doesn't give me a good impression of someone who would do that."

*Do cushion canned messages.* Instead of sending an impersonal informational file to someone who wants to know more about what you do, either add a customized introduction or send a personal "here's what's coming" message first. "I usually either send a canned message enclosed in my reply or I say that the following E-mail contains information about my firm or about a particular topic," says attorney Frederic Wilf. "The recipient knows that the information is canned but the accompanying personalized message takes the edge off."

*Do stick to straight text unless given permission to do otherwise.* Many people won't have the faintest idea of what to do with a so-called binary file—a program, program-specific file, or specially compressed file—that turns up in their E-mail. Even if they know how to unpack and read it, that's a lot of trouble to expect someone to go to, particularly for something like your résumé rather than the software patch that's going to allow them to meet a pressing deadline.

*Don't overburden your recipient.* "I call to get permission before I send a ten-page fax," says Susan RoAne. "You should do the same with E-mail." Anything longer than 20,000 bytes (seven or eight single-spaced pages) may not make it through an online service's gateway, according to Michael Strangelove. E-mail that goes on and on is tiring to read on the computer and taxing on the attention span.

*Do use discretion with multiple addressees.* Someone who doesn't reveal his or her E-mail address to every Dick, Jane, and Sally may not appreciate you listing it visibly when you send a single message to many people at once. Most E-mail systems have separate procedures for "carbon copies," where the list of recipients appears along with the message and "blind carbon copies," where the list is nowhere to be seen. Bother to send the "blind" kind of message to a list, especially where those on the list really deserve to remain anonymous to each other, as with people answering classified ads.

# 19 | Dousing the Flames

"As for your snotty little remarks—I'm not as petty, small, and vindictive as you. You're a vicious and pathetic person who twists the words of others for your own small ego. And, I'll tell you this, your attitudes, your snide posts, your egregious smugness and superciliousness disgust me."—Name withheld

Well, I'll tell you this: It's no fun finding words like these on one's computer screen first thing in the morning. I hope it never happens to you, because getting "flamed," as abusive computer messaging is known, can be a scorching experience. I had not received such a burst of venom since I was fourteen years old. It wreaked no lasting damage, but it helped me appreciate how important it is to be prepared for a phenomenon that can go far beyond ritual blade-to-blade combat with verbal swords. Certain factors in the process of communicating via computers seem to prod some people into emotional overtilt. But since engaging in flaming, even its tamer forms, can broil your business image, I'll explain why flaming occurs, how to handle flare-ups directed at you, and how to disengage yourself from provocations so that you don't fuel a searing exchange of insults.

## Hotheadedness in Cyberspace

In its mildest form, flaming involves an exchange of emotional remarks in stronger language than most of us normally use in everyday life. Yishai Almog, an Israeli-American psychologist and management consultant, points to four reasons why flaming easily gets going online. First, because there's no nonverbal context for someone's words, it's easy for the recipient to misunderstand a message and read into it a very different meaning than what was intended. Almog cites an example: "In face-to-face communication, when someone says 'Thanks a lot' you know from their tone inflection or facial expression whether that means 'I really appreciated that' or 'I hate your guts.' Online, you lose those multiple levels of communication." Second, emotions may get too intense for ordinary civil exchanges of words. As Almog puts it, "People communicate online in ways that are very intimate with respect to content, or very charged, so that the level of content is high, and a lot gets across substantively, but the channel of communication is too narrow to contain and convey all of what they're feeling." So arguments quickly escalate. Interestingly, when I asked sysops what were the perennial flame topics in their forums, I got answers like, for a desktop publishing forum, the "Macintosh versus IBM" debate and whether or not one should ever work on speculation, and for a PR forum, the ethics of doing public relations for a tobacco company like Philip Morris. These are issues where logical methods of persuasion rarely change anyone's mind, and therefore frustrations run high.

Third, says Yishai Almog, the asynchronous or time-delayed nature of message boards allows misunderstandings to set in without correction. "You don't have an immediate chance to check out what the other person meant the way you do on the telephone or in person, where you can ask, 'Wait a minute, are you saying . . . ?' and the person can respond, 'No, no, no! That's not what I meant.' If somebody sends you something that rubs you the wrong way, whatever starts getting stirred in you stays there. That built-in communication break can cause trouble, especially on a bulletin board, where one person responds to what they thought someone else meant, and then a whole series of people piggyback on that. Before you know it you have a free-for-all, with people interpreting an interpretation of an interpretation." And fourth, says Almog, the online world lacks clear expectations, limits, and sanctions against extreme behavior. "The medium encourages people to act out their psychological agendas in ways that are ordinarily curbed by social norms. On the Internet, there's no framework to contain the behavior, so that things can escalate freely. Other than the desirability of open and free expression, there is no agreed-upon set of norms."

Barb Tomlin, a former board leader on Prodigy and president of Westward Connections in Albuquerque, New Mexico, also suggests that many of the more offensive messages that get sent through cyberspace aren't really meant as communication. "We all have thoughts going around in our head that we wouldn't normally put on paper. But on the computer, it's like you're talking to yourself. Something in the little fuzzy ions around the characters releases thoughts that are actually self-talk." Almog calls it "dumping"—an attempt to vent and have an emotional impact. What I compare it with is those times when you are in a bad mood, someone cuts you off in traffic, and you let loose a stream of belligerent slurs about his or her driving (and perhaps parentage). Such venting may look and sound like communication, but it serves a very different purpose.

On the Internet, flaming can also serve as a means of vigilantism. Since no one owns or officially governs the network, morally self-righteous folks sometimes take on a policing role and use whatever weapons they have available. These include threats, complaints to the offender's service provider, "mail bombs"—the sending of dictionary-sized files repeatedly to an E-mail address—and invective that would send chills down the spine of a serial killer. The frontispiece of Michael Strangelove's book, *How to Advertise on the Internet*, features messages from three such characters promising to retaliate if they receive any unsolicited E-mail advertisements. "I'll mount a personal campaign to flood the mailbox of the person who sent it," one wrote. Retaliatory sabotage really can wreak havoc on your online marketing plans. Some well-known personages who have rubbed people the wrong way have become the victims of skilled imposters putting up odious messages under their name. Also, numerous self-appointed Internet watchdogs know how to create a "cancelbot" that automatically expunges all newsgroup messages from a given source. One so-far-anonymous entity called Cancelmoose goes around canceling any mass postings to twenty or more groups at once. Another individual named Axel Boldt maintains a "Blacklist of Internet Advertisers" listing offenders who have been sending unsolicited commercial E-mail or inappropriate commercial posts to newsgroups or mailing lists. Boldt includes personal names, phone and fax numbers, E-mail and postal addresses, and other details so that others outraged by the violators can take action.

Among the younger set, flaming appears to have developed into a competitive sport. Several Internet newsgroups, such as "alt.flame," provide a playing field for top-notch word sluggers to enjoy bashing matches for fun. But when an adult with professional standing wallops you with industrial-strength vilification, as happened to me and to *New Yorker* writer John Seabrook from a technology columnist for a major newspaper, something besides adolescent horseplay may be going on. "Unfortunately, not everyone who is chronologically an adult is also psychologically mature," says Yishai Almog. "A certain percentage of the population may appear to be adults but really are not. For example, an individual with a reputation to maintain who would send that kind of extreme message clearly has difficulty containing his emotions. As we know from phenomena like drive-by shootings, some people out there are volcanoes waiting to erupt."

## What to Do When It Happens to You

It's hard not to get shocked and troubled when vicious language meant for you shows up on your computer screen. Early in 1994, Seabrook, who had profiled Microsoft chairman Bill Gates for *The New Yorker,* received a flame much too obscene for me to quote comfortably in this book. "The flame seemed to put a chill in the center of my chest which I could feel spreading slowly outward," he later wrote. "My shoulders began to shake. I got up and walked quickly to the soda machines for no good reason, then hurried back to my desk." Not only were the words still on the screen, Seabrook couldn't wipe the nasty message out of his brain. He spent most of that day composing equally vile replies that he held back from transmitting and instead sent a subdued attempt at polite irony. In return came another fierce insult.

"When you happen to trigger the minefield, the last thing you should do is take it personally," advises Almog. "It's pointless to respond." Janet Attard, who administers forums on several online services, agrees. "The smartest—and the hardest—thing to do is simply to ignore a provocation," she says. "When someone attacks you, your natural impulse is to defend yourself. But the more you say, the longer the episode goes on, and flaming back will make you look unprofessional. On a bulletin board, often other users will come along and defend you, and if they don't, just one or two messages will get quickly forgotten. But if you respond in kind, it turns into something like rubbernecking on the highway—everyone comes along to see who's going to say what next to whom."

Freelance writer Angela Gunn remembers one particularly regrettable instance in which she jumped impetuously onto the field of combat with both dukes up. "In the Comics forum on CompuServe, someone said something about copyright that I replied to with a thoughtful post detailing both sides of the issue. Thinking that everyone knew who I was, which was stupid, I signed it, 'A.G., former 'zine publisher.' He came back on and started ranting at me as if I was some seventeen-year-old, and I wrote, 'Look, Buckwheat'—that's New York City slang, I hear it a lot—'you want a standdown? Here's my resume.' Then he really let loose. 'How dare you, you racist bitch . . .' He forgot that I couldn't see him on my monitor. How was I supposed to know he was African-American? It was an unfortunate choice of words on my part, and he overreacted."

I have seen apologies work wonders when it looked like things were going to heat up into that vehement an exchange. Once, having decided to buy a new dictionary, I listed my criteria and asked other writers which one they would recommend. I mentioned that I wanted it to include new American expressions but without giving a green light to what I considered overly permissive usage, like saying that "all right" could also be spelled "alright." Many writers

offered useful information, but one took me to task for expecting
dictionaries to dictate usage. Her use of the sentence, "You should
know better than anyone. . . ." set me off, and I replied, "Please!
Surely I have the right to buy whatever kind of dictionary I want."
Someone whose name I didn't recognize posted a message that
read, "Uh-oh, flame war coming :-) Be kind, everyone :-)," and just
while I was thinking that perhaps I should have known better than
to speak so sharply, I saw that the next message was an apology
from the woman who had admonished me. The entire affair ended
there.

What you most need in order to avoid fanning the flames is a
method of disengaging yourself from provocative messages on the
screen or of allowing yourself to sound off but keeping your finger
far away from the Send button. Chances are that if you wait to reply until the next time you go online, you'll be in a better position
to decide how to do so in a way consistent with your professional
image. Ask yourself, Is my pride worth the mayhem I'll cause? One
time I was so concerned about what I saw as a deceptive offer that
had been posted publicly that I could only prevent myself from getting involved by telling myself dozens of times, "It's none of your
business. It's none of your business." If you regret having sent a
message, find out if there's a way to delete it. On CompuServe you
can not only easily delete any of your own messages, you can also
delete an intemperate public message from someone else addressed
specifically to you. On other services you may have to ask a sysop
or board leader to get rid of your ill-considered post for you. "Tell
the sysop exactly where the message is, and remember that the
sysop doesn't live online and may not be able to delete it till the
following morning," says Janet Attard.

## Prevention Tactics

A few communication techniques will help you avoid triggering
or becoming a target of overly emotional messages online. Some
are variations of advice your parents probably taught you, while
others pertain particularly to the online environment.

*Stay out of no-win arguments.* On certain topics, like

whether or not all lawyers are scumbags, the chances of you sway-
ing opinions are just about nil. Save your energy for issues where
people are more likely to be interested in what you have to say. If
you know what makes the other person wrong, try explaining it
point by point rather than simply disagreeing. "This tactic is not for
the faint at heart," warns Angela Gunn. "You might have to go
back and defend yourself."

*Don't make personal remarks.* Call someone a jerk, an idiot,
an ignoramus, or a hick and it's safe to assume he or she will take
offense. Take issue with the substance of what he or she said, on
the other hand, and constructive dialogue can ensue.

*Notice what triggers misunderstandings or misplaced
outrage.* "People seem to have a hard time understanding the dry
humor typical of Vermonters," says computer consultant Gary
Ellenbogen of Winooski, Vermont. "I've learned to be careful about
that." Don't rely on symbolic grins or smileys to take the edge off
disrespectful remarks. I've seen one person make gratuitously nasty
comments and then add a "<g>," as if that would sweeten the
thought. It doesn't.

*Always begin by assuming you've misunderstood.* "Actively assume that you've put a more negative interpretation on a remark than was intended," says Yishai Almog. "Restate it in your
own words and ask the person who said it for a clarification." This
policy saves face for both you and your respondent and helps prevent the creation of unnecessary enemies. Similarly, if someone
flames you, tell yourself it has nothing to do with you personally,
and that it reflects more on them than on you. "It's equivalent to
you bumping someone and them yelling very loudly," Almog says.

*Sandwich a negative message between positive
comments.* I learned this from communication consultant Laurie
Schloff, with whom I wrote *Smart Speaking* and *He and She Talk.*
Instead of flying off the handle with "You sexist pig!" try: "You
made some valid points, but did you realize the phrase 'executives
and their wives' falsely assumes all executives are male? Acknowledging the accomplishments of women lets people know you're
aware of what's happening in today's business world."

*When appropriate, express criticism privately.* The old saying, "If you can't say anything nice, don't say anything at all" is as

appropriate for the business world as it is for the playground. Writer Lary Crews follows this policy, he says. "When I have anything negative to say, I say it by E-mail. If I put it on a message board on America Online, it's going to stay there for a long time."

**Add self-effacing apologies in advance.** If you're going to promote yourself in Internet newsgroups, avoid flames by doing it in a humble, self-deprecating way that excuses itself, advises Bryan Pfaffenberger, author of *The Usenet Book*. For instance: "Is it OK if I also mention my own book, *Guide for Tiddlywinks Tournamenters?* It includes a little section on competitive strategies that people say has been helpful to them."

**Apologize afterwards when appropriate.** If you provoke a mess with one of your messages, undo as much damage as you can with a sincere apology. I forgot to use the sandwich technique, above, when I E-mailed an author of one of the books referred to in Resources about a mistake I'd noticed in his book. He replied grumpily and defensively, and I apologized, acknowledging that I should have written, "I'm looking forward to reading your book. I couldn't help noticing, however, that you referred to X as a Y when she is a Z. If it's not too late to correct this, it will help your book's reception." The other author not only accepted my apology, but also took on part of the blame for the rift that had almost occurred.

**Never pretend to know more than you do.** Whether it's the black market in Bulgaria or the medical causes of "the bends" that you've ignorantly sounded off publicly about, chances are that someone will correct you, and not always in a face-saving way. Get your fingers busy doing something else when you're tempted to butt in with "facts" for which you have no basis.

**Do your homework.** Avoid antagonizing the regulars in an online area by "lurking" and listening for a while before asking one of the questions that they're tired of answering. Most newsgroups have a "FAQ"—Frequently Asked Questions (with answers)—file available that gets newcomers up to speed for constructive, welcomed participation.

## Other Psychological Hazards Online

Practically any psychological dynamic that occurs in our three-dimensional world can get going online as well, with similar consequences. Novelist Neal Shusterman of Irvine, California, encountered the Troublemaker-come-to-town Syndrome when he went looking around Prodigy for other writers with whom he could discuss serious professional issues. "Barb Tomlin, board leader of the Office Board, asked me to become a member representative and suggested I recruit people for professional discussions there. Like an idiot I posted a note on the Books Board that we were opening a new area on publishing over on the Office Board, and I got the bashing of my life." Shusterman hadn't considered the possibility that his well-meant invitation would be perceived as a threat to an online community. "About ten people riled up the others in thinking that I was trying to 'steal' people from their board. Rumors circulated that my agenda was to close down the Books Board, and no matter what I said, some people believed that I was Satan's second cousin. I had no idea that there was a sense of territoriality on the different boards because I was thinking in terms of interesting conversations. In my mind I was just an individual sitting at my computer and no threat to anyone."

Jealousies, rivalries, cliques, crushes, transference, and projection in viewing forum leaders as parental figures—if it happens anywhere it can occur in cyberspace. Shusterman also experienced online stalking, when he irritated someone who had been posting off-topic notes. "He started chasing me around the boards, leaving nasty notes wherever I went. Several people came to my defense, which made him more vicious. It was scary because he knew where I lived in California." I've both witnessed and experienced heckling—being badgered with disparaging questions, insinuations, and labels no matter what the topic. In the "Cyberbusiness" section of CompuServe's "Smallbiz" forum, one person kept disrupting discussions with irrelevant jibes at direct marketer Sheila Danzig. Elsewhere one particularly exasperating individual kept referring to me in his messages to others as "the brat." There's no magic remedy for such situations. When you are lucky, eventually hecklers and harassers go away. See Chapter 21 for cases in which unlucky folks experienced online threats becoming real offline, in what Barb Tomlin calls "geospace."

But occasionally an initially unpleasant episode has a happy ending. "I got into a flame war with a guy named Bill Beem," Angela Gunn recalls. "We took it into E-mail, and after going back and forth for a while, we got tired of it." Beem mentioned something about *PC Magazine,* where Gunn was then working, and the conversation shifted to a professional level. "He gave me a lead about a publisher looking for writers, and that led to my first published book, *Plug-N-Play Mosaic for Windows.*"

# 20 | Legal and Ethical Danger Areas

To hear some people talk, cyberspace is everywhere and nowhere, an intangible and thus legally untouchable world apart from nations, governments, and the earth that we inhabit. When you and I meet online, this line of thinking goes, we don't go head to head on your computer or on mine, or on some master monster mainframe in Virginia or Ohio, but in the realm of the imagination. We may need silicon, plastic, and metal devices to communicate electronically, but computer bytes themselves have no weight, no taste, no color, no physical size, and no geographical location. We meet in the ether, which no one owns or governs, and which therefore is invulnerable to national laws and traditional customs. We may be subject to the frontier justice meted out by self-appointed vigilantes but otherwise anything goes, including ordinarily outlawed crimes and cons.

Sorry—that's a dream.

Physicists proved long ago that there is no ether, once thought of as an all-pervasive massless medium through which electromagnetic waves traveled. Similarly, legal authorities familiar with online communication assure us that a realm invulnerable to human laws does not exist. Take heed! And if you want a thriving business with repeat customers and clients who sing your praises, you'd better cotton up to prevalent ethical expectations too.

# The Reach of the Law

"A lot of people have the misconception that cyberspace is somehow different from anyplace else, and it's really not," says Hilary Miller, a Greenwich, Connecticut, attorney who specializes in publishing law. "All the same rules about copyright infringement and defamation, for example, apply in exactly the same way for electronic communication as for newspapers, magazines, letters, paintings, or any other medium of expression." Because laws don't become null when you're using a modem to communicate, online you should be at least as careful as anywhere else not to violate others' legal rights and to safeguard your own prudently. According to Montclair, New Jersey, attorney Lance Rose, author of *Netlaw: Your Rights in the Online World,* online jurisdiction has less to do with exactly where a breach occurs than with whether a governmental court system has power over the parties involved. For example, if I posted material on a server in Sweden that violated some other Bostonian's rights, I could have to answer for it in a Massachusetts court, Rose says. And this would be so even if online messages did drift around in space without the aid of land-based computers and telephone lines. In this discussion I'm referring specifically to United States law, although many of the principles hold in other countries as well. Consult a knowledgeable lawyer for advice on any specific legal situation you face, but here's a general orientation to issues you should know about.

*1. Intellectual ownership.* Anytime someone creates a work and fixes it in tangible form, it's instantaneously covered by copyright law, which, with a few exceptions, gives the creator the exclusive right to distribute the work, copy it, perform it publicly, or to authorize others to do so. This is true whether or not the work carries a copyright notice, whether the tangible expression involves marks on paper or digital codes on a disk, and whether you happen upon it in print, in the airwaves, or on a computer network. In other words, almost all the words and pictures you encounter in cyberspace legally belong to someone else, and you must gain permission to publish, transmit, or otherwise reproduce the work. One exception, known as "fair use," allows you to quote brief portions of someone else's work—not the whole work—for purposes of commentary. You're almost always free to make a complete copy for your own private use as well. Also, when someone explicitly grants readers the right to upload and distribute the work elsewhere, you are of course free to do so. I should also note that when someone creates a work in the course of his or her regular employment, the copyright generally belongs to the employer, not the employee.

These concepts of ownership apply to software programs you might encounter online, text files, E-mail messages, newsgroup or forum postings, mailing list items, newspaper articles in online databases, pictures accessible through the World Wide Web or Gopher, and so on. Because of rampant infringements in the wired world, I know this will strike some of you as shocking or even unbelievable news. But neither "Everyone else does it" nor "I didn't know" excuses you from responsibility for respecting others' property rights. So let me restate the legal situation as simply as possible: You must seek permission from the copyright holder before you can legally republish on paper or distribute to other online arenas any significant proportion of a program, uploaded article, E-mail message, forum thread, picture, etc., that you encounter online. You also may not upload other people's material to the Internet or online services without their permission. Copyright laws have bite. In 1992, *Playboy* collected $500,000 from a BBS that was distributing images from the magazine without authorization.

The membership agreement you accept when you join an online service may contain additional rules about copyright. For instance, CompuServe members agree that "neither member nor its designated users may reproduce, redistribute, retransmit, publish or otherwise transfer, or commercially exploit, any information, software or other content which they receive through the Service." A violator gets one warning and upon repeating the misdeed, can get cut off from CompuServe and face legal action.

When it comes to your own work that you wish to protect, the prudent thing to do is to insert a copyright notice that lets people know they should understand that what they're reading or looking at is your property. A copyright notice should take the following form: Copyright 19xx Jane Author. You can abbreviate "copyright" to "copr.," says Hilary Miller, or replace it with the letter "C" within a circle, but a "C" within parentheses is not legally recognized as equivalent. If you do wish to authorize or even encourage certain kinds of distribution and reuse of your work, specify what you do and do not permit. For instance, every chapter in my electronic book, *Get Priceless Media Coverage for Pennies,* contains the following notice:

> Copyright 1994 Marcia Yudkin. You may reproduce this entire electronic book and pass it on as shareware. All other rights reserved.

To ensure that you'll be able to collect attorney's fees from the other side if you should ever sue for copyright infringement, you can register your copyright with the Library of Congress. Currently it costs only $20, and the form is easy to fill out. (Write to the Library of Congress, Washington, D.C. 20559 and request Circular R1 and Form TX.) Note that neither a copyright declaration nor registration truly *prevents* unauthorized exploitation of your work. "No one should post anything in a public place today, whether a Usenet newsgroup or a bulletin board conference or a public mailing list, with the thought that they're going to be able at a practical level to tightly control its distribution, unless they're a huge company like Paramount that's able to run after every violator and threaten to sue them," says Lance Rose. "In the future, artists' and creators' rights groups may be able to obtain similar enforcement for individuals and small businesses."

*2. Libel.* Despite the prevalence of insults online, you shouldn't get the impression that all's fair and safe in a war of words. The doctrine of defamation defines certain kinds of pronouncements as legally actionable. "The most harmful thing you can say is something that injures someone in their business or profession. For instance, if you call someone a crook whose reputation particularly depends on probity, like a banker—as opposed to, say, a ditch digger—that could be libel," says Hilary Miller. According to Edward Cavazos and Gavino Morin, authors of *Cyberspace and the Law,* libel involves written language that has a tendency to harm a specific person or company's reputation by attacking his, her, or its honesty, integrity, or sanity. A libelous message must be disseminated to someone else besides the one attacked, so that private E-mail can't fall into the category. There must be factual content, not merely general insults or a statement of opinion. Finally, libelous statements are necessarily false. "Declaring that 'Joe is a con artist' when, in fact, Joe has been found guilty of fraudulent activities, will not get you into trouble," write Cavazos and Morin. Nor will saying, "Watch out—I sent XYZ a certified check for $350 and he never sent the merchandise or refunded the money," if in fact that happened. But beware of writing, "XYZ is running the biggest scam on the Internet, cheating buyers right and left" if they only cheated you or if you're only furious for some reason with XYZ.

The degree of harm done may have to do with the size of the audience receiving the message as well as the contents of the message, so that it might seem like common sense to take a careful look at any broadsides you send off into cyberspace. Journalist Brock Meeks found himself facing a legal bill of $30,000 when he was sued for libel by an entrepreneur whose business practices he criticized in his widely disseminated online column, CyberWire Dispatch. Nevertheless, according to Mike Godwin, legal services counsel for the Electronic Freedom Foundation, relatively few people, online or off, get sued for libel. "For one thing, it's expensive, which means you either have to be rich, or you have to have such a convincing case that you can persuade a lawyer to take your case on a contingency-fee basis. For another, the long, drawn-out process of suing someone for damage to your reputation is almost always wearying and very rarely satisfying." Lance Rose also warns against extreme self-censorship. "If people are going to veer away from saying things that are controversial, even if they might not turn out to be libelous, then we're watching a demonstration of the 'chilling effect,'" he says. "The Supreme Court has said that defamation laws are limited so that people can speak freely. Keep in mind too that when someone is a pubic figure, a statement about him or her has to be not only false to be libel, but also said maliciously, with an intent to hurt the person, or with a reckless disregard for the truth. There's a strong First Amendment value in being able to discuss famous people and companies."

What should you do if someone is spreading negative, untrue rumors online about you or your company? "First," advises Hilary Miller, "find out who is doing it. Second, ask the person responsible to change their ways. And third, if that doesn't work, consult with an attorney. It's no different from any other medium."

*3. Free expression.* With our civics lessons a foggy memory, many Americans have the idea that our First Amendment gives us a near absolute right to free speech. Sorry, that's another misconception. The First Amendment to the U.S. Constitution prevents the *government* from interfering with our freedom of expression. Government cannot swoop down and stop you from expressing your opinions or disseminating pictures online, except where obscenity, child pornography, and a few other categories like threats against the President are concerned. Yet an online service, Internet service provider, or BBS can legally censor messages or deny access to U.S. citizens, as Lance Rose puts it, "for any reason, or for no reason at all." Thus an online system can "kill" messages containing any of a given set of prohibited words, forbid certain kinds of discussions, or terminate your membership if you make a verbal nuisance of yourself—without you necessarily having any legal recourse. The key is the rules set out in the service agreement you were asked to agree to when you signed up with the service. Because of our general belief in the value of fairness and a cultural/political bias against unreasonable censorship, it may help you to cry "Unfair!" when you think an online system is trying to shut you up, but you won't be entitled to help from First Amendment watchdog groups.

*4. Privacy.* Thanks to the 1986 Electronic Communications Privacy Act, you have a right to expect that your private E-mail remains for your eyes only. Exceptions include your employer in many circumstances having the right to inspect private messages within a company E-mail system; law-enforcement officials sifting through E-mail and transmissions pursuant to court orders; and an online system specifying in its user agreement that no messages are truly private on the system. According to the "Identity, Privacy and Anonymity on the Internet" Frequently Asked Questions file, you should not, however, expect much privacy from your system administrator, who usually has a variety of monitoring procedures in place to detect unauthorized use of the system, which can also reveal your patterns of usage and even recover your deleted messages. Still, if a system administrator were to reveal to another person private messages not addressed to him or her, you might have a basis for a lawsuit. The rules are complicated, so consult a lawyer.

5. *Online agreements.* Is a deal arranged and concluded through electronic communication legally valid? Yet another common misconception operates here, says Hilary Miller. "Most business in the world transpires without any written agreement, and in most cases the writing is merely evidence of the agreement rather than the deal itself," he says. "Very, very rarely are disputes about the formation of a contract—usually they're about the *performance* of the contract. And in those cases, whether there's a manual signature on a letter or just an electronic message containing the terms doesn't matter." Miller says that his retainer agreement for clients, which he asks them to hand-sign, includes a clause saying that an electronic communication between them is valid. "And I think that's enforceable," he adds.

6. *Commercial misrepresentation.* All the laws forbidding false or misleading advertising apply in the online environment, as do most other kinds of governmental regulations over commerce. In 1994 the Federal Trade Commission brought to heel a company advertising a purportedly "100 percent legal and 200 percent guaranteed" credit repair program that the agency found to be advocating illegal methods of credit repair. The same year, Missouri securities regulators caught up with a man who praised to the skies on Prodigy the stock of a public company without disclosing that he was the public relations manager of the company and the son of its president. Outside of the securities field, competitors of a company making believe that its messages about itself were posted by disinterested bystanders might be able to sue for unfair competition, says Lance Rose. See below for opinions on such practices from an ethical point of view.

7. *And . . .* This doesn't exhaust all the possible legal concerns. Consult *Netlaw* or *Cyberspace and the Law* (see Resources) if your business ventures might involve sexually oriented material, incite-

ment to break laws, hacking, killer-for-hire ads, use of celebrity names or images, or dissemination of others' trade secrets.

## Ethics in Cyberspace

Most of the ethical issues I have encountered in my online travels have to do with the withholding or distortion of information. Skimping on honest, frank disclosure can open you up to moral condemnation that may ultimately prove far more destructive to your business than even a barrage of flaming. If you don't see anything wrong with the practices described below, you need to recognize that many of your online and offline prospects do. And never assume you're clever enough to escape detection! Instead, where your own moral sensors don't sound an alarm, sift questionable tactics with the question, Would I feel completely comfortable having everyone online understand what I'm doing? Marty Winston, an assistant sysop on CompuServe's PR and Marketing forum, told me about running across a message along the lines of "Hey, I found this great thing, you've got to call so-and-so and ask for such-and-such." Winston's nose alerted him, and he called the telephone number posted in the message and asked for the person named as the one offering this seemingly disinterested hot tip. "She's on the phone right now," came the answer, corroborating his suspicion. Winston then asked for the company president, read him the posted message, and told him that selling under disguise was not allowed in the forum and it had better not happen again. Winston did not "out" the company by letting other forum members know what its employee had done, but that would be the logical recourse on the self-governing Internet.

Indeed, someone as prominent as *New York* magazine editor Kurt Anderson became the object of negative publicity in several print publications after he went on the Internet and praised a forthcoming cover story of his magazine. He signed his plug, "Kurt Anderson," but failed to mention that he held any position at the magazine. Alert cybernauts who did make the connection scolded him roundly for the ploy. The operative expectation is that if you have any sort of financial interest in a product, service, or company you mention, you should say so, to let readers know how to take your comments. A related kind of hooha broke out when a new employee of Microsoft named John Callan applied to join a high-tech journalists-only mailing list with the mystifying affiliation, "MSN News Service." Several journalists blasted Callan for trying to trick his way onto the list as a sort of spy for Microsoft (the "M" in "MSN") and Callan exacerbated the situation when he acknowledged that of course he would forward relevant messages from the members-only list up his corporate ladder. Because people disdain deception so much, it's worth bending over backward with disclosures and disclaimers when you really do lack any underhanded intent. If you wait until someone challenges you, you'll rarely be able to defuse the suspicions.

Probably the most ethically dubious practice I heard about was a scheme where a company gets accounts under different names from several different Internet providers and uses them to drum up discussion in newsgroups about their product without appearing to be advertising. As I explained in the chapters on schmoozing, if you answer someone else's question, you're not soliciting. Why wait for questions and positive interest to get a thread going, the reasoning runs, when you can stage the process yourself? Usenet expert Bryan Pfaffenberger called this "a very risky strategy. If word got around—as, for example, through a disgruntled employee—man oh man would you find yourself on the wrong end of flames!" Paul Edwards, system administrator of the popular Working from Home forum on CompuServe, condemned the subterfuge even more strongly. "Normally we have a 'two-strikes-and-you're-out' policy, but that's a one-strike offense. Anyone who did that on our forum would be permanently locked out. It's highly unethical." He likened it to "shilling," an old carnival ruse where an accomplice encourages gambling or buying by posing as an enthusiastic or successful customer.

Edwards also tsk-tsked about two other cases I knew of involving misleading publicity on bulletin boards. In one case a person was telling people who had expressed interest in the World Wide Web about the opportunity to get a "home page" for just $10 a month, consistently failing to mention that this was part of a multilevel marketing scheme. In another case someone was offering publication and royalties for a certain kind of business material, yet failed to mention in the initial message that authors would have to pay a significant fee to participate. "To me, anything where an important fact is concealed that when revealed would cause an individual to turn off is not good business ethics. You need to present the salient information up front. There's a strategy called 'the curiosity method,' where you describe the benefits of a business, get people to a meeting, and then tell them the name of the company, which makes people feel deceived. We cut that off at the knees whenever we see it."

The most ethically controversial tool on the Internet does not come up much in a business context, but it's worth knowing about the pros and cons in case you're tempted to use it. Several sites exist that will post your message to Usenet stripped of any clues to your identity. Sometimes you can also receive anonymous E-mail replies to such a post through the same site. Many Usenet regulars denounce anonymous posting, holding that one should be willing to stand up and acknowledge one's words. Others point to legitimate reasons for anonymity, like whistle-blowing on a corporation without fear of retaliation and the ability to get and offer candid advice on sensitive topics like sexual harassment. There's widespread agreement that you shouldn't use anonymity when your purpose is to break the law, flout Usenet taboos against commercial messages, or attack others' reputations.

Other ethical principles to remember include respecting clients' and correspondents' requests for confidentiality and being careful not to spread misinformation. Anne Stuart, senior writer for *CIO* magazine, told me that some publications have a rule that every bit of information coming from the Internet has to be independently verified. "Someone had apparently doctored the text of the Bible at one site, and in lots of places information online is out of date," she warns. Stuart also proceeds with caution when it comes to assuming that people really are who they say they are electronically. "When I initiate E-mail contact to the address on someone's stationery or business card, I feel pretty confident about their identity, but in other cases identity can be tricky, and I think it's better to call and check the situation out. Once I saw a post asking for contributions to a racist textbook, and it turned out that while the professor was on vacation, a student was using his ID and sneaking into his electronic mailbox." Stuart sensed that that situation was fishy, but where you intend to blast someone's conduct far and wide it might be only fair to do a little checking first.

# 21 | Practical Risks to Beware Of

In the classic story *The Wizard of Oz,* Dorothy discovered that where her house landed after the storm, strange and wonderful things were possible that would have been fantasy back home in Kansas. Some surprises, like the welcoming Munchkins, were pleasant, while others, like flying monkeys and witches on broomsticks, were utterly horrible. Similarly, it's important to recognize that in the brave new world of cyberspace, not everyone honors values like honesty and respect. Unsavory characters, mischief, and outright crimes can spoil your online journeys. To a great extent, however, you can minimize the dangers by taking some simple precautions.

## Personal Risks

The scariest stories I heard came from two women who experienced personal threats to their safety from people who learned of their existence online. When a woman I'll call Wendy happened to mention in a forum message that she lived in Chicago, another woman from Chicago posted a message expressing similar interests and suggesting that they get together. "We exchanged E-mail, and she sounded sane and interesting, so I gave her a call," recalls Wendy. "It was the most bizarre conversation. The one and only time I'd experienced anything like it was in a locked psychiatric unit. She expressed a lot of anger at certain people in the forum, and she sounded truly dangerous. I didn't want her showing up at my door." Wendy made some calls to mental health contacts and discovered that sure enough, this woman had been hospitalized for psychiatric problems. She also learned that several sysops of the forum had been receiving middle-of-the-night phone calls from the woman. "I called and begged CompuServe to delete an E-mail I had already sent her with my telephone number, but they said they couldn't do that except with a court order. Then the woman disappeared." Relieved, Wendy decided to proceed more cautiously in making offline contacts with online people. "Looking back, I think that if I'd carried on a little longer in E-mail she wouldn't have seemed so normal."

The other woman, whom I'll call Brenda, began receiving unwelcome sexual comments from a man by E-mail and then by telephone. "I was shocked and alarmed," Brenda says. "I have a publicly listed phone number, and at that time my address was listed too." The problem escalated. Although he lived in another state, the man told Brenda he was sending someone to her house to let her know he was for real. "He vandalized my car. I contacted the online service where this had all started, but when things happen offline, they can't help you." Brenda decided she wasn't going to be victimized by this jerk, and hired a private detective in another state to let *him* know that she knew where he was and to warn him to stop communicating with her. That worked. "It cost me about three hundred dollars, and the damage he had already done was much greater than that. Now I have caller-ID service, no listed address, and an immediate callback capability as deterrents."

Although these two incidents happened to women, men can experience genuine threats as well. As discussed in Chapter 19, Neal Shusterman was harassed online by another man who knew his home city, and a male attorney told me he had been threatened with bodily harm by someone who hated lawyers. Both Wendy and Brenda say that the best tactics for preventing real-world harassment are caution in giving out one's home telephone number and address, and arranging with the telephone company for one's home address to be omitted from directory information. Those who have a home-based business and want prospective customers and clients to be able to get in touch can insert a layer or two of security by giving out a post-office box address, making it difficult for people to find your street address, and acting as if you run a big company out of a conventional office. That way, you can have credibility and accessibility without sacrificing personal security.

If you're a small or home-based business, you might also want to avoid posting your address, fax, and phone numbers publicly when you're just asking for information. Send your contact information privately instead—unless you don't mind getting onto the lists of folks who will flood your mailbox and fax with silly moneymaking offers. One fellow told me, quite erroneously, that if you post a fax number online you are telling people it's fine to fax advertising to you. I'm sure he's not the only one with that misconception!

## Computer-Related Risks

"Security is the number one concern expressed by people interested in doing business on the Internet," says Dan Janal, a publicist for high-tech companies and author of the *Online Marketing Handbook*. So if you're worried that going online will expose your business to theft, sabotage, or electronic mayhem, you are not alone. Yet according to the experts I consulted, most of the fears you might have in this area are groundless if you're an individual or small firm connecting to the outside world via a personal computer. Here's why.

Even before the mass implementation of elaborate security systems that we're told are in the works, the risk of credit-card thievery online is minimal, says Rich Roth, an Internet connectivity consultant and the founder of On the Net in Georgetown, Connecticut. "It's the same level of risk as using a credit card at a restaurant." Suppose a customer wishes to E-mail you a credit-card order via her America Online account to your America Online mailbox. "An online system is basically a closed box, and that E-mail could only be intercepted by someone working for the company—as at the restaurant," Roth says. When unencrypted or so-called clear-text E-mail travels through the Internet, the risk is greater, as the mail passes through a number of gateways, at any one of which it might get bottlenecked. While waiting to be sent across an ocean via satellite, for example, data might sit in a queue for several minutes, where someone might be tempted to rifle through it. We could compare this to credit-card data passing through a procession of restaurants amidst a flood of bills, personal notes, and business data, increasing the chances of interception but only by an extraordinary patient or brilliant snooper. According to Roth, "The risk comes primarily from your own service provider and the one on the other end. Smaller providers are more likely not to have proper safeguards in place, but any provider is vulnerable to human mistakes or misdeeds. You can build a maximum security system and if a guard leaves a door open . . ."

On the World Wide Web, Roth continues, whatever slight transmission delay you see when you submit your credit-card data is the actual length of time—seconds—the information is vulnerable to snatching. "The risk of someone hanging around a site that takes orders waiting for a buyer to show up is very low. And when there is fraud, banks usually charge it back to the vendor. In fact, there's a bigger risk of a vendor selling to a bad card than of a buyer getting their credit-card information stolen and used." Although the widespread fears may be overblown, it's essential to recognize security trepidations and to provide alternative ways of taking payment besides E-mail or direct Web orders. You will lose sales if you just try to convince buyers at the point of sale about the safety of your enhanced security system—precisely when they are most inclined to worry.

Another common fear, fueled by highly publicized incidents, is of having one's computer broken into and private data stolen or the system damaged. Many of us read about the Christmas 1994 intrusion by notorious hacker Kevin Mitnick into the computer of security expert Tsutomu Shimomura and about the 1988 "worm" released by Cornell student Robert Morris, Jr., which clogged up many organizations' computers on the Internet for days. Here reality is even more divergent with perception if you're a small organization. Chances are you go online with a personal computer, a single machine not otherwise linked to any computer network. "There's no risk at all—none—if you dial up CompuServe or another online service in those circumstances," explains Rich Roth.

"Your individual computer probably isn't even capable of letting in an incoming call when you're dialing out. With a direct connection of your individual machine to the Internet via SLIP or PPP, there is a slight security risk, but it's pretty low." (The protocols "SLIP" and "PPP" make your computer a way station on the Internet, rather than a commuter to and from the service provider's station.) Where you have an internal network in your office that runs Novell NetWare or Windows NT, an outsider trying to break in through the phone lines couldn't get in because your network's operating system doesn't recognize Internet protocol. The real risk, experts concur, occurs with a corporate Unix-based system that offers information to the outside world as an Internet "host." In that case you do need sophisticated security protections that set up various kinds of technical barriers, particularly "firewalls," which are beyond the scope of this book.

According to Christian Crumlish, author of *A Guided Tour of the Internet,* if you access the Internet by dialing up to a service and using their software, your vulnerability has nothing to do with your own computer but rather with your account on the service. Someone who knew your password there could not only spy on your E-mail but also use your identity to place messages or run up a bill. The best security tactic in that case, Crumlish says, is changing your password frequently. Since a hacker can break into your account by automatically trying all the words in the dictionary, a secure password isn't an official word, but equally should not be your birthday, the name of your beloved or your pet, or some cute but guessable phrase like "letmein" or "knockknock." An electronic bandit can also learn your password by watching you type it. This rascal can also wreak mischief if you leave the machine unattended to, say, go to the bathroom while you're signed on. Or, when you have set up a script for an automatic sign-on, the scoundrel merely has to run the access program on your computer when you aren't around. A crook could also steal into your account by tricking you into revealing your password, so never give it out verbally for any reason. To further tax your memory or organization skills, experts recommend that you not use the same password for all of your accounts, so that someone who broke into one wouldn't be able to get into them all. Whew! Have you resolved to safeguard your passwords and computer yet?

And then there are so-called viruses—rogue programs that vandalize your computer from within. In December 1994, rumors spread about a "Good Times" virus that would erase one's hard disk and that one could contract on American Online simply by reading a certain message. Karyn Pichnarczyk of the U.S. Department of Energy's Computer Incident Advisory Capability investigated and issued an alert that this scare was a hoax. "As of this date, there are no known viruses which can infect merely through reading a mail message," she wrote to computer users worldwide. "For a virus to spread some program must be executed." In other words, so far as anyone knows, you cannot catch a computer virus by receiving and reading E-mail text or downloading and reading a text file—only by running a software program. A virus cannot take up residence within straight text, but it can within almost any kind of binary file or program. Take care especially, then, when receiving or fetching programs or when installing them from floppy disks. Even commercial software from large companies has occasionally been shipped containing infections. Inexpensive or free virus scanning programs that help you practice "safe computing"—if you remember to use them—are available widely online or at computer stores.

Finally, you face the risk of valuable, time-sensitive E-mail getting delayed or lost. Computer columnist John Dvorak reports that using MCI mail, he sent a series of three E-mail messages to one correspondent who received the third first, ten hours after it was sent, the first twenty-four hours after it was sent, and the second thirty-nine hours later. Another time, when messages seemed to be getting lost, not delayed, he called the MCI help desk and learned that a server had crashed during that time and many messages were indeed lost, with no notification of regular users. "Even one lost message is one too many" where important business is concerned, Dvorak complains. Similarly, Cliff Stoll, author of the true-life cyberspace thriller *The Cuckoo's Egg,* performed an experiment comparing the reliability of snail-mail postcards and E-mail. Of two months of daily postcards from Buffalo, New York, to Oakland, California, half arrived in two days, many in three, and one took as long as eight days. Whereas all the postal mail arrived, of the E-mail he sent to himself from five different accounts, "most letters arrived within two hours; some took up to two days," he reports. "Average delivery time: twelve minutes. But I discovered that five messages never made it. Three of them bounced, due to network problems or crashed computers along the way. The other two? Swallowed by the electronic abyss." It seems wise, then, to use the telephone, fax, or postal mail as a backup when you don't receive an E-mail reply you're expecting—or not to depend on E-mail at all when something has to get there positively, absolutely this afternoon.

## Business Risks

The old IBM slogan, "Think!" serves as a good guideline to follow before rushing ahead to "put your company online." According to Dallas investment banker Fred Richards, more businesspeople should carefully consider the consequences of posting information publicly about their company, given that they won't be able to control exactly who will be accessing it and with what motive. "We use the Internet primarily when we're looking into a field that's completely new to us," Richards says. "And lo and behold, we recently discovered just how amazingly stupid people can be. One company in England had its entire pricing schedule and distribution technique out there for anyone to see. He had contract offers up there too—thirty-five inquiries from customers all over the world. If you wanted to compete with them you'd have everything right there that you needed—without them knowing you had seen it. I showed this to six different bankers as well as the guy trying to raise money and they were all incredulous. Maybe a marketing or sales person did it without the CEO knowing. . . ." I kept this issue in mind in the early stages of researching this book, when it was important not to let competing writers, editors, and publishers know precisely what I was working on. Whenever I publicly asked for input on a topic, I avoided describing the angle of the book, although I did brief those I interviewed. Through the grapevine effect the news could still have reached someone in a position to "scoop" me, but at least I minimized the odds.

Besides unwittingly giving away your secrets, make sure you understand that by doing practically anything besides E-mail online you are opening up your business for public scrutiny. Fail to satisfy your customers and they have an effortless way to spread their discontent. Put out an announcement that provokes skepticism and, fairly or not, the questions will pop up. I once looked in on a thread where a company president was getting roasted for talking about his company's service in terms that professional publicists would not accept. "The guy was talking about going on the Internet and creating editorial interest with a 'proprietary' method," said CompuServe PRSIG assistant sysop Marty Winston months later. "My suspicions were raised, and I said, 'If this isn't what you're doing you'd better tell us, and if it is what you're doing, you'd better not do it.' It was like saying you had a miracle cure for cancer that worked through exposure to dangerous levels of radiation." In response to merciless challenges from Winston and others, the company president offered unconvincing stalls like "I need the permission of my board to tell you anything about that." Verbally it was the equivalent of five schoolyard tough guys piling onto one poor schnook, and I wasn't surprised to learn from Winston that the man didn't show up there again.

Note that the public, interactive nature of the online world makes this risk much more acute than in any other marketing medium. If you use direct mail to deliver a pitch that some recipients find fishy, rarely will any one of them be able to discuss it with more than one other prospect at a time. If they don't like it, they'll probably just toss it out. With ads or press publicity, half a dozen people sitting around a lunch room might share opinions, but this doesn't begin to compare with thousands or tens of thousands being able to pose objections and debate something fundamental about your business, like your price, product, or ethics.

A final business risk is falling prey to overpriced promoters, consultants, and providers. I have seen seminars that offer less than the information in this book being hawked at thousands of dollars a head and companies being told that they need to budget $50,000 plus a new full-time employee for the most minimal sort of Internet presence—which the entrepreneur down the road already has up and running for $50 a month. The best way to locate value in this frontier area is to go online, find a BBS or forum or newsgroup where people know more than you do, and ask, ask, ask. Exercise skepticism when it comes to offers that sound irresistible, or that try to terrorize you into acting right away. For example, I've seen come-ons like these:

"How to reach over a million ripe, virgin prospects with a classified ad all for less than a penny a day!" (A chance to pay $100 for an eight-week CompuServe ad that costs a member $10.40—and my calendar says that 8 weeks is 56 days, for $1.79 a day, not "less than a penny.")

"What will you do when your business is banned from the Internet?" (The context implies that if you don't obtain your own registered Internet domain name right away for $297, you won't be able to get onto the Internet—completely false.)

Caution, friends. Calm down and forget about the "gold rush" mentality. Unless you really don't mind spending eight times more than you have to, separate the rackets from the services that fairly help you onto the information highway in a way that makes sense for your business.

# 22 | Getting Addicted or Enslaved

A $200-an-hour executive management skills coach confessed that after he received a Prodigy start-up package as a gift, he became "completely fascinated" with the work dilemmas people were describing online, spending an hour or two every day reading and commenting on messages. "One Friday afternoon I signed on when I had a report for an existing client that I had to get out that day, and the next thing I knew three and a half hours had gone by! I wasn't procrastinating, I'd just gotten totally sucked in to these discussions that I didn't often run across offline. I barely got my report finished, and that scared me. I quit Prodigy and haven't used my modem since."

"I'm happy to help out with your book—just one request," replied another person I contacted. "*Please* don't tell anyone to contact me by E-mail, for my sake and the sake of my family. I don't want to be flooded. E-mail has consumed my life (100–150 messages a day). :-)"

As with almost any human activity, too much of a fun or useful thing holds a potential for trouble. You can fall victim to your own fascination with the byways of this incredible new world or people's eagerness to seek you out for business. Your involvement spins out of control, and either in volume or intensity, you get overwhelmed. "I expect there to be a twelve-step online addicts group forming soon," jokes Susan RoAne, author of *The Secrets of Savvy Networking*. "I just hope they don't have their meetings online."

## Help for the Obsessed

If you check your E-mail box ten times a day, find yourself dreaming about disputes among people you've met online, or aimlessly surf the World Wide Web for hours every day, it might be time to wonder if you have a problem. It's past time to wonder, of course, when you realize you've been racking up three-digit monthly online bills. Control *is* a problem for some people, says professional sysop Janet Attard, and the money factor doesn't force a solution as much as it used to. "When I first went online, in the eighties, I used a service that cost thirty-five dollars an hour during the daytime. To send manuscripts I was working on, it was still cheaper and faster than overnight mail, though, so I used it as a substitute fax machine. Now that the hourly rates have tumbled, people don't always cut back when they should. Because the online medium is interactive, you can get really tied up in it, but you can learn to control your usage the same way you learn not to watch TV all the time. You need to treat going online the same way you would treat any other kind of outreach to customers."

Self-help for online "addiction" begins with figuring out what exactly is happening that makes your cyberspace involvement a problem. Are you losing track of time and missing deadlines? Is it really someone else who's complaining about your time spent online? Do you have great fun at it but don't have any time for other activities you enjoy as well? Is there a compulsiveness about your online entanglements? Have you been getting emotionally overinvolved with the conflicts and connections that come to life through your computer screen? Is it the bills that pose the problem? Once you've isolated the difficulties, remedies should be easier to come by.

Anne Stuart, a senior writer for *CIO* magazine, told me that she sometimes spends so many hours at a time online that her vision begins to go double and she finally looks away at a window and gets shocked to see that it has gotten dark outside. "My husband is into it almost as much as I am, and we can be wrestling for control of our one telephone line," she says. Still, she doesn't see her involvement with numerous electronic penpals and participation on four work-related mailing lists as a problem. "I lose myself in it the way other people get absorbed in gardening or other hobbies. It's all related to my work as a writer, and I'm not on twenty-four hours a day or anything like that." When she used to subscribe to close to a dozen mailing lists, however, she did feel overwhelmed and out of control. "Sometimes, I'd turn my computer on and there'd be two hundred messages, and I didn't feel able to delete any of them without reading them. I've learned how to do that, though. I also cut back on the mailing list subscriptions even though I felt I was learning a lot, because it felt like I was working all the time." Stuart turns one particular subscription on and off according to whether or not she's drowning in E-mail.

So, what's the real problem *you're* concerned about?

*You lose track of time.* If overabsorption creates difficulties for you, rig up a system to remind you of the passage of time. Put an alarm clock near your computer and set it before you boot up. If you have two phone lines and a ringing telephone gets your attention more than an alarm, phone a friend before you go online and ask him to call you in exactly one hour. Entrepreneurs and inventors, how about a product that automatically logs you off after a preset length of time?

*You're in conflict with others.* Discuss the problem with the other person or people. Negotiate. Describe the pleasure and educational benefits you derive from being online, and the money you're making. Give in a little to keep the peace.

*You're simply overdoing it.* Set priorities, advises Anne Stuart. Realize that you don't have to respond to every item or contribute to every debate. Separate the indispensable forums and business matters from the optional ones and wean yourself from the latter when necessary.

*You can't stop signing on.* If you're spending more time online than off or your world of online relationships exceeds your other involvements in number and intensity, you might need professional counseling, says psychologist/consultant Yishai Almog. For less extreme compulsiveness, try rewarding yourself for checking your E-mail only five times a day, or three or two.

*You're overinvolved emotionally.* Take a vacation, leaving your laptop at home. One married man who had developed quite a roster of online girlfriends told me that he quit cold turkey. Hiking through high desert for two weeks, he was relieved to discover that he got along fine without his daily hours of "online sex."

*You're spending too much.* Switch to a service with unlimited access hours, if possible. Or invest in a so-called offline reader, which might cost you a bit up front but allows you to read and write messages without the money-clock ticking.

Sometimes just putting your attention on the problem leads to a change. When I asked to hear from online addicts on Prodigy, electronic publisher Jim Migneco of Vernon, Connecticut, wrote to me, in part: "Online, each time you open a door, you are entering a hallway with more doors and are tempted into opening another portal to yet another wondrous place—all without going outside! But 'going out' is exactly what is missing from cruising through cyberspace. Years ago, I never missed an opportunity to walk along the beach on a blustery, frigid January day or to hike through the woods with the smell of pines and burbling sound of a thousand-year-old brook. Now I spend entire Sundays in my swivel-rocker office chair in a virtual world where the only exercise I get is moving my right index finger on a mouse key. Sitting in front of a PC in a heated and air-conditioned condo, it doesn't matter much whether it's sunny or cloudy outside, winter or summer. Have I gotten too wrapped up in cyberspace? Yes! Writing about this has helped me realize that I must make the effort to step outside again and venture into cyberspace in moderation."

## Liberation from E-mail Slavery

The wired business folks I spoke with differed greatly in the volume of E-mail they found unmanageable. One handled 100 messages a day while another found 30 to 40 a week totally burdensome. *Newsday* columnist and public radio commentator Alice Bredin said she knew the cure and couldn't wait to hire an assistant to speed up the process. "I used to have an assistant who could provide my answers to commonly asked questions and then call me and ask about the rest. It's a huge investment of time to train someone to do that for you, because it takes about three months before they're efficient, but in the long run it will let you concentrate on more important things. All the businesspeople that I have interviewed who make tons of money know how to delegate." Bredin admits, though, that delegation holds pitfalls. "You have to tell the assistant to check with you if they're not one hundred and fifty percent certain of how they should respond. Once someone I used to work with got in touch, and my assistant sent back an ordinary reply instead of the 'Hi, How are you doing? How's Bill?' I would have written."

Brian Kilgore, a communications consultant from Toronto, argues that E-mail is no different from any other in-basket in an office. "If you're never going to get E-mail you don't want your assistant to see, and if you have someone smart enough to do it well, then delegating your E-mail handling is fine, just as with conventional mail. And when you travel without an electronic connection, wouldn't it be good to have someone pull the messages out of the machine back at the office and call you if anything important is there?" But Peter Lloyd, a creativity consultant based in Newport, Kentucky, says he's noticed telltale signs that his addressee isn't handling his or her own E-mail: "People who have others reading their E-mail for them answer less faithfully—or not at all. The worst is people who do not answer polite, businesslike E-mail messages which call for a response. It's as rude as not giving the time of day. Another dead giveaway is talking to the person on the phone and finding out they know nothing about something you E-mailed them. Even worse: They call and ask about something you've already E-mailed."

Chris White, a speaker and writer from Sacramento, California, says that when she receives the exact same reply two or three times, or when she gets a reply beginning "Dear Mr. White," she suspects someone else is typing the message. White expresses skepticism that E-mail assistants can do an adequate job: "Queen bees like to talk to other queens! If you're a worker, never been queen and never will, how can you know what's a queenly matter and what isn't?" I'll let Lloyd have the last word on this controversy: "If Microsoft mogul Bill Gates can read his own mail, no one has an excuse." Indeed, Gates has said that while almost nobody has his home telephone number, he lets his E-mail address be widely known and reads everything that lands there himself.

Before you decide to foist all your E-mail on someone else, consider these other solutions:

*Separate E-mail accounts.* Of several CompuServe accounts used by classified-ad whiz Sheila Danzig, one is her "private" account that her customers learn of only after they buy something from her, or if they meet her in one of the forums. "I answer all of the mail in my private account myself," she says. "A high school girl, Ali Davis, takes care of one hundred and fifty ad responses in about an hour and a half, answering the phone at the same time! It frees Ric, my director of operations, to take care of more pressing matters, and in turn, Ric frees me to do only the creative and troubleshooting ends of the business."

*Divided responsibilities.* Janet Attard of Centereach, New York, who serves as a sysop for six forums on three services, has an assistant who answers all the questions that fall within one particular topic and leaves the rest for her.

*Macros (scripts) for repeated situations.* Save time by developing explanations or other responses in files that you can call up and customize with your respondent's name and some other appropriate introductory comments before sending them. Make sure these canned responses sound natural, as if you really did write them on the fly.

*Priorities.* I'm told that you can program E-mail management software to follow any rules you can formulate for what should come to your attention first, later, and last. For instance, you might want to read messages from your boyfriend, sister, editor, and best friend first; then your top clients with pending projects; then others; finally stuff from mailing lists you subscribe to, with anything from that jerk in Portland who keeps on writing you getting automatically deleted. Other software can save you time by collecting your E-mail from different accounts automatically and presenting it to you all in one batch.

*Escapism.* Who says you have to respond to every message? argues Chris White. Or that you have to respond right away? Napoleon, it's said, opened his mail only once every three weeks. Much of it concerned problems that had already been solved in the meantime.

*Brevity.* Adopt the habit of writing only what needs to be said and no more: Yes. Tuesday at five. See you!

*Thoughtful scheduling.* "I used to answer E-mail at the end of the day when I was tired, but it requires a lot of energy to do it well," says Alice Bredin. "Now I do it whenever I have twenty minutes free, as a break or a filler." I enjoy turning my computer on in the morning and seeing who sent me messages overnight. It warms up my mind to reply while my mug of coffee is waking up my body.

*The Dave Barry solution.* I sent humorist Dave Barry an E-mail asking how he felt about being listed in Seth Godin's little book, *E-mail Addresses of the Rich and Famous.* Within minutes I received the answer: The account had been disconnected.

## But Don't Overcontrol

You might suppose that a good way to keep your online activities manageable is to determine which tasks regularly produce results and to drop the others. In the next chapter, however, you'll learn why in the long run that might not be helpful. Of the following four kinds of online business tasks, all contribute to a thriving business:

1. Incoming business such as orders and requests for information
2. Research—receiving or gathering data, ideas, news, perspectives that you can put to work in your business
3. Outgoing public marketing messages designed to attract business
4. Opportunity scouting

Ignoring #1 would be near suicidal. Forgetting about #2 would mean falling out of date. Overlooking #3 would soon cause inquiries and sales to dry up. Yet neglecting #4, which seems the most remote category, might mean missing the biggest payoffs of all. To understand the importance of online exploration, read on.

# 23 | Staying Open for Business

If you've ever run across conventional career counselors, you know that among their bag of tricks are questionnaires that ask you to fill in rows of spots with your number 2 pencil: Would you rather do A or B? Eventually you receive an assessment that explains why you, a lawyer, hate your profession. Your responses indicate that your most congenial careers, tied for first place, are: 1) hairdresser; and 2) cleaning lady.

I have no such predictions in store for you, but I did notice numerous themes running through my interviews with people benefiting on a regular basis from their online activities. Apart from the techniques I have described in previous chapters, these people tended to share certain attitudes and leanings. The common threads weren't personality characteristics or abilities so much as basic operating assumptions, long-settled habits, and even philosophical approaches to life. If you find yourself fundamentally at odds with these assumptions, you'll have a harder time catching on and may conclude that getting business online isn't for you. But if you recognize yourself in this profile, or are willing to try on these attitudes and put them into practice, you're likely to benefit more than others from your rambles through cyberspace.

## Open Mind, Fluid Boundaries

*Do you expect the unexpected?* Not one person I spoke with mentioned specific goals, plans, quotas, or hopes governing their online participation. Not one story along the lines of "I decided I would line up two new distributors and sell forty-five copies of my product—and I did" turned up. Instead of any fixed preconception of a payback from their time and money spent online, my successes talked of surprises, discoveries, connections that zigzagged into an unanticipated type of deal. For example, when Robert Savage, an information broker specializing in international trade based in Woodstock, Vermont, joined the Italian forum on CompuServe, he sent an introduction to all three of the sysops thinking that perhaps he'd make a book of his about Italy available in the forum library. One of the sysops, a British publisher specializing in Italian themes, suggested putting the material into his magazine. Upon hearing about the magazine, Savage proposed becoming its distributor for the United States. And upon hearing more about the sysop's publishing company, Savage mentioned an unpublished novel he had written about Italy, which the publisher asked to review. "One thing leads to another," Savage told me with a smile in his voice.

The way in which people look for and find opportunities online resembles scouting more than hunting, browsing more than searching, and cruising more than driving. They have a relaxed, fuzzy focus rather than a sharply defined intention, and they're equally prepared to come out with nothing or with a coup worth celebrating. "It's an open-ended thing—maybe something good will come out of it, maybe not," Savage says. "You wait and see how things progress. There are a lot of dead ends—and a lot of deadbeats out there—but if only a few leads work out, you're ahead." Compare this with the pleas I've seen from marketing managers for hard-and-fast numbers they can use to bolster proposals to take their company online.

*Are you curious?* An inquiring mind can take you through some pretty interesting twists and turns. Robert Savage once saw a message about a well-known multilevel marketing company planning expansion into Europe. Instead of going on to the next message with his reflexive recoil from multilevel marketing, he took the opportunity to ask what it was all about. "They put me in touch with someone higher up in the organization, to whom I happened to mention my CD-ROM project. A trip to Florida ensued to discuss it, and he's now scrambling around trying to find investors for it." Similarly, Robert Bixby, an international marketing consultant based in Santa Cruz, California, told me about his delight at learning about a free source of international trade leads. "I did the download and worked the leads for quite a while, with no success," he says. "There was a little note, however, about a chamber of commerce in Russia newly online. I contacted them, we traded mail back and forth, and I ended up doing a research project for them. There hasn't been any work since, but Yuri and I stay in touch and have become friends. I think it's mainly a matter of keeping your eyes open."

*Do you trust your intuition?* After his weekly conference for professional speakers had run on America Online for a year, Wally Bock was unable to point to any hard evidence that it was bringing in more subscribers to his newsletter, *Cyberpower Alert!,* or paying off in some other concrete way. Yet he had no plans to discontinue the schmooze sessions. "My gut says it works—it's part of how I establish expertise," Bock says. "My invitation list has grown from twelve to one hundred forty people, but there's really no way to quantify your relationships with people. That's what reputation is." When I mentioned to consultant Jeff Senné that the word *intuition* kept coming up in my interviews, he commented, "Intuitive people can take in the future and the past, and aren't stuck with the five senses or the way things are now. So it wouldn't surprise me if a great many of the people excited about the online world are intuitive." In a realm where A leads to Q and Q to C-squared, instincts may be a more reliable guide than logic.

*Can you spot and act on opportunities?* Here too entrepreneurs and professionals out on their own have an edge over employees who need layers of approval for each move. But more than self-employment comes into play here. You could be "just" a solo accountant serving clients or an accountant who also publishes, becomes a partner in a software venture, and advises Hong Kong entrepreneurs on how to set up an American branch office. I encountered many more of the latter type than the former during my research. It's less a matter of being multitalented than of having a flexible conception of business activities appropriate for you. Paulette Ensign doesn't see many of her colleagues in professional organizing getting as much out of being online as she does, some because they don't create products, and others because "they spend untold hours giving advice and never toss out a lasso." If you have or would contemplate multiple income streams, the online world offers very promising fishing.

*Are you willing to blaze a trail?* So many marketing strategies for the online environment remain untried that you may need to go forward with the spirit of a pioneer. In 1993 Laura Fillmore, creator of the Online Bookstore, acquired first serial rights to a story from Stephen King's new book, *Nightmares and Dreamscapes,* and offered it for sale on the Internet. The idea generated "a vast amount of smoke, a tremendous marketing boost for the printed book, lots of noise, but not enough in per-copy sales to pay for the phone bills for setting up the deal." Nevertheless, Fillmore regards the venture as a valuable learning experience that demonstrated a way to do things that wouldn't work. "Who wants to be a sheep?" she adds. "The Internet is a meritocracy of the mind, where you can get recognition for your ideas and for doing something different. A company can spend millions there and get nothing back, but someone else can spend almost nothing and the word about it spreads everywhere."

*Do you value accessibility?* A perennial query in the business forums on CompuServe concerns Jay Abraham, a marketing consultant who runs $5,000 seminars and charges $3,000 an hour for private advice. Is he worth it or is he not worth it?—opinions fly back and forth so regularly that I began to wish Abraham himself would show up to give the masses a taste of his caviar-class talent. But when I thought about it more, it became clear to me that staying out of reach bolstered his ability to remain one of the world's most highly paid consultants. The same goes for those who pride themselves on being a well-kept secret. If you like or depend on working behind closed doors, electronic schmoozing—or online anything—probably isn't worth your time.

*Can you accept the reality of intangibles?* Plenty of people steadily cash in on goodwill, reputation, and word of mouth, without knowing exactly which former client's praise, which publicity appearance, which thirdhand mention influenced someone new to buy. Chris Brandlon, who formerly worked with Jay Abraham, disagreed with my reasoning in the previous paragraph, giving another reason certain people reject online marketing: "Since there's no way of quantifying the net impact on one's business of a typical talk-show appearance, media release, or online forum participation, there is no basis for asserting that this is a productive way to build a business. It's not that Jay Abraham is trying to maintain a 'Man Behind the Curtain' façade, it's that 'getting his name out' is a 'soft fuzzy' concept that cannot be tallied and costed on a per- basis, giving him a clear picture as to whether a piece of programming in question is working." Well, the means may not be quantifiable, but the greenbacks earned by the people I've quoted in this book were real enough!

*Do you subscribe to the motto, "Nothing ventured, nothing gained"?* Or to "It never hurts to ask"? Many of my sources showed a definite tendency to reach for the long shot. Stamps journalist/entrepreneur Dick Sine once described an idea online very roughly and almost tongue-in-cheek said he'd like to find some investors. The next day he received a private message from a man who said he might indeed want to invest $10,000 in the project. Likewise, consultant/speaker Nikki Sweet sometimes searches the CompuServe directory for CEOs whose names she has encountered in her reading. When she couldn't get through to one of these CEOs by phone she E-mailed him and received a reply the next day along the lines of "Wow, isn't this E-mail a great invention? The answer to your question is, Please feel free to call me any time, here's my private telephone number."

*Do you proceed in a spirit of contribution and reward?* I asked myself what was the difference between the discreditable Green Card Lawyers, Canter and Siegel (see Chapter 17), and Lary Crews (see Chapter 12), whom I applaud, since both took the risk of venturing forth without any official permission. My answer is that Canter and Siegel's motivation was sheer reward, while Crews focused on the contribution first. Reasonably enough, however, he wasn't willing to subsidize his volunteering indefinitely, and a fairer arrangement came his way because the nature of his contribution became so clear. In a myriad of ways, the interactive spirit of the online world rewards givers, not takers.

*Are you patient?* Copywriter Al Bredenberg of Cornwall, Connecticut, says that business seems to develop more slowly on the Internet than in the traditional business world. "People contacting me online want help with concepts and may not have a specific project in mind. It takes a lot more discussion before we get something definite going. In contrast, when someone calls in response to one of my ads in an industry journal or directory, that usually leads to immediate work. On the Net, inquiries are also more likely to come from out in left field, like a guy asking me if I can help him sell king salmon on the Net. I kind of like that."

*Do you get a kick out of trying new things?* Computer consultant Lawrence Seldin of East Patchogue, New York, decided to use his vacation to master the procedure of posting to Internet newsgroups. "The very first night, I got twenty book orders from the Internet," he told me, still amazed months later. "I couldn't quite understand what was happening, but my mailbox was filling up with orders for my book, *Power Tips for the Apple Newton.*" He had just as much fun posting to CompuServe forums where he happened to be interested in the topic, like the Journalism and QuickBooks forums, and having people ask him upon seeing his signature line if he did consulting. "I got several clients that way, from hanging around places I enjoy," Seldin says. This is decidedly different from the attitude, "I'd better find three new paying clients this month—or else!" A relaxed approach not only fosters success in online marketing, I believe, but also makes it likelier that you'll stick with it.

## Planning for Success

I don't want to leave the impression that online marketing is all haphazard serendipity. Despite the unpredictability, you need a focused plan of action. A good way to begin developing such a plan would be to reread this book, notebook in hand, listing tactics and approaches that might make sense for your business. Keeping your overall marketing goals in mind, translate those possibilities into a series of action steps. For instance, after noodling around on the Internet for several months, copywriter Al Bredenberg formulated a plan which in part read like this:

Goals:
• To increase client base through new Internet marketing efforts.
• To develop a new service as a writer of Internet marketing messages.
• To serve business and industry by providing information in my areas of expertise.

Ongoing activities:
• Participate in forums and discussion groups, as a way to provide information, make contact and promote my services.
• Set up an affordable World Wide Web page, ftp and gopher sites and E-mail capabilities to disseminate my marketing presence.
• Prepare a series of free reports as a service and as a soft-sell marketing effort. Find ways to distribute these reports and make them available online.
• Regularly initiate discussions and dialogue that increase exposure by raising questions, conducting surveys, participating in discussions, etc.
• Develop organized methods to follow up leads, respond to inquiries, keep site information up to date, etc.
• Evaluate and test the success of the efforts.

If you haven't yet gone online at all, here is one way to proceed step by step toward a successful online marketing program:

1. Sign up for a trial membership in at least one of the major commercial online services (CompuServe, American Online, Prodigy).
2. Learn how to send and receive E-mail, read bulletin board messages, post messages, and download files. Also test out the Internet features (especially World Wide Web, Gopher, newsgroups) available on that service.

3. Formulate your online marketing goals, including the occupations, interests, age groups, geographical groups, etc., of prospects you wish to reach. After reviewing this book, list possible ways of achieving those goals.
4. Prepare and refine any materials you'll need for your marketing efforts, such as ad copy, a signature file, articles to upload, an electronic sales letter, or follow-up piece, and make any necessary technical arrangements, such as with an Internet or mailbot provider.
5. Implement your plan, and give it at least four months before evaluating results.

Although I can't give you help on technical questions, I can coach you on strategy and help you develop online lures that work. I can also help you achieve publicity in paper or broadcast media for your online programs. And if you became intrigued by the creative perspectives expressed earlier in this chapter, you'll enjoy my bimonthly printed newsletter, *The Creative Glow: How to Be More Original, Inspired & Productive in Your Work.*

Here's how to find out more about my coaching services, online seminars, audiotapes, books, and newsletter. I'd also love to hear about how you implemented the ideas in this book.

By mail:     Marcia Yudkin
             P.O. Box 1310
             Boston, MA 02117
By phone:    (617) 266-1613
By fax:      (617) 871-1728
By modem:    overview via mailbot: info@yudkin.com
             for a personal reply: yudkin@world.std.com
             Or, on CompuServe: 75200,1163

Courage, and good luck!

# Glossary

***acronyms, online***   Any unfamiliar group of capital letters you encounter online might be one of these. For instance, "BTW" means "by the way," "PMJI" means "pardon me for jumping in" and "TIA" "thanks in advance." Unless you deliberately want to make *newbies* (see below) feel unwelcome, don't use these yourself.

***article***   What Internet newsgroups call a posted message.

***ASCII***   Pronounced "askee," this stands for "American Standard Code for Information Interchange" and denotes a standard set of 128 characters that can be recognized and displayed by any computer, whether a Macintosh, IBM-compatible, or mainframe. "Pure ASCII text" includes only the letters and numbers on a standard computer keyboard and a few more generic symbols and commands, but no special codes used only by a specific program.

***autoresponder***   Also called a "mailbot," this signifies an E-mail address programmed to automatically return a fixed marketing message to anyone who corresponds with it. Convenient—but make sure you have a "live" E-mail address too, where you personally respond to questions or requests.

***baud rate***   Usually used interchangeably (wrongly so, the experts say) with "bps," this indicates the sending and receiving speed of a modem. "9600 baud" is much faster than "300 baud." Some online services have different telephone-access numbers for different baud rates.

***BBS***   The universal nickname for Bulletin Board System, the small-scale and often noncommercial versions of the commercial online services, frequently operated as hobbies or home businesses. Most offer users' files, message boards, and live chat. Increasingly BBSs offer access to and from the Internet as well as direct-dial connections.

**binary files**   In contrast to *ASCII* files (see above), binary files include graphics, programs, or codes specific to a particular program, such as WordPerfect or Lotus 1-2-3. If you attempt to read a binary file in your word processor it will look like a bunch of nonsense. Avoid E-mailing or posting binary files unless you're sure your recipient or target audience knows what to do with them.

**bit**   Short for "binary digit," this is the "0" or "1," or "on/off" electrical state that comprises the basic unit of information for computers. Eight bits make up a "byte."

**bps**   Bits per second. A measurement that shows how many bits a modem can transfer in a second. In 1995, 14,400 bps was considered fast, 28,800 bps superfast, and 2,400 bps painfully slow for file transfers, although 2,400 bps is plenty fast for *real-time* (see below) online conversation.

**browser**   A program such as lynx, Mosaic, or Netscape that allows you to visit sites and read information on the *World Wide Web* (see below).

**bulletin board**   This can mean either a special-interest discussion group on a commercial service, as on Prodigy, or a stand-alone bulletin-board system.

**byte**   Eight bits, or the number of basic units of computer information that convey an alphabetical letter ("01000001" equals "a," for instance). Larger units of information are measured in kilobytes (a thousand bytes), megabytes (a million bytes), and so on.

**cancelbot**   A program used by cyberspace vigilantes to delete messages throughout *Usenet* (see below) from posters deemed to be abusing their Internet privileges.

**chat**   Interacting online with at least one other party who is also logged in and typing away at that time. Also called "live conferencing."

**client**   In the computer world, this may not mean a person or company you provide services for but a computer that connects to a remote computer somewhere else (a "server" or "host"), which contains files and programs that the first computer can then use.

The person working at the "client" computer can then perform functions as if that remote computer were sitting on his or her desk.

*compressed files*   As the word suggests, computer files can be squished so that they take up less storage space. To use them, though, you then have to unsquish them, with a program such as PKUNZIP or uncompress.

*conference*   Either a live group chat session online or, as with the Great Britain–based CIX service, a special-interest message board or forum.

*cyberspace*   Term coined by science fiction writer William Gibson, which denotes the nonphysical universe in which those networked by computers and modems feel they are interacting.

*dial-up account*   An account that gives you inexpensive access to the Internet by means of the much larger computer of your Internet service provider.

*domain name*   The part of an Internet E-mail address that specifies the organization of a user. For instance, in "nightly@nbc.com," "nbc.com" is the domain name for the National Broadcasting Company; ".com" shows that it is a commercial organization. If you hanker for your own domain name, apply for one through your Internet service provider.

*DOS*   Disk Operating System, or the set of commands that perform basic functions on IBM-compatible computers. If a software program is DOS-based, you'll probably start it from a screen prompt that looks something like "C:\>."

*download*   In contrast to *uploading* (see below), downloading involves transferring files from a remote computer to your own.

*E-mail*   Electronic mail—private messages sent almost instantaneously from one computer user to another and which are easy to reply to, forward, or save.

*electronic book*   A collection of information organized attractively on a disk or in compressed form in "chapters" rather than in one long plain string of text. Sometimes abbreviated as "E-book."

*emoticon*   Combinations of traditional typewriter symbols used to convey emotions, such as ";-)" for winking or ":-O" for surprise (turn your head sideways and you'll get it). Some businesspeople (like me) consider these hokey and clichéd.

*encryption*   Computerized coding of a message to conceal its meaning so that only authorized recipients can read it. Currently the United States government considers some digital encryption tools "munitions" and controls their export.

*FAQ*    Frequently Asked Questions—a digest of common questions and their answers that Usenet *newbies* (see below) are supposed to retrieve and read to prevent wasting the time and taxing the patience of the regulars.

*firewall*    A security system for organizational computer networks designed to control the ability of outsiders to access proprietary information or perform other mischief in the system from afar.

*flaming*    Internet jargon for electronically hurling insults and verbal abuse at people deemed idiotic, obtuse, annoying, or depraved. When lots of people get into the act, it becomes a "flame fest."

*forum*    An online special-interest group with message boards, libraries of information, and conference facilities.

*Freenet*    A no-charge public gateway to the Internet.

*freeware*    Software or electronic text packets that can be downloaded, distributed, and used for free. Contrasts with *shareware* (see below), which is free for trial purposes only.

*ftp*    Acronym for "file transfer protocol." A command-based system for fetching files from remote locations on the Internet.

*Gopher*    A menu-based system for reading or fetching text files from anywhere on the Internet. Much easier to use than *ftp* (see below). Through your Internet service provider, you can make information available to cybernauts via Gopher.

*handle*    Virtually all chat systems, most Internet providers, and some commercial online services allow you to select a nickname by which you'll be known. Your real name may or may not be available for discovery.

*home page*    An "electronic billboard" that you can post about your business via the *World Wide Web* (see below), and link to others' home pages anywhere on the Internet.

*hotspot*    A link on the *World Wide Web* (see below) that, when clicked, sends the user to another site.

*HTML*    Hypertext markup language, the coding system that produces *World Wide Web* (see below) pages.

*hypertext*    A nonlinear system of nesting information that allows you to find out more about certain items if and only if you're interested. On the *World Wide Web* (see below), hypertext links can transport you from one site to another.

*interface*    The visual and functional façade with which you interact via your computer screen. When a service has "improved its interface," that means it has made it more attractive on-screen and easier to use.

*Internet*    The international network of computer networks that links organizations and individuals on every continent, including Antarctica. Although the U.S. Department of Defense created much of its initial infrastructure and procedures, no one now owns or governs the Internet.

*link*    A function that takes a user with just one click from one page on the *World Wide Web* (see below) to another that may be based in a computer system ten thousand miles away.

*log on* (or *log in*)    To start a session on a computer service by entering your account number and password. When you're finished, of course, you "log off."

*lurker*    Someone who reads messages regularly without actively participating.

*lynx*    A program available through many Internet providers that allows you to browse text on the *World Wide Web* (see below). In the place of pictures you'll see something like "[IMAGE]."

*mailbot*    An electronic mailbox programmed to do something automatically with all incoming messages, such as sending back a canned set of information or forwarding the mail to another address. Also called an autoresponder.

*mailing list*    On the Internet, a system for exchanging ideas on a given topic by sending discussion notes to a central location for E-mail distribution to subscribers to the list. Some mailing lists have a moderator who screens contributions; others are unmoderated. It's best to "lurk" (see *lurker* above) in a mailing list first before participating.

*modem*    Short for "modulator-demodulator," this is a telecommunications device that is either installed within your computer or attached outside it and that connects your computer, via telephone lines, to the Internet, BBSs, or online services.

*moderated*    A newsgroup or mailing list where contributions are screened for relevance and informational (versus promotional) content.

*Mosaic* A program that enables you to view images *and* text on the *World Wide Web* (see below). Compare with "lynx," above.

*Net* The affectionate nickname for "Internet."

*Netiquette* Desirable and acceptable behavior on the Internet.

*Netscape* Another program that enables you to view images *and* text on the *World Wide Web* (see below).

*newbies* A not-so-affectionate nickname for newcomers to the Internet.

*newsgroup* A special-interest message area on the section of the Internet known as *Usenet* (see below), similar to a *forum* or a *bulletin board* (see above).

*newsreader* A program that allows you to sort through, choose for reading, reply to, and forward messages in Internet *newsgroups* (see above).

*offline reader* A program, often created by a third party, that saves you online time and money by enabling you to log on, grab your messages, and log off for you to read them at your leisure.

*online service* A subscription-based service that you can connect with via modem for news, games, information, forums, and more. Usually you pay a monthly access fee and extra for the hours you spend online.

*post* To send a message for public viewing to a *newsgroup, forum,* or *mailing list* (each defined above).

*PPP* Point to Point Protocol, an alternative to *SLIP* (see below) that also puts you directly on the Internet using ordinary telephone lines.

*protocol* A specific set of rules with which two computers can communicate.

*real time* Pronounced with emphasis on "real." The mode in which events such as online conversation actually occur, as opposed to the delayed communication of E-mail or message boards.

*roundtable* GEnie's word for an online special-interest group.

*scroll* What text does when it moves up and then off the computer screen. On CompuServe, "scroll rate" is the rate at which new messages force old ones off the board.

***server***    A "master computer" that provides information services to other computers called *"clients"* (see above) that dial into it.

***service provider***    An organization that, usually for a fee, connects you to the Internet. Many service providers offer additional services such as getting you a *domain name* (see above), setting up *mailbots* (see above), and providing storage space for your *World Wide Web* pages (see below).

***shareware***    "Try-before-you-pay" software, much of which equals in quality better-financed "pay-first" commercial software.

***signature***    Standard sign-off you create to use as boilerplate for the close of your *Usenet* (see below), *mailing list,* or *forum* (see above) postings.

***SLIP***    Serial Line Internet Protocol, or one way to connect directly to the Internet rather than through the server of your Internet provider, using ordinary telephone lines. More powerful and expensive than a *dial-up account* (see above).

***smiley***    Pictures composed of punctuation marks to be read sideways (e.g., ":-(" ) and that many people use online to perform the function of tone of voice or facial expression.

***snail-mail***    Postal, paper-and-envelope-type mail.

***spamming***    The widely despised practice of mass posting an advertisement in irrelevant *newsgroups* (see above) on the Internet. The term originated in a Monty Python comedy skit before the information superhighway became a household world—but the *flaming* (see above) you'll get if you try it won't be funny.

***sysop***    Short for "system operator," a person in charge of an online area, either a *forum* (see above), a section of a forum, or a whole *BBS* (see above).

***telnet***    A service program that allows users to log onto the Internet by modem or use a remote computer site on the Net. Also called "remote log-in."

***thread***    In *newsgroups* and *forums* (see both above), a series of replies to an initial post, organized in chronological order in isolation from other threads.

***Unix***    The user-unfriendly operating system of most Internet *server* (see above) computers.

***upload***    The opposite operation to *downloading* (see above), "uploading" involves transferring files from your own computer to a remote computer system, usually to make them available for others to read and/or use.

***URL*** Universal Resource Locator—an "address" on the *World Wide Web* (see below) that begins with "http://."

***Usenet*** The anarchic collection of special-interest *newsgroups* (see above) on the Internet.

***virtual*** Not physical in nature. A "virtual bank" has an E-mail address instead of walk-up tellers; a "virtual corporation" provides services to clients without physical interaction among its members.

***virus*** A mischievous or malicious program embedded within another one that wreaks mild to catastrophic damage on your computer after you "catch" it (download and use it).

***Web*** Nickname for the *World Wide Web* (see below).

***Windows*** The mouse-based Microsoft operating system for IBM-compatible personal computers.

***World Wide Web*** The section of the Internet resembling electronic billboards, through which you can navigate without learning special commands. Since 1994, it has been growing wildly in popularity.

# Resources

## All About Modems

Glossbrenner, Alfred, *The Little Online Book,* Berkeley, CA, Peachpit Press, 1995. How to install and troubleshoot your modem, hot-wire your hotel room, quickly scope out a BBS, and more. Glossbrenner is blind to business needs, though: his definition of "keyboard commerce" is just "shopping, banking and stock trading," and he has a whole chapter describing downloading but no instructions for uploading your own files.

Kinkoph, Sherry, *The Complete Idiot's Guide to Modems & Online Services*. Indianapolis, IN, Alpha Books, 1994. This breaks down the process of using modems and fax-modems into easily comprehensible steps. Includes a great troubleshooting chart and a tour of BBSs, the online services, and the Internet.

Shipley, Chris, *How to Connect: Driver's Ed for the Information Highway.* Emeryville, CA, Ziff-Davis Press, 1993. From an award-winning technical writer, this book contains clear, easy-to-understand explanations of all the major concepts in the online world, and step-by-step instructions for installing modems, signing on to services, and sending E-mail.

# Ah, the Internet!

Angell, David, and Brent Heslop, *The Internet Business Companion*. Reading, MA, Addison-Wesley, 1995. Recommended for companies that wish to set up their own server system on the Internet, providing information to be accessed through E-mail, ftp, Gopher, or the World Wide Web.

Crumlish, Christian, *A Guided Tour of the Internet*. Alameda, CA, Sybex, 1995. Don't be fooled by the full-color cartoons: This is a well-organized tutorial on all the major Internet functions, chock full of solid tips. Highly recommended for beginners.

December, John, and Neil Randall, *The World Wide Web Unleashed*. Indianapolis, IN, Sams Publishing, 1994. At 1,058 pages, this outsized book reads like an overgrown dissertation, but Part V contains useful theoretical and practical issues to think about in designing a home page for the World Wide Web.

Ellsworth, Jill H. and Matthew V., *The Internet Business Book*. New York, John Wiley, 1994. Good checklist for choosing an Internet provider. Contains a few examples of offering information on the Internet, but about two-thirds of the book covers using the Internet for research, with dozens of business and government data bases and document source lists, along with how to access them.

Ellsworth, Jill H. and Matthew V., *Marketing on the Internet: Multimedia Strategies for the World Wide Web*. New York, John Wiley, 1995. If you want to splash your company onto the World Wide Web, this book contains much of the technical advice you'll need, from coding your page in HTML to publicizing your location appropriately. Especially useful: pictures of home pages opposite their HTML coding.

Hoffman, Paul E., *Internet Instant Reference*. Alameda, CA, Sybex, 1994. Arranged encyclopedia-style, this resource on the Internet will come in handy if you get lost in Unix. Includes complete technical instructions for Internet mail, ftp file transfers, Gopher, several different newsreader programs, lynx access to the World Wide Web, and more. Not recommended for getting started.

Kehoe, Brendan, *Zen and the Art of the Internet: A Beginner's Guide,* third edition. Englewood Cliffs, NJ, Prentice Hall, 1994. A nice orientation to what the Internet has to offer, for nontechies, with a mild anticommercial bias.

Peal, David, *Access the Internet!* Alameda, CA, Sybex, 1994. This cute, user-friendly book is a great investment if you can run its Netcom-linked Netcruiser software, included with the book, and connect locally to the national Netcom Internet access service. Buried deep in the book is the information that you need a "386" machine or better to run the software, and nowhere does it tell you how to find out in advance if Netcom has a local access number for your area.

Pfaffenberger, Bryan, *The Usenet Book: Finding, Using and Surviving Newsgroups on the Internet.* Reading, MA, Addison-Wesley, 1995. This book can save you a lot of frustration. Most valuable features: exactly how to master the user-unfriendly newsreader programs on a Unix system; list of newsgroups with archived info available; eye-opening reviews of more than 300 specific newsgroups—but only one focused on business.

Resnick, Rosalind, and Dave Taylor, *The Internet Business Guide: Riding the Internet Superhighway to Profit.* Indianapolis, IN, Sams Publishing, 1994. A mix of technical instructions and strategic considerations for medium-sized to large businesses considering Internet connections.

Rose, Dr. Donald, *Minding Your Cybermanners on the Internet.* Indianapolis, IN, Alpha Books, 1994. If you can stand Rose's sophomoric sense of humor, this offers guidelines for civil, effective communication online that Internet old-timers consider common sense.

# Finding, Creating, and Using BBSs

Allen, S. Carol, *How to Successfully Run a BBS for Profit.* Yucca Valley, CA, InfoLink, 1993. I have not seen this, but it is highly recommended by sysops.

Hedtke, John, *Using Computer Bulletin Boards,* 3rd edition. New York, *MIS:Press,* 1995. How to log on to and explore eight common types of electronic bulletin-board systems, detect and eradicate a virus, set up your own BBS, and more.

*Boardwatch Magazine.* A monthly magazine about the BBS world, geared toward sysops, those already technically adept and political conservatives. Contains extensive BBS listings, mostly from North America. Available by subscription or in computer stores, larger newsstands. For subscription info: 800-933-6038; subscriptions@ boardwatch.com; http://www.boardwatch.com.

*Computer Shopper.* A hefty computer shopping guide packed with ads, some articles on buying and using computers, and state-by-state BBS listings. Appears monthly, available in some convenience stores and office supply stores, as well as at newsstands and by subscription. For information: 800-274-6384; http://www.ziff.com.

# Electronic Books and Shareware Distribution

Haynes, Colin, *Paperless Publishing.* New York, Windcrest/ McGraw-Hill, 1994. Cutting-edge techniques and resources for presenting and distributing information online or on disk. Includes a disk containing four electronic-book publishing programs for DOS and Windows: Dart, Multimedia Workshop, Softlock, and Writer's Dream.

Hudgik, Steve, *Make Money Selling Your Shareware.* New York, Windcrest/McGraw-Hill, 1994. Lots of resources, surveys, and advice that applies to using an electronic book as a marketing device.

Schenot, Bob, *How to Sell Your Software*. New York, John Wiley, 1994. I found the suggestions and case studies on shareware marketing in the previous self-published version of this book valuable and thought provoking. His catalog of persuasive methods for getting customers to send money is entertaining, eye-opening, and relevant for anyone using a "freebie" marketing strategy.

Shareware Distribution Network. A donation-supported service that will upload your electronic book to the FidoNet BBS network. For complete instructions, send a self-addressed stamped envelope to SDN International, 13 Douglas Drive, Meriden, CT 06451.

## What's Happening in Cyberspace

*Internet World*. Straightforward technical, feature, and interview articles about the Internet, published monthly. For subscription info: 800-573-3062; iwsubs@kable.com; http://www.mecklerweb.com.

*Netguide*. My favorite of all the magazines about cyberspace: literate, stylish writing; sociological, philosophical, and people-oriented perspectives along with opinionated what's-happening listings; assumes no more technical interest in computers than you'd have in your VCR. Monthly. Subscription info: 800-829-0421; netmail@ netguide.cmp.com; http://www.cmp.com/NetGuide/home.html.

*Online Access*. Covers the BBS scene and online services as well as the Internet. Monthly. Subscription info: 800-366-6336; 74514.3363@compuserve.com.

## On Marketing

Caples, John, *Tested Advertising Methods*. Fourth Edition. Englewood Cliffs, NJ, Prentice Hall, 1974. Dated examples, but timeless and deliciously specific advice on copywriting that gets results.

Godin, Seth, *eMarketing: Reaping Profits on the Information Highway*. New York, Perigee, 1995. If you've got a lot of money to invest in marketing technology, read this book for creative uses of fax machines, video, audio, computer databases, BBSs, and the Internet. Most examples come from companies the size of Procter & Gamble.

Janal, Daniel S., *Online Marketing Handbook: How to Advertise, Publicize and Promote Your Products and Services on the Internet and Commercial Online Systems.* New York, Van Nostrand Reinhold, 1995. Step by step, how to put your company online. Emphasizes product sales and serving shoppers. Strong on World Wide Web marketing and public relations possibilities; good info on how to negotiate a forum for your company on an online service.

Hoge, Cecil C., Sr., *The Electronic Marketing Manual: Integrating Electronic Media into Your Marketing Campaign.* New York, McGraw-Hill, 1993. Ideas and resources relating to online advertising, geared toward larger companies. Many candid case studies.

Ott, Richard, *Creating Demand.* Burr Ridge, IL, Irwin, 1992. Whether you're selling online or traditionally, read this book to understand the psychological underpinnings of buying behavior.

RoAne, Susan, *The Secrets of Savvy Networking.* New York, Warner, 1993. Highly readable, humorous, and sensible guide to making business connections face to face. Much of RoAne's advice applies online as well.

Strangelove, Michael, *How to Advertise on the Internet.* Ottawa, Ontario, Strangelove Enterprises, 1994. This book looks homemade but it's packed with creative ideas for Internet marketing. Especially useful: screen shots of more than 150 World Wide Web home pages. Excellent Internet resource lists for online marketers.

Yudkin, Marcia, *Six Steps to Free Publicity—and Dozens of Other Ways to Win Free Media Attention for You or Your Business.* New York, Plume/Penguin, 1994. Practical tips for making your business newsworthy and getting print or broadcast publicity without spending a bundle.

*Cyberpower Alert!* Wally Bock's candid, no-hype monthly electronic newsletter on cyberspace developments and online marketing for speakers, consultants, and writers. For subscription info: BockTalk@aol.com; 510-835-8522.

*The Online Marketing Letter*. Eight times a year, get the lowdown on what works and what doesn't in selling online—and why—from Jonathan Mizel. He's a highly skilled copywriter, generous in describing the details of his online marketing enterprises. For information: jmizel@hooked.net; JMizel@aol.com; 415-677-7909.

## Online Law

Cavazos, Edward A., and Gavino Morin, *Cyberspace and the Law: Your Rights and Duties in the On-Line World*. Cambridge, MA, MIT Press, 1994. Compact, readable summaries of American legal issues concerning contracts, copyright, libel, obscenity, and crimes involving computer networks. Contains the full text of the U.S. Electronic Communications Privacy Act and other federal and state laws covering computer rights and crimes.

Rose, Lance, *Netlaw: Your Rights in the Online World*. Berkeley, CA, Osborne/McGraw-Hill, 1995. Illuminating, in-depth window on the culture and legal controversies of cyberspace. Essential reading if you operate a BBS or moderate any online area; highly recommended for others.

## General Reflections on Cyberspace

Heim, Michael, *The Metaphysics of Virtual Reality*. New York, Oxford University Press, 1993. I don't know where else you'll find Heidegger (twentieth-century German philosopher) and hypertext on the same page. Philosophical reflections on the way we experience computer technology.

Kroker, Arthur, and Michael A. Weinstein, *Data Trash: The Theory of the Virtual Class*. New York, St. Martin's Press, 1994. "In the beginning was the Word, but in the end there is only the data byte."

A hip exploration of digital life, but don't venture in unless you enjoy portentous combinations of five-syllable words.

Rheingold, Howard, *The Virtual Community: Homesteading on the Electronic Frontier*. New York, HarperCollins, 1993. Cultural, social, and political aspects of the online world, from a long-time member of The Well. Engaging; international perspective.

Stoll, Clifford, *Silicon Snake Oil: Second Thoughts on the Information Highway*. New York, Doubleday, 1995. From an Internetter of fifteen years' experience, reflections on cyberspace as an illusory nonplace and on the addictive glut of unnecessary online information. "Life in the real world is far more interesting, far more important, far richer than anything you'll ever find on a computer screen."

*Wired*. The relentlessly neon color scheme of this monthly magazine fooled me for years. Not until I encountered back issues archived online did I realize it carries articles about the legal, social, and economic implications of technology. For subscription info: 800-769-4733; subscriptions@wired.com; http://www.hotwired.com.

## Commercial Online Services

America Online. Tollfree in U.S. and Canada: 800-827-6364; Phone: 703-448-8700.

Compulink Information eXchange (CIX). Phone in U.K.: 0181-390-8446; Fax in U.K.: 0181-390-6561; E-mail: cixadmin@cix.compulink.co.uk.

CompuServe Information Service. Toll-free in U.S. and Canada: 800-848-8990; Tollfree in United Kingdom: 0800-289-458; Phone: 614-529-1340; Fax: 614-529-1610; E-mail: sales@cis.compuserve.com; World Wide Web: http://www.compuserve.com.

Delphi Internet Services. Toll-free in U.S. and Canada: 800-695-4005; Phone: 617-491-3342; Phone for Delphi UK: 0171-485-5964; Fax: 617-491-6642; E-mail: info@delphi.com; World Wide Web: http://www.delphi.com.

eWorld. Toll-free in U.S. and Canada: 800-775-4556; Toll-free in United Kingdom: 0800-896-206; Phone: 408-974-1236; Fax: 408-974-0551; E-mail: askeac@eworld.com; World Wide Web: http://www.eworld.com.

GEnie. Toll-free in U.S.: 800-638-8369; Toll-free in Canada: 800-387-8330; Phone: 301-251-6475.

Prodigy Service. Toll-free in U.S. and Canada: 800-776-3449; E-mail: info99A@prodigy.com; World Wide Web: http://www.astranet.com.

The Well. Phone: 415-433-4335; E-mail: info@well.com; World Wide Web: http://www.well.com.

## Internet Service Providers

Pretty soon there will be a Yellow Pages category for this sort of business, but it hasn't arrived yet in most areas. Here are other ways to find a service provider with local access for your area: Ask around on a commercial online service or local BBS; check the ads in the business section of your nearest city's newspaper; call a local computer store or computer consultant and ask. I haven't provided these listings because they'd necessarily be spotty, outdated, and incomplete. See below for up-to-the-minute lists available online.

## Online Information Resources

How to get FAQs (Frequently Asked Questions), including the FAQ about FAQs:

  most are periodically posted in the newsgroup news.answers
  ftp to rtfm.mit.edu/pub/usenet
  send E-mail to mail-server@rtfm.mit.edu with a message of
    "help"
  on the World Wide Web, http://www.cis.ohio-state.edu/
    hypertext/faq/usenet/FAQ-List.html

How to find lists of Usenet newsgroups:

> ftp to ftp.uu.net:/networking/news/config/newsgroups.Z
> posted regularly to the newsgroups news.lists, news.groups, and news.answers
> send E-mail to mail-server@rtfm.mit.edu with the message "send usenet/news.announce.newusers/A-Guide-to-Social-Newsgroups-and-Mailing-Lists"
> most of the commercial online services have lists, though incomplete ones

How to find lists of mailing lists:

> send E-mail to mail-server@sri.com with the message "send netinfo/interest-groups"
> ftp to rtfm.mit.edu, in the directory /pub/usenet/news.lists
> some of the commercial online services have lists, though incomplete ones

How to find lists of service providers:

> send any E-mail message to info@merit.edu
> on the World Wide Web, visit http://amazing.com/faq.html or ftp://ftp.einet.net/pub/INET=MARKETING/WWW=SVC=providers

# INDEX